PHOTOSHOP CS4
Volume 2: Visual QuickStart Guide

Elaine Weinmann
Peter Lourekas

Peachpit Press

Photoshop CS4, volume 2:
Visual QuickStart Guide

Elaine Weinmann and Peter Lourekas

Peachpit Press
1249 Eighth Street
Berkeley, CA 94710

510/524-2178
510/524-2221 (fax)

Find us on the Web at: www.peachpit.com
To report errors, please send a note to errata@peachpit.com
Peachpit Press is a division of Pearson Education

ISBN-13: 978-0-321-63503-7
ISBN-10:   0-321-63503-5
9 8 7 6 5 4 3 2 1
Printed and bound in the United States of America

Acknowledgments

Nancy Aldrich-Ruenzel, publisher, supports the core strengths of Peachpit Press while cultivating new subject areas and technologies. This book was in the idea stage for many years, and we're grateful for her help in nurturing it to fruition.

Victor Gavenda, our technical editor at Peachpit, ever so carefully tested the book in Windows, with a great sense of humor.

Lisa Brazieal, expert production editor at Peachpit, ironed out the preflight kinks in our files as she readied them for press, then sent them to Courier Printing.

Nancy Davis, editor-in-chief; Gary-Paul Prince, promotions manager; Keasley Jones, associate publisher; and many other terrific, hardworking people at Peachpit contribute their respective talents.

Elaine Soares, photo research manager, and Lee Scher, photo research coordinator, of the Image Resource Center at Pearson Education, the parent company of Peachpit Press, quickly procured the stock graphics from Shutterstock.com that we requested.

Rebecca Pepper did a thorough and thoughtful job of copy editing.

Steve Rath generated the index.

Scout Festa did the final round of proofreading.

Krista Behrend of Datacolor provided us with technical and product support for our Spyder3Elite display calibrator.

For creating a great product that's a pleasure to use and write about, and for helping beta testers like ourselves untangle the mysteries of Photoshop by way of the online forum, kudos to John Nack, senior product manager for Adobe Photoshop; Vishal Khandpur, senior prerelease program associate for Adobe Photoshop; and other members of the Adobe Photoshop CS4 beta team.

Most important, our love and gratitude to Alicia and Simona, for just being who they are (a great pleasure!).

— Elaine Weinmann and Peter Lourekas

Introduction

Why another book on Photoshop?

Adobe Photoshop has so many features, we couldn't stuff all the topics we wanted to cover into volume 1 of our *Visual QuickStart Guide* on the subject. Such a robust application deserves a sequel. In this second volume, we cover many topics that are too complex for beginning users to tackle, and expand on topics that we only touched upon in the first one, such as Camera Raw, retouching, and advanced techniques for creating selections and layer masks — to name but a few. We'll show you not only how individual features work (e.g., the mechanics of creating selections and masks), but how they work in the context of executing real-world, multistep tasks.

Is there a prerequisite to using this book?

This book is geared for users who have a basic proficiency and working knowledge of Photoshop. If you want to brush up on some of your basic skills or incorporate more shortcuts into your workflow, see Chapter 4: Using Photoshop, as well as the lists of shortcuts and Quick Summary reference guides to essential tasks that are located in various chapters throughout the book. For example, you'll find a guide to choosing colors on page 94, and a summary of Layers panel features on pages 96–97 (for more summaries, refer to the table of contents; for shortcuts, see "shortcuts" in the index).

How this book is organized

The following breakdown will give you a bird's-eye view of how the Adobe Photoshop application and its pals, Adobe Bridge and the Adobe Camera Raw plug-in (both of which ship with Photoshop), fit into the "bigger picture." It will also give you an idea of how this book is organized, from calibrating your display to choosing color settings to using Bridge and Camera Raw, and then, of course, to the many image-editing and image-processing controls in Photoshop. The chapter topics progress in a natural order, from essential skills to specialized techniques.

Chapter 1: Color Management

To ensure that the color in your digital images remains consistent, from its initial input through its various editing phases onscreen to its final output, be sure to calibrate your display and choose color management settings. Don't skip this chapter!

Chapter 2: Bridge

Adobe Bridge serves as a conduit among the programs in the Adobe Creative Suite. In addition to being the most convenient vehicle for opening files into Camera Raw or Photoshop, Bridge also lets you rate, sort, examine, and compare your image thumbnails; assign keywords and other metadata to your files; locate your files by their current rating or other criteria; and create photo galleries for the Web. If you want to streamline your work sessions, set aside some time to learn more about Bridge — it will be time well spent.

Chapter 3: Camera Raw

Raw files from a digital camera must be converted by the Camera Raw plug-in ("Camera Raw" for short) before they can be opened and edited in Photoshop. But the ever-improving Camera Raw is more than just a converter; it's also a powerful adjustment tool. We'll show you how to use it to crop and straighten your photos; correct under- and overexposure, color casts, and chromatic distortion; remove noise, dust marks, and red-eye; and apply sharpening — among many other tasks — and then open your photos into Photoshop. You should take advantage of the Camera Raw plug-in, not just because it has a user-friendly interface and a smorgasbord of controls, but also because the settings you apply remain editable and the original digital photos remain unaltered (akin to traditional film negatives). If you shoot digital photos, you should use Camera Raw.

Chapters 4 to 15: Photoshop

From Chapter 4, which is a reference guide to the fundamental features of Photoshop, through the last chapter in the book, you'll be immersed in Photoshop, in all its power and glory. Among the many topics covered are color and tonal corrections; in-depth montaging, masking, tinting, retouching, and filtering techniques; creating type and vector shapes; saving and loading presets; recording and playing actions; and finally, executing output-related tasks, such as applying output sharpening and choosing print settings.

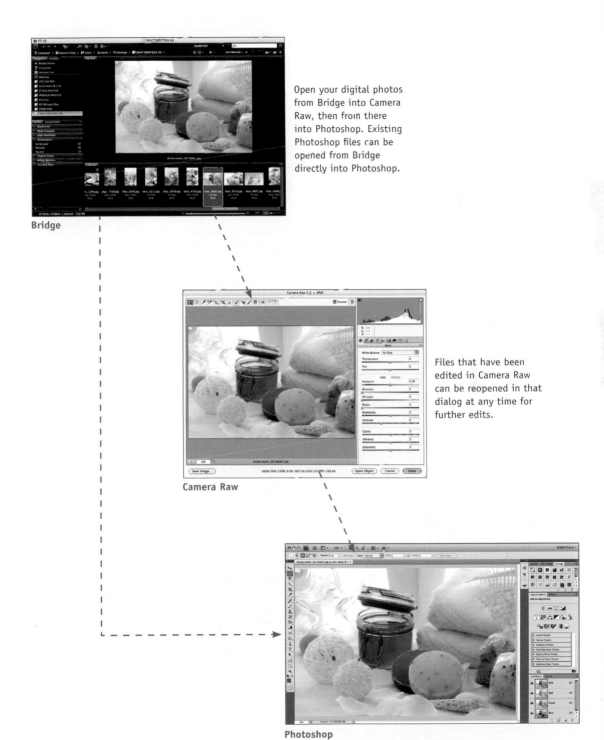

Bridge

Open your digital photos from Bridge into Camera Raw, then from there into Photoshop. Existing Photoshop files can be opened from Bridge directly into Photoshop.

Camera Raw

Files that have been edited in Camera Raw can be reopened in that dialog at any time for further edits.

Photoshop

How this book can help you

The feature set of Photoshop has grown with each upgrade of the program, from its first release by Adobe Systems Incorporated in 1990 to its current incarnation. The sheer number of tools and commands can be intimidating — not to mention the wealth of settings that can be chosen for them. It can be a challenge for even an experienced user to sort out the most useful features from the rest. And to add to the confusion, some features overlap or are downright redundant. To perform a simple process like cropping, for example, should you use the Crop tool in Camera Raw or Photoshop, or the Crop, Trim, or Crop and Straighten command in Photoshop? Or suppose you want to lift a figure or object from its background and put it on a new background. Should you isolate it with a selection tool or command, or by using a Quick Mask?

When you're faced with a particular task, one command might help you get the job done efficiently and easily, whereas another might be tedious to use or marginally successful. What makes one method or sequence superior to another? Speed, power, accuracy, and flexibility. Whether you want to refine a photograph (such as correct for under- or overexposure) or be adventurous with filters and creative montaging, with some forethought and planning — and some new skills garnered from this book — you will be able to accomplish your goals.

You can have it your way

Every photographer has a unique sense of aesthetics, and from a practical standpoint, every photography or design project poses unique challenges. We suggest you follow our step-by-step instructions to the letter the first time around, as you might follow recipes in a cookbook. Once you've mastered the techniques, feel free to concoct your own "technique recipes" as needed, to suit the images or assignments that you're working on.

Our photos or yours?

One approach, when following the step-by-step instructions in this book, is to use the low-resolution practice photos that we've made available for you to download (see the sidebar on page x and the directory on pages xi–xiv). An advantage of this approach is that you'll be able to monitor your progress closely by following the sequence of figures in the book.

Another approach is to use photos from your own inventory or that you download from a stock house. This offers the advantage of enabling you to practice on high-resolution files. Our instructions are generic enough to apply to different photos, provided you have access to a reasonably diverse assortment of subjects (e.g., landscapes, still lifes, portraits), and to some imperfect photos that need correction.

Stick with it

Although learning software is often fun, at times it can also be maddeningly confusing or frustrating. Not only do you need to learn how commands and features work (no easy accomplishment in itself), but to become really proficient, you need to learn when, for what purpose, and in what sequence it's best to use them. With patience, practice, and perseverance, fundamental editing steps and sequences will become second nature, and you will evolve into a pro user of Photoshop. You'll even experience occasional moments of clarity (between moments of cursing under your breath!) when a feature that had been trying your patience becomes comprehensible and everything, well... clicks.

Whether you want to become more technically proficient in Photoshop to give your photos a more professional edge or you want to explore it further to discover new creative avenues and tools, we hope this book helps you reach your personal goals. Equally important, we hope it makes your experience of using the program more enjoyable and rewarding.

— Elaine Weinmann and Peter Lourekas

Chapters at a glance

CONTENTS

★ Indicates topics which cover new (Photoshop CS4) features

Contents

REGISTER THIS BOOK!

Purchasing this book entitles you to more than just a couple of pounds of paper. If you register the book with Peachpit Press, you're also entitled to download copies of most of the images used throughout the book, which you can use to practice with as you follow the step-by-step tutorials. To get started, go to www.peachpit.com/photoshopcs4volume2.

This takes you to the book's page at the Peachpit Press website. Once there, click Register your book to log in to your account at peachpit.com. (if you don't already have an account, it takes just a few seconds to create one, and it's free).

After logging in, you'll need to enter the book's ISBN code, which you'll find on the back cover. Click Submit, and you're in! You'll be taken to a list of your registered books. Find *Photoshop CS4, volume 2: Visual QuickStart Guide* on the list, and click Access to protected content to get to the download page.

Please note that these images are low-resolution—not suitable for printing—and they are copyrighted by their owners, who have watermarked them to discourage unauthorized reproduction. They are for your personal use only, not for distribution.

INSTRUCTORS! READERS!

The Adobe Creative Suite upgrades approximately every year and a half. Although that pace leaves us huffing and puffing, we also welcome the challenge and innovations that each revision cycle presents us with. At the very least, our jobs are never boring. Moreover, compulsive perfectionists that we are, each upgrade also presents us with yet another opportunity to improve, refine, and redesign our books.

Is there a topic that you would like us to cover, or cover more in depth, or clarify, or explore from a different angle? Have you discovered a special workflow or sequence of commands that you'd like to share with us—and potentially with other readers? Let us know via email, by visiting the book's Web page (see "Register this Book!" above) and clicking the Feedback link.

Downloadable images

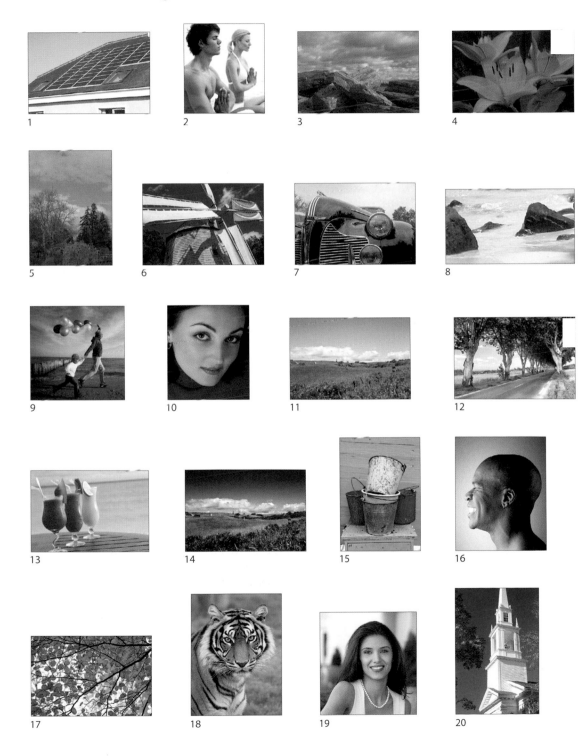

21

22

23

24

25

26

27

28

29

30

31

32

33

34

35

36

37

38

39

40

41

42

43

44

45

46

47

48

49

50

51

52

53

54

55

56

57

58

59

60

61

62

63

64

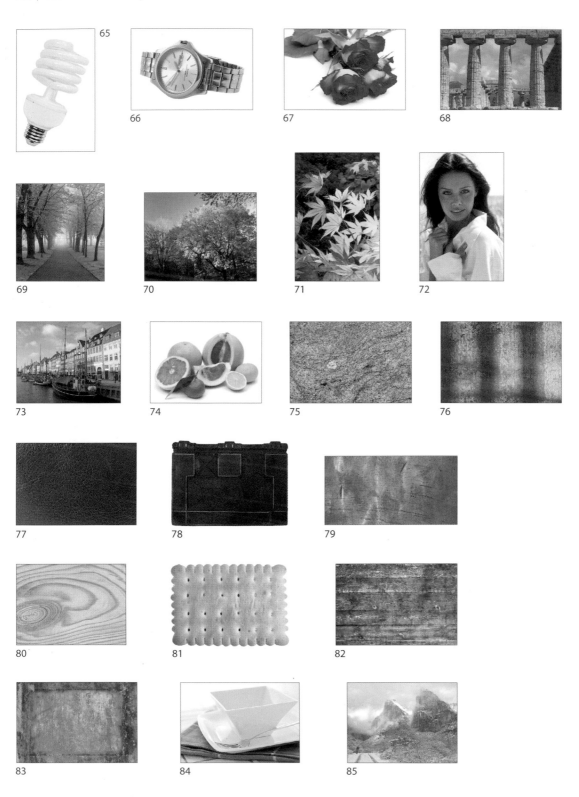

65

66

67

68

69

70

71

72

73

74

75

76

77

78

79

80

81

82

83

84

85

Although you may be tempted to start editing your images right away, you should make sure your display is properly calibrated and choose the appropriate color management settings first.

What is color management?

Each device in your workflow reads colors differently, from the camera to the display in Adobe Photoshop and finally to the printer. As a result, the colors you see through the viewfinder in your camera may not look the same on your computer display, let alone on a printout. A color management system can solve most of these color inconsistencies by acting as a color interpreter. It knows how each device and program interprets color and adjusts colors, if necessary, to keep them as consistent as possible when you shift your file among various devices and programs. With the proper color management settings in place, your colors will display and output more accurately.

Each device can capture and reproduce only a limited range (gamut) of colors, which is known as its color space. The mathematical description of the color space of each device is stored in a type of file called a color profile and is the key feature of any color management system. Each input device, such as a camera, embeds a color profile into the image files it produces. Photoshop then uses this embedded profile to determine how to display the document colors, or if a file doesn't have a profile, Photoshop uses data from the current working space instead (a color space that you've chosen for Photoshop) to display the document color.

To enable you to maintain color consistency throughout your workflow, in this chapter we'll show you how to set the color space of your digital camera to Adobe RGB, calibrate your display, choose the same color space for Photoshop, acquire the proper profiles for your intended printer and paper type, and finally, use those profiles to view a soft proof of your document onscreen. We recommend using the Adobe RGB (1998) color space because it encompasses a wider range of colors than the sRGB color space and is particularly well suited for inkjet printing.

In Chapter 15, color management will come into play once again as you learn how to choose the correct output profile for an inkjet printer.

COLOR MANAGEMENT

1

IN THIS CHAPTER

Setting your camera to the Adobe RGB color space

Most digital SLR cameras, and most of the high-end, advanced amateur digital cameras, have an onscreen menu that enables you to customize how the camera processes digital images. In this task, we'll demonstrate how to set a camera to the Adobe RGB color space using the example of a Canon EOS 40D, but you can follow the same basic procedure to set the color space for your camera model.

If you shoot photos in the JPEG format, you should choose Adobe RGB as the color space for your camera, regardless of the camera model. If you shoot raw files, these steps are optional, because you'll assign the Adobe RGB (1998) color space when converting your photos via the Adobe Camera Raw plug-in.

To set a camera to the Adobe RGB color space:

1. On the back of the camera, click the Menu button to access the menu on the LCD screen, then press the right arrow to select the Shooting Menu tab.**A**

2. Press the down arrow to select the **Color Space** category.**B** Press the Set button to shift to the submenu on the right (on a Nikon camera, press the proper arrow key instead).

3. Press the down arrow to select **Adobe RGB.C–D**

4. Press the Set button (on a Nikon, press the right arrow), then press the **Menu** button to exit the Menu screen.

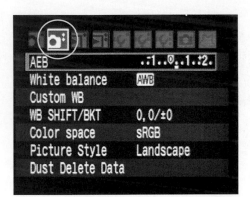

A On the Menu screen for our Canon camera, we chose the Shooting Menu tab.

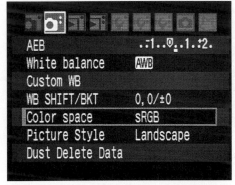

B We used the down arrow to select the Color Space category (we will press Set to get to the submenu).

C We chose Adobe RGB from the submenu (then will press Set to assign that option).

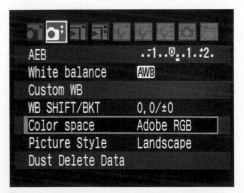

D Adobe RGB is now established as the color space for our camera.

Calibrating your display

Display types

There are two basic types of computer displays: CRT (cathode ray tube, as in a traditional TV set) and LCD (liquid crystal display, or flat panel). The display performance of a CRT fluctuates due to its analog technology and the fact that its display phosphors (which produce the glowing dots that you see onscreen) fade over time. A CRT display can be calibrated reliably for only around three years.

An LCD display uses a grid of fixed-size liquid crystals that filter color coming from a backlight source. Although you can adjust only the brightness on an LCD (not the contrast), the LCD digital technology offers more reliable color consistency than a CRT, without the characteristic flickering of a CRT. The newest LCD models provide good viewing angles, display accurate color, use the desired daylight temperature of 6500K for the white point (see below), and are produced under tighter manufacturing standards than CRTs. Moreover, the color profile that's provided with an LCD display (and that is installed in your system automatically) usually describes the display characteristics accurately.

➤ Both types of displays lose calibration gradually, and you may not notice the change until the colors are way off. To maintain color consistency, try to stick to a regular monthly calibration schedule.

Understanding the calibration settings

Three basic characteristics are adjusted when a display is calibrated: The brightness (white level) is set to a consistent working standard; the contrast (dark level) is set to the maximum value; and finally, a neutral gray (gray level) is established using equal values of R, G, and B. To adjust these characteristics, calibration devices evaluate the white point, black point, and gamma in the display.

➤ The white point data enables the display to project a pure white, which matches an industry-standard color temperature. Photographers normally use D65/6500K as the temperature setting for the white point.

➤ The black point is the darkest black a display is capable of projecting. All other dark shades will be lighter than this darkest black, thereby ensuring that shadow details display properly.

➤ The gamma defines how midtones are displayed onscreen. A gamma setting of 1.0 reproduces the linear brightness scale that is found in nature. Yet human vision responds to brightness in a nonlinear fashion, so this setting makes the screen look washed out. A higher gamma setting redistributes more of the midtones into the dark range, where our eyes are more sensitive, producing a more natural-looking image. Photography experts recommend using a gamma setting of 2.2 in both Windows and the Mac OS.

Buying a calibration device

The only way to properly calibrate a display is by using a hardware calibration device. Such a device will produce a profile with the proper white point, black point, and gamma data settings for your display. The Adobe color management system, in turn, will use this data to display colors in your Photoshop document with better accuracy.

If you're shopping for a calibration device, you'll notice a wide range in cost, from a colorimeter that will run you between $100 and $300 to much more costly, but more precise, high-end professional gadgets, such as a spectrophotometer. Instead of relying on subjective "eyeball" judgements, the colorimeters and step-by-step wizard tutorials that are included with these devices will enable you to achieve more accurate calibration.

Among moderately priced calibrators, our informal reading of hardware reviews and other industry publications has yielded the following as some of the current favorites: Spyder3Pro and Spyder3Elite by Datacolor; Eye-One Display 2 by X-Rite; and hueyPRO, which was developed jointly by Pantone and X-Rite.

The steps outlined here apply loosely to all three of the hardware display calibrators that are mentioned on the previous page. We happen to use Spyder3Elite.

To calibrate your display using a hardware device:

1. Set the room lighting to the usual level that you use for work. If you have a CRT, let it warm up for 30 minutes, to allow the display to stabilize.

2. Increase the brightness of your display to its highest level. In the Mac OS, if you have an Apple display, choose System Preferences > Displays and drag the Brightness slider to the far right. For a third-party display, or any display in Windows, use either an actual button on the display or a menu command in the OnScreen Display (OSD).

3. Launch the calibration application that you've installed, then follow the straightforward instructions in the "step-by-step wizard" screens. Proceed from one screen to the next, choosing options as you go.**A**

   The important information that you need to tell the application is: what type of display you have (CRT or LCD); the desired white point (choose D65/6500K); and the desired gamma (choose 2.2 for both Windows and Macintosh). If you're calibrating a CRT display, you may

see a few more instructional screens requesting more display setting choices.

4. After entering your display information, you'll be prompted to drape the hardware calibration sensor (the colorimeter) over the monitor. For an LCD, remember to clip on the baffle that's included with the device to prevent the suction cups from touching and potentially damaging the screen. Follow the instructions to align the sensor with the image onscreen (**A**, next page). Click OK or Continue to initiate a series of calibration tests, which will take around 5 or 10 minutes to complete.

5. After removing the calibration sensor, you'll be prompted to name your new display profile (**B**, next page). Include the date in the profile name, so you'll be able to tell which profile is the latest. The application will place the new profile in the correct location for use by your Windows or Macintosh operating system. The wizard will step you through one or two more screens (**C**, next page), then you're done. Upon launching, Photoshop will automatically be aware of the new display profile.

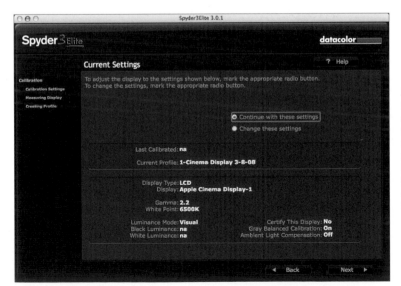

A We launched the Sypder3Elite application, then answered questions on two consecutive screens to tell the wizard software what features are present on our LCD monitor, clicking Next to get from one screen to the next. The resulting settings appeared on this Current Settings screen.

When this Measuring Display screen appeared, we aligned the colorimeter with the onscreen image, then clicked Continue to start the actual calibration process. (Note: Although the Spyder3Elite instructions state that the sensor can either be attached with suction cups to or draped over the LCD monitor, we play it safe by doing the latter.)

When the calibration was finished, we clicked Next, and this Specify Profile Name screen appeared. We included the monitor name and the current date in our profile name.

After we clicked Next again, this SpyderProof™ screen appeared. We clicked Switch to compare the pre- and postcalibration results, then clicked Next a last time to exit the software.

Choosing a color space for Photoshop

Next, you will choose a color space for Photoshop. If you use the program primarily for print work (whether outputting from a desktop printer or a commercial press), you can choose a color settings preset by following the simple steps below.

To set the color space to Adobe RGB (1998):

1. Choose Edit > **Color Settings** (Ctrl-Shift-K/ Cmd-Shift-K). The Color Settings dialog opens.**A**

2. Choose Settings: **North America Prepress 2** (foreign readers, choose an equivalent for your output device and geographic location). This preset changes the RGB working space to Adobe RGB (1998); it also sets the color management policies to the safe choice of Preserve Embedded Profiles, so each file you open in Photoshop will keep its own profile.

3. Click OK. (Note: The Adobe RGB (1998) color space includes more colors in the CMYK print range than the sRGB color space, which is designed for online output. For some reason, Adobe feels compelled to keep sRGB as the default RGB working space in the Color Settings dialog, which can spell disaster for print output.)

DOCUMENT-SPECIFIC COLOR

Photoshop supports document-specific color, meaning that each document keeps its own color profile. The profile controls how colors in the file look when you preview and edit them onscreen, and how they're converted upon output. If a document lacks an embedded profile, Photoshop will generate a preview based on the current working space. An RGB document without an embedded profile will be assigned the current RGB working space — Adobe RGB (1998), if you follow the instructions on this page — whereas a CMYK document without a profile will be assigned the current CMYK working space.

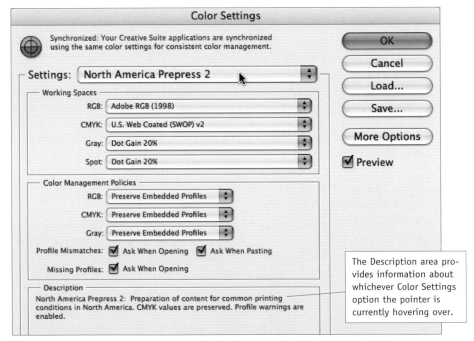

The Description area provides information about whichever Color Settings option the pointer is currently hovering over.

A North America Prepress 2 is chosen from the Settings menu in the Color Settings dialog.

For commercial printing, you can ask your print shop to recommend a Settings menu preset or a list of suggested settings. Even better, find out if they can supply you with a color settings (.csf) file that contains the correct Working Spaces and Color Management Policies settings for their press. If they send you a .csf file, all you need to do is install it in the proper location, as we show you here. Once installed, you'll be able to access it via the Settings menu in the Color Settings dialog.

To install custom color settings as a preset for the Creative Suite:

1. In Windows, put the file in C:\Documents and Settings\[user]\Application Data\Adobe\Color\Settings. (To learn how to display the Application Data folder, refer to Windows Help.)

   In the Mac OS, put the file in Users/[user name]/Library/Application Support/Adobe/Color/Settings.

2. To access your newly saved settings file, relaunch Photoshop, choose Edit > **Color Settings**, then choose the .csf file name from the **Settings** menu.

If your print shop supplies you with a list of recommended settings for the Color Settings dialog box—but not an actual .csf file—you can choose and then save that collection of settings as a .csf file.

To save custom color settings as a preset:

1. Choose Edit > **Color Settings** (Ctrl-Shift K/ Cmd-Shift-K). The Color Settings dialog opens.

2. Choose the recommended menu options and check the recommended boxes.

3. Click **Save**. In the Save dialog, enter a file name (we recommend including the printer type in the name, for easy reference), keep the .csf extension and the default location (the Settings folder), then click Save.

4. The Color Settings Comment dialog opens. Enter the name of the print shop and the printer type, to help you identify the preset, then click OK.

5. Note that the new settings preset is now listed on the Settings menu. Click OK to exit the Color Settings dialog.

Acquiring a printer profile

Thus far, you've learned how to set your camera to the Adobe RGB color space, calibrate your display, and specify Adobe RGB (1998) as the color space for Photoshop. Next, you need to acquire the necessary printer profile (or profiles) so you can incorporate color management into your specific printing setup.

To download a printer profile:

1. Most printer manufacturers have a website from which you can download either a profile for a specific printer/paper combination or a printer driver that contains a collection of specific printer/paper profiles. Be sure to choose a profile that matches the particular printer/paper combination that you're planning to use.

    If you have an Epson Stylus Photo inkjet printer, you can follow the images on this page to navigate through the epson.com website.**A–D**

    You could also download a profile for a specific printer/paper combo from the website for a paper manufacturer, such as ilford.com or museofineart.com.

    Note: The profiles for the newest printer models may not be available yet on these sites. Check back periodically.

2. After visiting the website, follow the installation instructions for the file you downloaded. To use the newly installed profile to proof a document onscreen, see the following page.

A On the Epson homepage for your geographic region, click Drivers & Support, then click Printers.

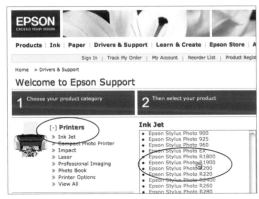

B Click Ink Jet, then scroll down and click your printer model on the list.

C On the page for the printer model, click the link below Drivers & Downloads for your platform. On the Drivers & Downloads page, click the Premium ICC Profiles for [printer name] link.

D On the Premium ICC Printer Profiles page, click the profile for your chosen paper type.

Proofing a document onscreen

In this final step in the color management setup, you'll create a custom preset for soft proofing, using settings for your specific inkjet printer and paper, then use that preset to view a soft proof (onscreen simulation) of how your colors will look in print.

To simulate an inkjet print onscreen:

1. Open an RGB image, then from the View > **Proof Setup** submenu, choose Custom. The Customize Proof Condition dialog opens.**A**

2. Check Preview, then from the **Device to Simulate** menu, choose the color profile for your particular inkjet printer and paper (the profile that you either downloaded from a website or that your printer driver installed).

3. Uncheck **Preserve RGB Numbers** to have Photoshop simulate how the colors will look when converted to the chosen profile. This option is available only if the color mode of the output profile chosen from the Device to Simulate menu matches the mode of the current file (e.g., if your image is in RGB Color mode and will be output to an RGB printer).

4. From the **Rendering Intent** menu, choose the **Perceptual** or **Relative Colorimetric** option to control how colors will change as the image is shifted from one profile to another. You can evaluate each intent via the preview. (For a description of the intents, see the sidebar on the next page.)

Check **Black Point Compensation** to improve the printing of blacks. With this option on, the full dynamic range of the image color space is mapped to the full dynamic range of the printer's color space. With this option off, blacks in the image may display or print as grays. We recommend checking this option when outputting a file to an inkjet printer.

5. *Optional:* For the Display Options (On-Screen), if available, check Simulate Paper Color to preview the white of the printing paper, as defined in the printer profile. For this simulation to work, the chosen printer profile must include the specifications for your printing paper.

6. To save your custom settings, click **Save**, enter a name (keep the .psf extension and the default location as the Proofing folder), then click Save. Your proofing preset is now available on the Customize Proof Condition menu, and also at the bottom of the View > Proof Setup submenu.

7. Click OK. View > **Proof Colors** will be checked automatically, enabling you to view the soft proof onscreen. Also, the Device to Simulate profile will be listed in the document title bar.

Note: A soft proof is merely an onscreen simulation of your print output. Colors in the file won't actually be converted to the chosen profile until you either change the document color mode (e.g., from RGB to CMYK) or send the file to print.

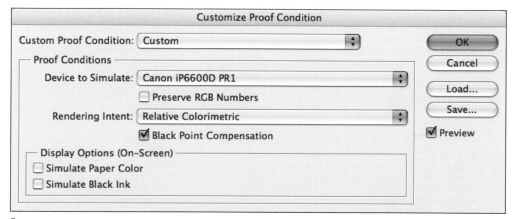

A To establish which printer the soft proof will simulate, in the Customize Proof Condition dialog, choose your printer model as the Device to Simulate.

Photoshop can also create a soft proof of your file to simulate how the RGB colors will look when printed with CMYK inks on a commercial press.

To proof colors for commercial printing:

1. Open your document, then from the View > **Proof Setup** submenu, choose **Custom**. The Customize Proof Condition dialog opens.

2. Check Preview, then from the **Device to Simulate** menu, choose the color profile for the type of commercial press and paper stock the file will be printed on. Click OK.

3. The View > **Proof Colors** feature will be checked automatically. You can uncheck it at any time to turn off soft proofing (Ctrl-Y/Cmd-Y).

➤ The Working CMYK option on the Device to Simulate menu in the Customize Proof Condition dialog is automatically set to the current CMYK Working Space that is specified in Edit > Color Settings.

Moving on

If you followed the instructions in this chapter, you've successfully completed the first (and most lengthy) part of the color management setup. You set your camera to the Adobe RGB color space, calibrated your display, chose Adobe RGB (1998) as the color space for Photoshop, acquired the proper profile for your inkjet printer and paper type, and created a soft-proof setting using that profile. You'll need to focus on color management once more when you prepare your file for printing. In Chapter 15, you'll learn how to let Photoshop handle color conversions for an inkjet printer, using the printer profiles that were used for soft proofing.

The benefit of using color management is that it helps ensure color consistency among all the devices in your workflow—from camera to display to printer. Now, as you use Photoshop to enhance your photos, you can be confident that the colors in your printout will closely match what you see onscreen.

In the next chapter, you'll learn how to download your digital photo files, then use Adobe Bridge to locate, sort, organize, preview, and manage them. And don't miss Chapter 3, which covers the powerful Camera Raw plug-in. Camera Raw lets you apply extensive adjustments to your photos before opening them into Photoshop.

THE RENDERING INTENTS

➤ Perceptual changes colors in a way that seems natural to the human eye, while attempting to preserve the overall appearance of the image. It's a good choice for continuous-tone images.

➤ Saturation changes colors with the intent of preserving vivid colors, but in so doing it compromises color fidelity. It's a good choice for charts and business graphics, however, which normally contain fewer colors than continuous-tone images.

➤ Absolute Colorimetric maintains color accuracy only for colors that fall within the destination color gamut (i.e., the color range of your printer), but in so doing it sacrifices the accuracy of colors that are out of gamut.

➤ Relative Colorimetric, the default intent for all the Adobe predefined settings in the Color Settings dialog, compares the white, or highlight, of your document's color space to the white of the destination color space (the white of the paper, in the case of print output), and shifts colors where needed. This is the best Rendering Intent choice for documents in which most of the colors fall within the color range of the destination gamut, because it preserves more of the original colors.

You shot some photos with your new digital camera. Now what?

Starting on this page, you'll learn how to download images from a digital camera to a computer. The remainder of the chapter is devoted to the Adobe Bridge application, which lets you preview and open images into Photoshop and Camera Raw* (and also works with the other programs in the Adobe Creative Suite). You will customize the Bridge window for your needs; preview, examine, rate, sort, filter, and stack image thumbnails; open files into Photoshop; embed metadata into your files; use the Find command to locate files; create thumbnail collections; and choose Bridge preferences.

Downloading photos

When you shoot digitally, your camera stores the photos on a removable memory card, such as a CompactFlash (CF) or Secure Digital (SD) card. To get the photos from your camera into a computer, you can remove the memory card and insert it into a card reader device, then download the photos via a USB or FireWire cable, depending on which connection your card reader supports (FireWire is faster).

For downloading photos, we use the Photo Downloader application, which is included with Bridge 2 and later. We recommend using Photo Downloader instead of the default system application in Windows or Macintosh for several reasons: it's fully integrated with Bridge, it lets you download raw digital photos, it provides simple but useful file management and naming controls, and it lets you embed copyright information into your photo files.

Continued on the following page

USING BRIDGE

2

IN THIS CHAPTER

*To open images into Camera Raw, see page 42.

To download photos via Photo Downloader:

1. Take the card out of your camera and insert it into the appropriate slot in your card reader.

2. Plug the card reader into your computer. If the default system application for acquiring photos launches, exit/quit that application.*

3. Launch **Adobe Bridge** (see page 15), then click the **Get Photos from Camera** button ⬛ at the top of the Bridge window.★

   The Photo Downloader dialog opens. If an alert dialog appears and you want to make Photo Downloader the default capture application, click Yes; if not, click No.

4. From the **Get Photos From** menu in the Source area, select your card reader or camera.

5. Click **Advanced Dialog** to display advanced options.**A**

6. In the **Save Options** area, do the following:

   To change the save location, click **Browse/ Choose**, then navigate to the desired folder. Click OK/Choose to select that folder and return to the Photo Downloader dialog.

   To create a new subfolder for the photos within the folder you just selected, choose a naming convention from the **Create Subfolder(s)** menu (**A**, next page) or choose **Custom Name** and type a folder name in the field below. If you prefer not to create a subfolder, choose None.

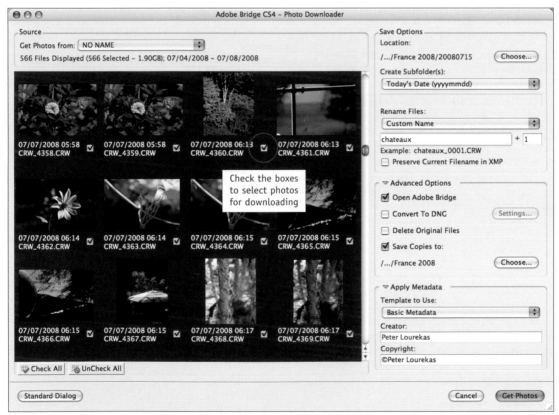

A This Advanced dialog of the Photo Downloader contains many of the same options as the Standard dialog, plus metadata features and the option to specify which photos are to be downloaded.

*In Windows, the first time you connect a camera or card reader, a dialog may open, offering a list of steps to take. Choose Download Images using Adobe Bridge CS4 and Always Do the Selected Action, then click OK. Skip to step 4, above.

To assign names and short sequential numbers to your files to replace the long default numbers that your camera assigned, on the **Rename Files** menu, choose **Custom Name**, then enter a name and a starting number.**B** Use a short but descriptive name to help you locate the files via searches. Consider including the date of the shoot in the name; having this unique file name will prevent the files from being overwritten unintentionally. A sample of the name displays in the Example field.

Note: Some camera models create a small .thm file for each raw photo, which contains nonessential image data and will be hidden in Bridge by default. If you want these files to be downloaded, keep the box checked below all the .thm thumbnails.**C**

7. *Optional:* Check **Preserve Current Filename in XMP** to preserve the option to access the original file names in the future.

8. In the Advanced Options area, check **Open Adobe Bridge** to have the photos display automatically in a new window in Bridge when the downloading process is completed.

Continued on the following page

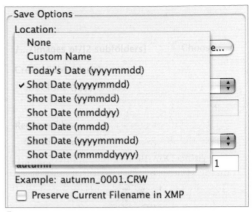

A To name your folder with the shot date of the photo, choose a Shot Date option on the Create Subfolder(s) menu. A subfolder will be created for each date found among the selected photos, and photos will be placed into folders labeled with corresponding dates.

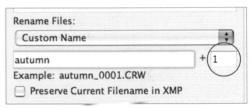

B Via the Custom Name option, you can rename your photos and include an identifying number. By default, the dialog displays the next number after the one that was assigned to the last downloaded file. Either keep that number to continue the sequential numbering or enter a new starting number.

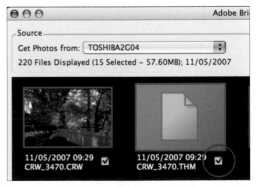

C If your camera model creates .thm files that you wish to download along with your photos, keep the box below the .thm thumbnails checked.

WHAT IS DNG?

Photographers wonder what the best file format is for saving digital photos — for the present and future — so they can be accessed and printed over, say, a 20-year period or longer. Currently, there is no one standard raw format; each camera maker has its own proprietary method for creating raw files. And should a manufacturer discontinue its proprietary method, raw photos from their cameras could then be incompatible with commonly used image-editing software.

DNG, an open-standard file format that was developed by Adobe, may someday become a popular long-term solution. It preserves all the raw, unprocessed pixel information that the camera records. Adobe has made the coding for DNG publicly available ("open standard") to other interested companies with the desire that it will be adopted for a wide range of hardware devices and software applications. In the future, hopefully, DNG files will be universally readable.

9. *Optional:* If you like to be selective about which raw photos are converted to the DNG format (as we do), use the Save Options dialog in Camera Raw. Or if you prefer to convert all the raw photos you're downloading to this format now, check Convert to DNG. (To learn more about DNG, see the sidebar on the previous page). This format is not recommended for digital photos that are captured as JPEG or TIFF.

Click **Settings**. The DNG Conversion Settings dialog opens.**A** Do the following:

To enable a thumbnail to display for a DNG file, it must contain a JPEG preview. Choose a size from the JPEG Preview menu. Medium Size produces an adequate preview without greatly increasing the file size.

Check Compressed (Lossless) to decrease the file size with no loss of image detail.

For the Image Conversion Method, click Preserve Raw Image to maximize the amount of original data that's preserved and available for reediting.

For Original Raw File, we don't recommend checking Embed Original Raw File (which would embed the large raw file into the DNG file), because doing so would increase the file size substantially, and because we trust that Adobe and other companies will continue to provide support for the DNG format. Check this option only if you must preserve access to the original raw image.

Click OK.

10. In the Photo Downloader dialog, be sure to check **Save Copies To**, then click Browse/ Choose to send copies of your photos to a designated external hard drive. This is your emergency backup!

11. In the **Apply Metadata** area, if you've created a metadata template already (see page 31), choose it from the Template to Use menu; otherwise, manually enter Creator and Copyright info to be added to the metadata of all the photos you're downloading. (The metadata info displays in the Metadata panel in Bridge.)

12. Do either of the following:

To download all the photos from your memory card, click **Check All**.

To download specific photos, below the thumbnail window, click **UnCheck All**, then check the box below each photo to be downloaded. Or click, then Shift-click a sequence of photos (and any corresponding .thm files), then check the box for one of them; a check mark will appear below all the selected photos.

13. Click **Get Photos** to begin the downloading process. When it is completed, the Photo Downloader application quits automatically. If you checked the Open Adobe Bridge option, your photos will display in a new window in Bridge; if not, navigate to the folder you chose in step 6 (see step 1 on page 18).

14. Before you proceed to managing your photos in Bridge, insert a blank DVD-R disk into your computer and burn copies of them to the DVD as a permanent archive. (In the Mac OS, you can do this via drag-and-drop in the Finder.) For more information, see the Help file for your system.

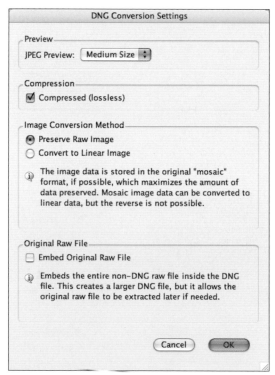

A In the DNG Conversion Settings dialog, choose options to control how your raw photos will be converted and archived to the DNG format.

Taking a look at Adobe Bridge

With its ability to display large thumbnail previews of files from all the Adobe Creative Suite applications, Adobe Bridge is the best vehicle for opening files into Photoshop—and for opening raw photos into Camera Raw—plus it offers a host of other useful features. You can use Bridge to preview, examine, rate, and sort thumbnails; organize thumbnails into expandable stacks; assign keywords and other metadata to make your files more searchable; embed copyright notices; and view data (metadata), such as the specific shooting conditions the digital camera recorded into your photos.

To launch Bridge: ★

Do one of the following:

On the Application bar in Photoshop, click the **Launch Bridge** button ▩ (Ctrl-Alt-O/Cmd-Option-O).

In Program Files\Adobe\Adobe Bridge CS4 in Windows or in Applications/Adobe Bridge CS4 in the Mac OS, double-click the **Adobe Bridge CS4** application icon.▩

In the Mac OS, click the **Adobe Bridge CS4** icon ▩ on the **Dock**.

The Adobe Bridge window opens.**A**

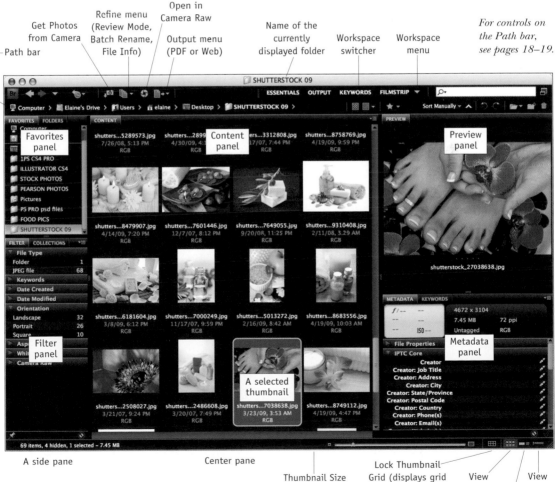

Get Photos from Camera

Refine menu (Review Mode, Batch Rename, File Info)

Open in Camera Raw

Output menu (PDF or Web)

Path bar

Name of the currently displayed folder

Workspace switcher

Workspace menu

For controls on the Path bar, see pages 18–19.

Favorites panel

Content panel

Preview panel

Filter panel

A selected thumbnail

Metadata panel

A side pane

Center pane

Thumbnail Size slider

Lock Thumbnail Grid (displays grid lines between full thumbnails)

View Content as Thumbnails

View Content as List

View Content as Details

A Features of the Bridge window are identified above. You'll learn their function throughout this chapter.

Choosing a workspace for Bridge

To reconfigure the Bridge window quickly, choose one of the predefined workspaces. (To create and save custom workspaces, see pages 23–24.)

To choose a workspace for Bridge: ★

Do one of the following:

In the workspace switcher on the toolbar, click **Essentials**, **Keywords**, **Filmstrip**, **Metadata** (List View for the thumbnails), **Preview**, **Light Table**, **Folders**, or a user-saved workspace.**A** (To display more workspace names, pull the vertical bar to the left. **B**)

From the **Workspace** menu on the workspace switcher, choose a workspace **C** (and **A–C**, next page).

Press the **shortcut** for one of the first six workspaces on the switcher (as listed on the Workspace menu): Ctrl-1/Cmd-F1 through Ctrl-6/Cmd-F6. The shortcuts are assigned automatically to the first six workspaces on the switcher based on their current left-to-right order.

➤ The Output workspace is used for different purposes than the other workspaces. To use it to create a Web gallery, see pages 342–347.

To change the order of workspaces on the switcher: ★

Drag a workspace name to the left or right.

Right-click/Control-click a workspace name and choose a different name from the context menu.

A Click a workspace on the workspace switcher.   Workspace menu

B To reveal more workspace names, drag the vertical bar to the left.

C The Filmstrip workspace features a large preview of the currently selected thumbnail.

A In the Essentials workspace, all the panel groups are showing, and the Center pane is wider than the side panes.

B In the Preview workspace, the Metadata and Keywords panels are hidden to make room for a larger preview, and the thumbnails display vertically (rather than horizontally, as in the Filmstrip workspace).

C The Light Table workspace allows you to display the largest number of thumbnails in a folder, because the Content panel occupies the entire Bridge window.

► To resize the thumbnails for any workspace, drag the Thumbnail Size slider, which you'll find at the bottom of the Bridge window.

Previewing images in Bridge

In Bridge CS4, there are controls on the toolbar for navigating to and opening folders, A in addition to controls in the Folders and Favorites panels.

To select and preview images in Bridge: ★

1. Do any of the following:

   In the **Folders** panel, navigate to the folder to be opened. Scroll upward or downward, or expand or collapse any folder by clicking the arrowhead.

   Display the contents of a folder by clicking its icon in the **Folders** panel or by double-clicking its thumbnail in the **Content** panel. Note: If folder icons aren't displaying, choose View > Show Folders (to make the check mark appear).

   To step back or forward through recently viewed folders, click the **Go Back** button or the **Go Forward** button at the top of the Bridge window. A

   Click a folder that you've placed in the **Favorites** panel (see the sidebar on the next page).

   Choose from a list of Favorites or Recent Folders on the **Go to Parent or Favorites** menu at the top of the Bridge window.

   Click a folder name on the **Path** bar (Window > Path Bar).

   From one of the menus on the **Path** bar, choose a folder. If another submenu displays, click yet another folder; repeat until you arrive at the desired folder.

   ➤ To display all the thumbnails for files in the current folder, including the files in any nested subfolders, choose Show Items from Subfolders from its menu. To restore the original hierarchy, click the Cancel Show Items from Subfolders button.

2. In the **Content** panel, do either of the following:

   Click an image thumbnail. A colored border will appear around it, and data about the file will be listed in the Metadata panel (if displayed). An enlarged preview of the image will also display in the Preview panel (if displayed).

   To select multiple nonconsecutive thumbnails, Ctrl-click/Cmd-click them; B or click the first thumbnail in a series of consecutive thumbnails, then Shift-click the last one.

   ➤ When thumbnails are grouped in a stack, the first thumbnail in the stack has a number in the upper left corner. To display all the thumbnails in a stack, click the number; to collapse the stack, click the number again (see page 27).

   ➤ To preview thumbnails in the Content panel sequentially, press the arrow keys on the keyboard.

   ➤ You can rearrange individual or multiple-selected thumbnails by dragging them.

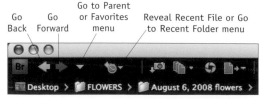

Go Back | Go Forward | Go to Parent or Favorites menu | Reveal Recent File or Go to Recent Folder menu

A These are the navigation controls on the Path bar.

B Ctrl-click/Cmd-click to select multiple image thumbnails.

You can control whether thumbnails and the preview render quickly but at low resolution, or more slowly but at high resolution.

To choose preview quality options: ★

From the **Thumbnail Quality and Preview** menu ▦ on the Bridge toolbar, choose a preference for the thumbnail quality: **A**

Always High Quality, the default setting, displays high-resolution thumbnails and previews, whether the thumbnails are selected or not, but renders them the most slowly.

Prefer Embedded (Faster) displays low-resolution thumbnails and previews, and is a suitable choice when you need to display many images quickly.

High Quality on Demand displays high-resolution thumbnails and previews for selected thumbnails only. This option is a good compromise between the other two. It's a good choice when you're downloading a large number of photos.

➤ For lower quality but faster previewing, click the Browse Quickly by Preferring Embedded Images button ▦ on the Bridge Path bar, which enables the Prefer Embedded (Faster) option. Click the button again to restore the current setting on the Thumbnail Quality and Preview menu.

➤ The Generate 100% Previews option on the Thumbnail Quality and Preview menu saves actual-size JPEG versions of thumbnails to disk, to produce higher-quality previews for the loupe and for 100% view in Slideshow mode. This option consumes a considerable amount of disk space, so we prefer to keep it unchecked.

PLAYING FAVORITES

➤ Via check boxes in the Favorite Items area of Edit/ Adobe Bridge CS4 > Preferences > General, you can control which folders appear in the top part of the Favorites panel.

➤ To add a folder to the user-created list in the lower part of the Favorites panel, drag the folder icon from the Content panel (in the center pane) or from the Desktop into the Favorites panel, and release the mouse when the pointer with a "+" displays; or click the folder and choose File > Add to Favorites.

➤ To remove a folder from the list of Favorites, click it, then choose File > Remove from Favorites.

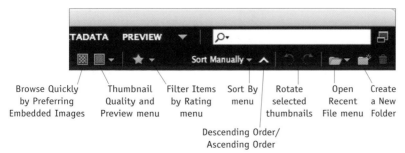

Browse Quickly by Preferring Embedded Images · Thumbnail Quality and Preview menu · Filter Items by Rating menu · Sort By menu · Rotate selected thumbnails · Open Recent File menu · Create a New Folder

Descending Order/ Ascending Order

A These controls are available on the right side of the Path bar in Bridge.

To compare image previews:

1. In Bridge, click or choose the **Filmstrip** or **Preview** workspace.

2. In the **Content** panel, Ctrl-click/Cmd-click two or more thumbnails.**A**

3. Large versions of the selected thumbnails will display in the **Preview** panel.

4. *Optional:* Ctrl-click/Cmd-click to add more thumbnails to the panel; Ctrl-click/Cmd-click a selected thumbnail (Content panel) to deselect it and remove it from the Preview panel.

To display a full-screen preview of an image thumbnail: ★

Press **Spacebar** to display a full-screen preview of the currently selected thumbnail and hide the Bridge window temporarily. Press Spacebar again to redisplay the Bridge window.

➤ Click the full-screen preview to display it at 100% view; click it again to restore the preview to its full-screen size.

To inspect picture details with a loupe:

1. To make the loupe (a magnifier) appear, click an image in the Preview panel or click the frontmost image in Review mode (see the following page).**B** Note: If the loupe doesn't appear, it's because Ctrl-click/Cmd-click Opens the Loupe When Previewing or Reviewing is checked in Preferences > General (for Bridge; see page 37). If this is the case, Ctrl-click/Cmd-click the image to make the loupe appear. ★

2. Click an area to be examined. By default, pixels display in the loupe at 100% view (the zoom level is listed below the preview image). Press + to zoom in on the loupe display or – to zoom out. To examine a different area, click that area or drag the loupe to it.

3. *Optional:* If you're previewing two images with two loupes, you can Ctrl-drag/Cmd-drag either loupe to move them in unison.

4. Click the loupe to remove it.

B You can use the loupe to inspect fine details.

A We Ctrl/Cmd clicked two image thumbnails to compare them in the Preview panel.

In Review Mode, multiple large image previews display on a black background.**A** You can cycle through the images in carousel fashion, or remove them to narrow down the selection for grouping as a stack (see page 27) or as a collection (see pages 35–36).

To view images in Review mode: ★

1. Open a folder of images; or click a thumbnail stack; or select five or more image thumbnails by clicking with Ctrl/Cmd or Shift held down.

2. From the **Refine** menu  at the top of the Bridge window, choose **Review Mode** (Ctrl-B/Cmd-B). The selected images will appear as large previews, and the Bridge window will be hidden temporarily.

3. To rotate the carousel, do any of the following:

   Drag any image preview to the left or right.

   Click a non-enlarged image preview to bring it to the forefront.

Click (and keep clicking) the Go Forward or Go Backward button in the lower left corner, or press the left or right arrow key.

4. To examine the frontmost (enlarged) image with a loupe, click that image. Drag the loupe to move it; click the loupe to remove it.

5. To take the frontmost image out of the carousel, click the down-pointing arrow in the lower left corner, or drag it to the bottom of your screen. This won't delete the actual file.

6. To exit Review mode, press Esc, or click the in the lower right corner.

7. After exiting Review mode, click any image thumbnail to deselect the rest.

A We Ctrl/Cmd clicked several image thumbnails, then pressed Ctrl-B/Cmd-B to display them in Review mode.

Opening files into Photoshop

You can open as many files into Photoshop as your currently available RAM and scratch disk space allow. (Note: To open a raw or JPEG digital photo into Camera Raw, see page 42.)

To open files from Bridge into Photoshop:

1. Select one or more image thumbnails (Shift-click or Ctrl-click/Cmd-click to select multiple thumbnails), then press Ctrl-O/Cmd-O or right-click/Ctrl-click and choose **Open**. Photoshop will launch, if the program isn't already running, and the image(s) will appear onscreen.

2. The Embedded Profile Mismatch alert dialog will appear if the file's color profile doesn't match the current working space.**A** Click **Use the Embedded Profile (Instead of the Working Space)** if you must keep the document's current profile, or for better consistency with your color management workflow, click **Convert Document's Colors to the Working Space** to convert the profile to the current working space. Click OK.

   If the Missing Profile alert dialog appears,**B** click **Assign Working RGB: Adobe RGB (1998)** to assign the profile that you chose as your working space when you chose color management settings in Chapter 1.

   Note: If you double-click a thumbnail, the file or selected files will open into Photoshop or Camera Raw, depending on the file type, the status of the **Double-Click Edits Camera Raw Settings in Bridge** option in Bridge Preferences (see page 37), and the current **JPEG and TIFF Handling** settings in the Camera Raw Preferences dialog (see page 40).

➤ To get to Bridge from Photoshop, click the Go to Bridge button [Br] on the Application bar.★

To reopen a recently opened file:

Choose the desired file name from the **Open Recent File** menu ▬ on the right side of the Path bar.★

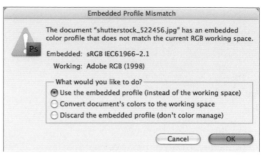

A If the Embedded Profile Mismatch alert dialog appears, indicate whether you want to use the embedded profile or convert the file to the current working space.

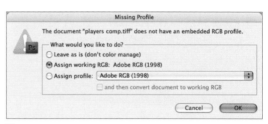

B If the Missing Profile alert dialog appears, click Assign Working RGB to convert the file to the current working space.

DECIPHERING THE BADGES

You may see one or both of these icons in the upper right corner of some of your image thumbnails:

BADGE	WHAT IT SIGNIFIES
⬆	The file was opened and modified in Camera Raw
⬚	The file was opened and cropped in Camera Raw

OTHER WAYS TO GET IMAGES INTO PHOTOSHOP

You're not limited to using images from a digital camera, although doing so will let you take advantage of the powerful, nondestructive adjustment controls in the Camera Raw plug-in. Other options are to scan imagery, such as original artwork or photographs, on a flatbed scanner; scan transparencies on a slide scanner; download stock photos from an online resource; or place or drag and drop files from Adobe Illustrator. (And remember, you can create images, patterns, or textures from scratch in Photoshop by using various tools and filters.)

Customizing the Bridge window

To further customize the Bridge workspace, you can resize, move, or minimize any of the panels. And if you save your new layout as a user-created workspace (see the instructions on the next page), you'll be able to access it again quickly at any time.

To customize the Bridge panes and panels:

Do any of the following: **A**

To make a panel or panel group **taller** or **shorter**, drag its horizontal bar upward or downward.

To make a whole pane **wider** or **narrower**, drag its vertical bar sideways; the adjacent pane resizes accordingly.

When a side pane contains multiple panels, you can **minimize** (or expand) any panel group by double-clicking its tab.

To move a panel into a different **group**, drag the panel tab (name), and release the mouse when the blue drop zone border appears around the desired group.

To display a panel as a separate **group**, drag its tab between two panels, and release the mouse when the horizontal blue drop zone line appears.

To resize the thumbnails, drag the **Thumbnail Size** slider or click the **Smaller Thumbnail Size** button ▭ or **Larger Thumbnail Size** button. ▭

➤ To hide (or show) the side panes, press Tab or double-click the vertical bar between two panes. To display just the Content panel in a compact window, click the Compact Mode button ◱ in the upper right corner of the Bridge window; click it again to restore the full window.

➤ To change the background shades for the Bridge interface, see page 37.

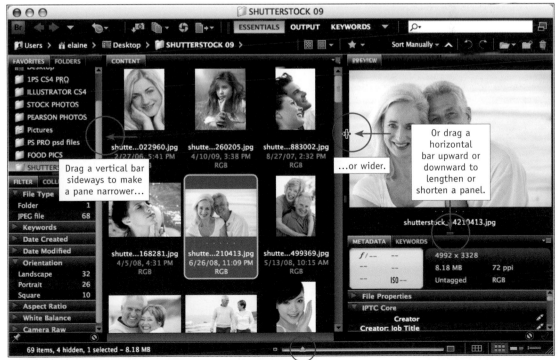

A You can customize any of the preset Bridge workspaces to suit your needs.

Thumbnail Size slider

Saving custom workspaces

If you save your customized workspaces, you'll be able to access them again quickly at any time and will avoid having to set up your workspace each time you launch Bridge.

To save a custom workspace for Bridge: ★

1. Choose a size and location for the overall Bridge window onscreen, arrange the panel sizes and groups as desired, choose a thumbnail size for the Content panel, choose a sorting order from the Sort By menu at the top of the Bridge window (see page 26), and click the desired View Content button (see page 31).

2. From the **Workspace** menu on the workspace switcher, choose **New Workspace**. The New Workspace dialog opens.**A**

3. Enter a Name for the workspace, check Save Window Location as Part of Workspace and/or Save Sort Order as Part of Workspace (both are optional), then click Save.

   Note: Your new workspace will be listed first on the workspace switcher, and will be assigned the first shortcut (Ctrl-1/Cmd-F1). To change the order of workspaces on the bar, drag any workspace name sideways to a different slot. The shortcuts are assigned automatically based on the current left-to-right order of the workspaces.

➤ To delete a user-saved workspace, from the Workspace menu, choose Delete Workspace. From the menu in the dialog, choose the workspace to be deleted, then click Delete.

Resetting the Bridge workspace

When you make a manual change to a saved workspace, the change sticks with that workspace even when you switch back and forth between workspaces. For example, if you were to change the thumbnail size for the Filmstrip workspace, click the Essentials workspace, then click back on the Filmstrip workspace, the thumbnail size you chose for it would remain (for Filmstrip only). Via the commands for resetting workspaces, you can restore the default settings either to a specific predefined (Adobe) or user-saved workspace, or to all the predefined workspaces.

To reset a Bridge workspace: ★

Do either of the following:

To restore the default settings to a preset or user-saved workspace, display that workspace, then choose **Reset Workspace** from the Workspace menu.

To restore the default settings to all the predefined (Adobe) workspaces, choose **Reset Standard Workspaces** from the Workspace menu.

A Use the New Workspace dialog to name your custom workspace and choose options for it.

Developing a workflow for managing digital photos in Bridge

Basic setup tasks

► Create and **save custom workspaces** for different purposes that incorporate the panels, panel sizes, and thumbnail sizes that you use most often. Arrange them on the switcher in the order in which you are most likely to use them. For example, you could choose the Essentials workspace, enlarge the thumbnails and the Preview panel, and save that configuration as one custom workspace, then choose the Filmstrip workspace, customize it to your liking, and save that configuration as another workspace.

► Create **metadata templates**, including a basic, all-purpose template for embedding your customary contact and copyright information.

► Enter **IPTC metadata** via the Metadata panel, and keywords via the **Keywords** panel.

A suggested workflow

The following is the workflow we typically follow in Bridge. You can use this scenario as a general guideline to develop a sequence that works for you.

► Use the **Photo Downloader** to rename your photos, embed copyright info, and choose an external hard drive for your backup copies (you can also convert files to the DNG format at this time).

► From the **Thumbnail Quality and Preview** menu ■ on the Path bar in Bridge, choose Always High Quality.

► **Display** your **folder** of downloaded photos, then get up and stretch while Bridge generates the thumbnail previews.

► Embed creator contact and copyright information in all the photos by applying your **metadata template**.

► Choose the **Light Table** workspace via the Workspace switcher or menu to fill the Bridge window with your photo thumbnails. Press Ctrl-T/Cmd-T to hide the metadata.

► Select the obvious losers, press Alt-Delete/Option-Delete to apply a **reject** rating to them (see the next page), then choose View > **Show Reject Files** (to remove the check mark) to hide them from view.

► Choose the **Preview** workspace (or a user-saved workspace that has similar characteristics), then select, view, compare, and examine shots of the same scene or subject one, two, or three at a time.

► Assign **star** ratings to thumbnails: first to the obvious winners and then to the maybes. You can do this via shortcuts or via the context menu in the Preview panel or in Review mode, or via shortcuts in Slideshow mode.

► To examine image thumbnails, do any of the following: Press the **Spacebar** to display the currently selected thumbnail as a full-screen preview; select five or more thumbnails and press Ctrl-B/Cmd-B to display them in **Review** mode; or click the preview image to inspect a minute detail with the loupe.

► **Raise** or **lower** any of the star **ratings** as you discover subtle differences among the photos.

► Assign descriptions and keywords to selected thumbnails via the **Metadata** panel (IPTC Core category) or the **Keywords** panel.

► Via the **Filter** panel, filter thumbnails by **Rating**, **Keywords**, or other criteria.

► Organize thumbnails into **stacks** and/or collections based on common similarities, such as their subject matter.

► Open one or more photos into **Camera Raw** (see the next chapter) for exposure corrections and other adjustments.

MOVING FILES OR FOLDERS VIA BRIDGE

If you need to move or copy a file or folder from one location to another, in Bridge, right-click/Ctrl-click and, from the Move To or Copy To submenu, choose a folder, or select Choose Folder to open a navigation dialog.

Rating and sorting thumbnails

Using star and reject ratings, the Filter panel, and a sorting method, you'll be able to narrow the display of thumbnails down to the best of the lot, and quickly locate the ones you need.

To rate thumbnails:

1. Click a thumbnail or select multiple thumbnails that you consider to be "in the running," then press Ctrl-1/Cmd-1 to assign a **star** rating to them. You can assign further ratings in a hierarchy by pressing Ctrl/Cmd 1, 2, 3, 4, or 5.

2. To apply the **Reject** rating to selected thumbnails that you want to remove from view but not actually delete from your hard drive, press Alt-Delete/Option-Delete (not Ctrl/Cmd-Delete!). Use the View > **Show Reject Files** command to show or hide rejected thumbnails.

➤ To quickly remove a Reject or star rating from selected thumbnails, press Ctrl-0/Cmd-0.

➤ To apply ratings in Slideshow mode, see pages 28–29.

The current sorting order controls the sequence in which thumbnails display in the Content panel. It applies to all folders and thumbnails, not just to one folder in particular.

To choose a sorting order: ★

From the **Sort By** menu on the Path bar, choose a sorting order (such as By Date Created).**A** Thumbnails (except those in stacks) will be rearranged in the Content panel.

➤ Click the Ascending Order ▲ or Descending Order ▼ arrowhead to reverse the order.

Filtering thumbnails

The Filter panel lists data specific to files in the current folder, such as their star ratings and date created. You can control which thumbnails display by checking specific criteria. A thumbnail must match all checked criteria in order to display.

To filter the display of thumbnails: ★

Do either of the following:

On the **Filter Items by Rating** menu on the Bridge toolbar,**B** check the desired criteria.

On the **Filter** panel, check listings within one or more categories, such as Labels or Ratings, to display only thumbnails that meet those criteria.**C** For example, to display only files that have a Reject rating, check Reject in the Ratings category; to display thumbnails that were assigned specific keywords, click those keywords (see page 33). (To redisplay hidden thumbnails, click to remove the check mark.)

OTHER FILTER PANEL OPTIONS	
TASK	**METHOD**
Control which categories can display in the panel	Check or uncheck options on the panel menu ▤
Apply the current panel criteria when displaying other folders	Click the Keep Filter When Browsing button 📌
Remove all visible check marks from the panel	Click the Clear Filter button ⊘ or press Ctrl-Alt-A/Cmd-Option-A

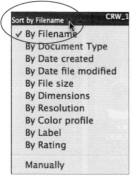

A Choose a sorting order for thumbnails from the Sort By menu on the Path bar.

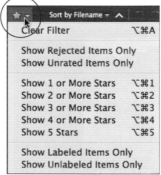

B Filter the display of thumbnails via the Filter Items by Rating menu.

C Because we checked the two-star option under Ratings in the Filter panel, only thumbnails matching that criterion display in the Content panel.

Using thumbnail stacks

Another good way to control how many thumbnails display at a given time is by grouping them in stacks (say, in categories, such as landscapes, shots of the same subject, etc.).

To create a stack:

1. Shift-click or Ctrl-click/Cmd-click to select multiple thumbnails. The first one you click will become the "stack thumbnail" (it will display at the top of the stack).

2. Press Ctrl-G/Cmd-G or right-click/Control-click and choose Stack > **Group as Stack**. The number in the upper left corner of a stack indicates how many thumbnails it contains.

To select the thumbnails in a stack:

Do either of the following: **A**

To **select** and **display** all the thumbnails in a stack, click the stack number. Click it again to collapse the stack. The stack stays selected.

To **select** all the thumbnails in a stack while keeping the stack **collapsed**, Alt-click/Option-click the stack thumbnail (not the number).

To rearrange thumbnails within a stack:

To **move** a thumbnail to a different position in an expanded stack, click it to deselect the other selected thumbnails, then drag it to a new position (as shown by the colored drop zone line).

To move a whole stack:

1. Alt-click/Option-click a stack that's in its collapsed state, to fully select it.

2. Drag the image thumbnail (not the border).

➤ If you drag the top thumbnail of an unselected stack, you'll move just that thumbnail, not the whole stack.

To add a thumbnail to a stack:

Drag a thumbnail into a stack.

To remove thumbnails from a stack:

1. Click the stack number to expand the stack.

2. Click a thumbnail (to deselect the other thumbnails), then drag it out of the stack.

To ungroup a whole stack:

1. Click the stack number to expand and select all the thumbnails in the stack.

2. Press Ctrl-Shift-G/Cmd-Shift-G or right-click/Control-click and choose Stack > **Ungroup from Stack**. The stack number and border will disappear, and the ungrouped thumbnails will be repositioned according to the current sorting criterion.

SHORTCUTS FOR STACKS		
TASK	**WINDOWS**	**MAC OS**
Group as stack	Ctrl-G	Cmd-G
Ungroup stack	Ctrl-Shift-G	Cmd-Shift-G
Open stack	Ctrl-right arrow	Cmd-right arrow
Close stack	Ctrl-left arrow	Cmd-left arrow
Expand all stacks in folder	Ctrl-Alt-right arrow	Cmd-Option-right arrow
Collapse all stacks in folder	Ctrl-Alt-left arrow	Cmd-Option-left arrow
Select all thumbnails in stack, keep stack collapsed	Alt-click the stack thumbnail	Option-click the stack thumbnail

A The stack of image thumbnails in the top row is collapsed, whereas the stack in the bottom row is expanded.

Using Slideshow mode

In Slideshow mode, images in the currently selected folder display in succession as full-screen previews on an uncluttered background.**A** You can rate or rotate the images while viewing them.

To preview images in Slideshow mode:

1. Display a folder of images or select multiple image thumbnails or a stack, then do either of the following:

   Press Ctrl-L/Cmd-L (View > Slideshow).

   To choose options for the slideshow before viewing it, choose View > **Slideshow Options** (Ctrl-Shift-L/Cmd-Shift-L). Choose options in the Slideshow Options dialog (**A**, next page), then click Play.

2. While the slideshow is playing, you can use the shortcuts listed onscreen to execute various commands, or if you find the list to be obtrusive, press H to hide it and refer to our sidebar on the following page instead.

   For example, you can press **L** to open the **Slideshow Options** dialog, then preview the effect of different **When Presenting**, **Show Slides** options on the current slide.

   Or to open a raw photo into **Camera Raw**, press **R**. The slideshow will resume playing when you click Done in the Camera Raw dialog.

3. To exit Slideshow mode, press **Esc**.

A In Slideshow mode, the current image fills the whole screen. Press H to show or hide the list of commands.

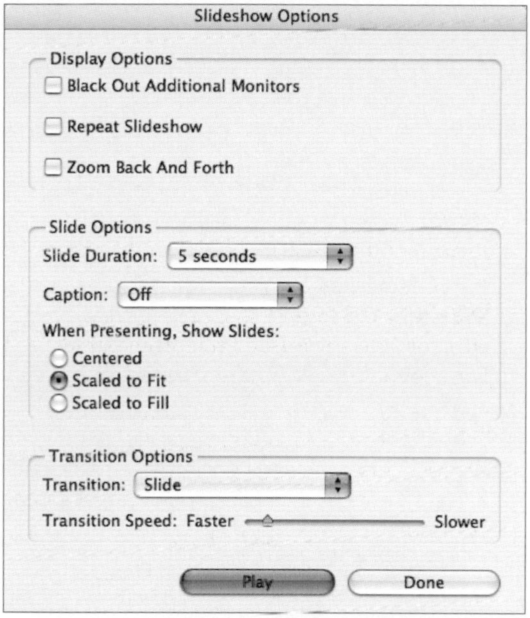

Slideshow Options

Display Options

☐ Black Out Additional Monitors

☐ Repeat Slideshow

☐ Zoom Back And Forth

Slide Options

Slide Duration: [5 seconds ⬍]

Caption: [Off ⬍]

When Presenting, Show Slides:
○ Centered
◉ Scaled to Fit
○ Scaled to Fill

Transition Options

Transition: [Slide ⬍]

Transition Speed: Faster ━━△━━━━━ Slower

(Play) (Done)

A Choose Display, Slide, and Transition options for your slideshow in the Slideshow Options dialog.

SHORTCUTS FOR SLIDESHOW MODE

TASK	SHORTCUT
Enter Slideshow mode	Ctrl-L/Cmd-L
Hide or show the shortcuts	H
Apply a rating	1–5
Apply a label	6–9
Increase the current rating by 1	. (period)
Decrease the current rating by 1	, (comma)
Clear the current rating	0 (zero)
Open the file into Camera Raw	R (click Done in Camera Raw to redisplay the paused slideshow, then press the Spacebar to resume playing it)
Open the file into Photoshop	O
Open the Slideshow Options dialog (from Slideshow mode)	L
Pause (blank the screen) or unpause	B
Pause the current slide onscreen/resume playing the slideshow	Spacebar
Zoom in or out	+ or –
Display the previous slide or PDF page	Left arrow
Display the next slide or PDF page	Right arrow
Jump from a PDF page to the previous (or next) slide	Ctrl-left (or right) arrow/ Cmd-left (or right) arrow
Rotate the preview 90° counterclockwise	[
Rotate the preview 90° clockwise	]
Exit Slideshow mode	Esc

Working with metadata

Data about the camera settings you use is embedded into your digital photos by the camera; other data (called "metadata") is embedded into your files by Bridge; and you can assign still other data ("user data") manually, such as contact information for viewers and searchable descriptions and keywords. Metadata is viewed and assigned via the Metadata panel.

To view a file's metadata:

1. Click a file thumbnail.

2. The placard* **A** at the top of the **Metadata** panel lists which camera settings were used to capture the photo, as well as file specifications, such as the pixel dimensions and file size.

   The **File Properties** category **B** lists other information about the file, such as the name, format, date created, and date modified. Click an arrowhead to expand or collapse that category.

   If a digital photo is selected, the Camera Data (EXIF) category lists which camera settings were used to capture the photo, in more detail than in the placard. This data was embedded into the photo by your camera.

▶ Data entered in the Creator and Copyright fields in the Photo Downloader is listed in the IPTC Core category.

▶ Once a photo is edited in Camera Raw, those settings are listed in a separate Camera Raw category and are updated each time further edits are made in Camera Raw.

▶ The metadata sticks with a file, and with any copies of the file that are created via File > Save As.

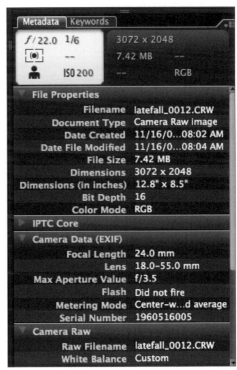

B Use the Metadata panel to view detailed information about the currently selected image.

> **CONFIGURING THE METADATA PANEL**
>
> ▶ To change the point size of the listings in the Metadata panel, choose Increase Font Size or Decrease Font Size from the panel menu.▾▤
>
> ▶ Via Bridge Preferences > Metadata, you can control which fields display in the IPTC Core and other categories in the Metadata panel (and to conserve panel space, check Hide Empty Fields).

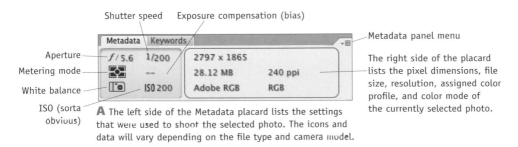

Shutter speed Exposure compensation (bias)

Aperture
Metering mode
White balance
ISO (sorta obvious)

Metadata panel menu

The right side of the placard lists the pixel dimensions, file size, resolution, assigned color profile, and color mode of the currently selected photo.

A The left side of the Metadata placard lists the settings that were used to shoot the selected photo. The icons and data will vary depending on the file type and camera model.

**If the placard is hidden, choose Show Metadata Placard from the Metadata panel menu.*

Instead of repetitively entering user data for individual photos, you can put general information, such as the creator and a copyright notice, in a custom metadata template and then apply the template to multiple photos at once.

To create a metadata template:

1. Do either of the following:

   From the Metadata panel menu, ▾☰ choose **Create Metadata Template**.

   Choose Tools > **Create Metadata Template**.

2. In the Create Metadata Template dialog, **A** enter a **Template Name**.

3. Click in the Creator, Copyright Notice, or other fields and enter general data that applies to all or most of your photos (you can press Tab to jump from one field to the next).

4. Click Save.

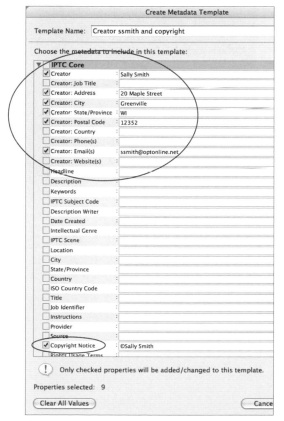

A In the Create Metadata Template dialog, enter basic creator or copyright notice information to be applied to your photos.

The quickest way to apply metadata is via a template. (To assign additional data subsequently by using the Metadata panel, see the next page.)

To apply a metadata template:

1. Click, then Shift-click, consecutive thumbnails, or Ctrl-click/Cmd-click nonconsecutive ones.

2. From the **Metadata** panel menu (or the Tools menu), do either of the following:

   Choose a template name from the **Append Metadata** submenu to add that metadata while preserving any existing metadata.

   Choose a template name from the **Replace Metadata** submenu to add metadata to blank fields and replace existing metadata with the template metadata (this option removes data).

   The Metadata panel updates.

   ➤ You can also assign a metadata template in the Photo Downloader dialog (but remember, you have to create the template first).

To edit a metadata template:

1. From the **Edit Metadata Template** submenu on the Metadata panel menu or Tools menu, choose the template to be edited.

2. The Edit Metadata Template dialog opens; it's exactly like the Create Metadata Template dialog. Edit the existing data or enter additional data, then click Save.

USING THE VIEW CONTENT BUTTONS ★

To control the format in which metadata displays in the Content panel, do the following:

➤ In the lower right corner of the Bridge window, click a View Content button: View Content as Thumbnails (minimal file data), View Content as Details (more file data), or View Content as List (small icons with columns of data). When View Content as List is chosen, you can change the column order by dragging any column header to the left or right.

➤ When content is being viewed as thumbnails, you can toggle the display of metadata on or off by pressing Ctrl-T/Cmd-T.

View Content   View Content   View Content
as Thumbnails   as Details   as List

Via the IPTC* Core category of the Metadata panel, you can embed user-created metadata into your files manually. For example, you can assign information pertaining to a specific photo shoot (such as the location, the country, or a description) or assign keywords to make your files easier to sort, run searches for, and filter out by category.

Before assigning any metadata manually, examine your photos, assign star and reject ratings to them, and apply a basic metadata template to them. Then you'll be ready, as per the following instructions, to assign Description and Keywords data to progressively smaller numbers of photos—a general category to the largest bunch, then narrower and more specific categories to smaller groups.

To add metadata to files manually:

1. Display and select multiple, related photos.

2. In the **Metadata** panel, expand the **IPTC Core** category by clicking the arrowhead.

3. Click to the right of **Description**, then enter descriptive data about the selected photos.**A**

4. In the **Keywords** field, enter keywords, separated by commas or semicolons, to help you identify, locate, and filter your photos. Click in (or press Tab to get to) any other fields, and enter data.

5. To embed your data into the selected images, click the **Apply** button ✔ in the lower right corner of the panel.

➤ Any keywords that you enter in the Keywords field will also be listed individually in the Other Keywords category in the Keywords panel and, for the images you selected, will have check marks.

➤ We think the easiest way to embed user data in Bridge is via the Metadata panel, but if you prefer to use the File Info command, select one or more files, then choose File > File Info. Click a tab to display related entry fields, then enter data. Data entered in the IPTC or Description tab will also be listed in the IPTC Core category in the Metadata panel. That is, data entered or edited in one location automatically updates in the other.

IPTC is an information standard that is used for transferring and publishing text and images.

A Enter user data in the IPTC Core category in the Metadata panel.

FILTERING THUMBNAILS VIA KEYWORDS

Because keywords that are applied to an image display in the Keywords category on the Filter panel, you can filter the display of images by checking specific keywords in that panel.

➤ The Filter panel is dynamic, in that its categories (e.g., File Type, Keywords) change depending on what data is available for files in the current folder. ★ For example, if you haven't applied ratings to any thumbnails In the current folder, you won't see a Ratings category. Should you apply a rating to a thumbnail, a Ratings category will appear.

Assigning keywords to files

Keywords (identifying text) are used by search utilities to locate files and by file management programs to organize them. Here you can create main-level keywords (such as events, people, places, things, themes, etc.), and nested subkeywords within those categories, and then assign them to your files. You can also locate files in Bridge by using the Find command with specific keywords as search criteria or display them by checking specific keywords in the Keywords category in the Filter panel.

To create keywords and subkeywords:

1. To create a new main-level keyword category, in the Keywords panel, click the **New Keyword** button, then type the keyword.**A** ★

2. To create a nested subkeyword, click a main-level keyword category, click the **New Sub Keyword** button, type a word, then press Return/Enter. You can also create sub-subkeywords. ★

➤ You can move (drag) any subkeyword into a different main-level keyword category.

To assign keywords to files:

1. Select one or more file thumbnails. If keywords have already been assigned to those files, the words will be listed at the top of the panel; you can assign additional ones.

2. Check the box for one or more subkeywords.**B** (Although you can assign main-level keywords to files, they won't be of much use in a search.)

➤ If keywords are contained in a file that you import into Bridge, they will be listed in the Other Keywords category in the Keywords panel. If you want to add them as permanent subkeywords, right-click/Control-click each one individually and choose Make Persistent from the context menu.

➤ You can also assign keywords via the File Info dialog. Select one or more thumbnails, then from the Refine menu on the Bridge toolbar, choose File Info. In the Description tab of the dialog, enter the desired keywords, separated by semicolons or commas (watch out for typing errors!). ★

A We created a new main-level keyword called "Spa products," kept that category selected, then used the New Sub Keyword button to add new subkeywords to it.

B We clicked the thumbnail for a photo, then assigned subkeywords to it via the check boxes.

USING THE KEYWORDS PANEL	
TASK	**METHOD**
Rename a subkeyword	Click the word, choose Rename from the Keywords panel menu, then type a name (this won't alter any already embedded data).
Delete a main-level keyword or subkeyword	Click the word, then click the Delete Keyword button (if the word had been assigned to any files, it will now be listed in italics).
Find a keyword or subkeyword on the list	Start typing the word in the search field at the bottom of the panel.

Searching for files

To find files via Bridge: ★

1. In Bridge, choose Edit > **Find** (Ctrl-F/Cmd-F). The Find dialog opens.**A**

2. From the **Look In** menu in the Source area, choose the folder to be searched (the current folder is listed by default). To select a folder that isn't on the list, choose Look In: Browse, locate the folder, then click OK/Choose.

3. From the menus in the **Criteria** area, choose search criteria (e.g., file name, date created, label, rating, particular camera settings), choose a parameter from the adjoining menu, and enter data in the field. To include additional criteria in the search, click the ⊕, then choose and enter more search criteria.

4. From the **Match** menu, choose If Any Criteria Are Met to find files based on one or more criteria, or choose If All Criteria Are Met to narrow the selection to files that meet all the criteria.

5. *Optional:* Check Include All Subfolders to also search through any subfolders within the folder you chose in step 2.

6. *Optional:* Check Include Non-indexed Files to search through files that Bridge hasn't yet indexed (any folder Bridge has yet to display). This will slow down the search.

7. Click Find. The search results will display in the Content panel and also in a temporary folder called Search Results: [name of source folder] **B** on the Path bar and on the Reveal Recent File or Go to Recent Folder menu  on the Bridge toolbar.

8. To save a copy of the search results to a permanent file group, follow the steps on the next page, or to cancel the search results, click the ⊠.

➤ To discard the current search results and begin a new search, click New Search.

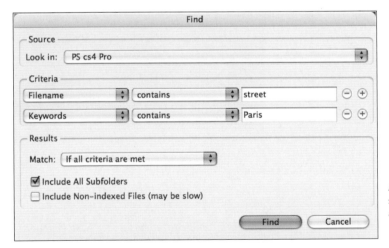

A Use the Find dialog to search for and locate files according to various criteria.

QUICK SEARCH ★

If you know the name of the file you're looking for, type it in the search field 🔍▾ on the right side of the Bridge toolbar, then press Enter/Return.

B After you click Find, the contents of the temporary Search Results folder display in the Content panel. The parameters used for the search and the name of the folder that was searched are listed as the Find Criteria.

Creating and using collections

The collection features in Bridge offer a useful way to group and access file thumbnails without actually having to relocate them. There are two kinds of collections: a Smart Collection that you create from the results of a Find search, and one that you create by dragging thumbnails manually into a collection folder.

To create a Smart Collection: ★

1. Click the tab for the Collections panel (if the panel is hidden, choose Window > Collections Panel).
2. Perform a search by using the Edit > **Find** command (see the preceding page). When the search is completed, click the **Save as Smart Collection** button at the top of the Content panel.**A**
3. A new Smart Collection folder appears in the top part of the Collections panel.**B** To rename it, type in the highlighted field, then press Enter/Return.

To display a collection: ★

Click its icon in the Collections panel.

What's smart about Smart Collections is that if you run a new search for a collection based on either new criteria or a new search folder, the collection contents update automatically.

To edit a Smart Collection: ★

1. In the **Collections** panel, click the icon for an existing Smart Collection.
2. At the top of the Content panel or in the lower left corner of the Collections panel, click the **Edit Smart Collection** button.**C**
3. The Edit Smart Collection dialog opens. Enter a new folder to be searched and/or new search criteria, then click Save.
4. The results of the new search will display in the Content panel, and the thumbnails matching the new criteria will replace the old ones in the same collection. Note: If you rename an actual file or move it from the folder that was used in the search, it will also be removed from the collection.

A Click the Save as Smart Collection button to create a Smart Collection.

B The new Smart Collection displays on the Collections panel. Rename it in the highlighted field.

C To edit a Smart Collection, click a Smart Collection folder in the Collections panel, then click the Edit Smart Collection button at the bottom of the panel.

Bridge also lets you create a nonsmart collection without running a search, and you can add to it simply by dragging thumbnails into it.

To create a nonsmart collection: ★

1. Do either of the following:

   On the **Content** panel, select the thumbnails to be placed into a collection. On the **Collections** panel, click the **New Collection** button, then click Yes in the alert dialog.

   While viewing files in **Review mode** (Ctrl-B/ Cmd-B), drag any files you don't want in the collection out of the carousel, then click the **New Collection** button.

2. On the panel, rename the collection,**A** then press Enter/Return.

To add files to a nonsmart collection: ★

1. Display the **Collections** panel.

2. Drag one or more thumbnails to an existing collection folder.**B**

A Click the New Collection button to create a new collection, then rename it in the highlighted field.

B Drag thumbnails to a collection folder to add them to that collection.

To remove a thumbnail from a collection: ★

1. On the **Collections** panel, click a collection folder to display its contents.

2. Select the thumbnails to be removed, then click **Remove from Collection** at the top of the Content panel **C** (or right-click/Control-click a thumbnail and choose Remove from Collection).

➤ Beware! If you apply the Delete command to a thumbnail in either type of collection, the actual file it represents is deleted from your hard drive.

If you rename a file or move it from its original location, Bridge tries to update the link to any nonsmart collections the file is a member of. If the program is unable to do so, follow these steps instead.

To relink a missing file to a collection: ★

1. On the **Collections** panel, click a folder to which you want to relink a file or files.

2. Next to the Missing File Detected alert at the top of the Content panel, click **Fix**.**D**

3. In the **Find Missing Files** dialog, click Browse, locate and click the missing file, click Open, then click OK.

C Click Remove from Collection to take a selected thumbnail out of the currently selected collection.

D Click Fix to relink a file that's missing from a collection.

Choosing preferences for Bridge (Choose Edit/Adobe Bridge CS4 > Preferences or press Ctrl-K/Cmd-K)

General Preferences A

Appearance

Choose a value between Black and White for the overall **User Interface Brightness** (for the side panels) and for the **Image Backdrop** (the area behind the Content and Preview panels).

Choose an **Accent Color** for highlighted items.

Behavior

Check **When a Camera Is Connected, Launch Adobe Photo Downloader** to make the Downloader the default system utility for acquiring photos (this option is for Mac OS only).

Check **Double-Click Edits Camera Raw Settings in Bridge** to have raw files open into Camera Raw (hosted by Bridge) when double-clicked.

If **Ctrl-click/Cmd-click Opens the Loupe When Previewing or Reviewing** is checked, you have to Ctrl/Cmd click an image preview to make the loupe display. With this option unchecked, you can make the loupe appear by clicking the preview without using the shortcut. ★

For **Number of Recent Items to Display**, enter the maximum number of folders (0–30) that can be listed at a time on the Open Recent File menu ◥▨ on the Path bar.

Favorite Items

Check which items and system-generated folders you want listed in the **Favorites** panel by default.

Thumbnails Preferences B

Performance and File Handling

Note: To implement Performance and File Handling changes, you must purge the folder cache (Tools > Cache submenu).

For **Do Not Process Files Larger Than**, enter the maximum file size that Bridge can display as a thumbnail (the default value is 1000 MB). Large files preview slowly.

Details

From the **Additional Lines of Thumbnail Metadata** menus, choose which categories of file information you want listed below or next to the image thumbnails in the Content panel.

Check **Show Tooltips** to allow tool tips to display when you rest the pointer on Bridge features, such as image thumbnails.

Continued on the following page

A The General Preferences in Bridge

B The Thumbnails Preferences in Bridge

Playback Preferences ★

See Adobe Bridge Help.

Metadata Preferences

Check which metadata categories are to display in the **Metadata** panel.

Check **Hide Empty Fields** to streamline the Metadata panel.

Check **Show Metadata Placard** to display camera data at the top of the Metadata panel.

Keywords Preferences ★

Check **Automatically Apply Parent Keywords** to have the parent keyword apply automatically when a subkeyword check box is clicked in the Keywords panel (we keep this option off). If this option is on and you want to override it (to apply just a subkeyword), Shift-click the keyword.

For **Write Hierarchical Keywords**, click a Delimiter option to tell Bridge how to separate keywords when exporting files. **Read Hierarchical Keywords** applies to keywords from imported files.

Labels Preferences

Check whether to **Require the Control/Command Key** [to be pressed] **to Apply Labels and Ratings** to selected file thumbnails. You can change the label names here, too, but not the colors.

File Type Associations Preferences

These settings tell Bridge which application to use when opening files of each type. Don't change these settings unless you know what you're doing!

Cache Preferences

Options

Keep 100% Previews in Cache saves a large JPEG preview to disk for faster previewing when using the loupe and when previewing images in Slideshow mode at 100% view. This option uses significant disk space, so we keep it unchecked. ★

Check **Automatically Export Caches to Folders When Possible** to have Bridge export the cache that is created when thumbnails are generated to the folders those images are stored in.

Location

Click **Choose** to specify a new location for the Bridge cache.

Manage

If you have a very large hard drive, you can use the **Cache Size** slider to increase the maximum number of items that can be stored in the cache. ★

Click **Compact Cache** to allow previously cached items that are no longer available to be removed from the cache, for improved performance. ★

Click **Purge Cache** to purge all cached thumbnails and previews from the central database to free up space on your hard disk, or if Bridge is having trouble displaying your thumbnails.

Startup Scripts Preferences ★

Depending on your usual workflow, check which **Startup Scripts** you need to have running on a regular basis and, to improve performance, uncheck the ones you don't. (Read the description below the script name.) Changes to these preferences take effect upon relaunch.

Advanced Preferences

Note: Most Advanced Preferences changes take effect upon relaunch.

Miscellaneous

Check **Use Software Rendering** to turn off hardware acceleration for the Preview panel and for Slideshow mode.

Check **Generate Monitor-Size Previews** to have Bridge generate previews in a dual-monitor setup based on the resolution of the larger monitor. ★

Check **Start Bridge at Login** to have Bridge launch automatically (into stealth mode) at startup. ★

International

Choose a **Language** for the Bridge interface and a language for the **Keyboard**.

Output Preferences ★

Check **Use Solo Mode for Output Panel Behavior** to show one category of Output settings at a time.

Check **Convert Multi-Byte Filenames to Full ASCII** to define Chinese and Japanese file names using the ASCII character system, to prevent problems when transferring files.

Check **Preserve Embedded Color Profile** to preserve any embedded profiles in files being output as PDF contact sheets or presentations.

➤ If you need to reset the Bridge preferences, hold down Alt/Option as you relaunch Bridge. In the alert, check Reset Preferences, then click OK.

The Adobe Camera Raw plug-in lets you apply powerful correction commands to photos before opening them into Photoshop, and is a digital darkroom in and of itself. Learning how to use this plug-in is essential if you want to maximize the potential of your digital photos. In this chapter, you'll choose Camera Raw preferences; correct white balance, exposure, contrast, and luminance problems; apply split toning; sharpen, crop, and straighten; use Camera Raw tools to apply local adjustments; blend dual exposures; process multiple photos; import photos as Smart Objects; and more!

Why use Adobe Camera Raw?

Advanced amateur and pro digital SLR cameras let you capture photos as raw files, which has many advantages over capturing them in the JPEG or TIFF format. For JPEG and TIFF, the camera applies internal processing to the original pixels, such as sharpening, white balance, and color adjustments. With raw files, you get only the raw data that the camera captured onto its digital sensor, giving you full control over subsequent image correction. Raw files must be converted by the Camera Raw plug-in before they can be opened and edited in Photoshop. The plug-in can process raw files from most of the current camera manufacturers, as well as JPEG and TIFF files.

With Camera Raw, you not only get a converter, you also get powerful adjustment controls. Camera Raw adjustments (e.g., exposure, white balance, hue/saturation, noise reduction) are less destructive than similar commands in Photoshop, and preserve more of the original pixel data in your photos. Furthermore, many Camera Raw features, such as the sharpening controls, produce better results and are easier to use.

The Camera Raw conversion redistributes tonal values from the highlight areas of the tonal range (which contain an abundance of pixel data) to the shadow areas (which usually contain insufficient pixel data). This helps prevent posterization and a loss of detail in the shadow areas that may result from applying tonal adjustments in Photoshop.

Camera Raw edits made to raw files are stored as a series of instructions, which in turn are saved either in a sidecar file or in the Camera Raw database, whereas instructions for edits made to JPEG and TIFF files are

Continued on the following page

Note: Settings listed in the captions in this chapter were chosen for photos that are approximately 3000 x 2000 pixels.

CAMERA RAW

3

IN THIS CHAPTER

saved in the file itself. Regardless of the photo's file type, when you open it from Camera Raw into Photoshop, the instructions are applied to a copy of the file, leaving the original digital file intact. This is one of the key advantages to using the Camera Raw plug-in: Even after applying corrections, the original capture file is preserved (like a traditional film negative). You can reopen a photo into Camera Raw and modify or remove any of your corrections at any time. Note: This chapter has been written for version 5.3 of Camera Raw.

Although the instructions in this chapter apply to raw and JPEG files, if your camera is capable of shooting raw files, we recommend choosing that option. Regardless of your format choice, however, you should process your photos and apply tonal and color corrections to them in Camera Raw before opening them into Photoshop. (A third file format option, camera-generated TIFFs, are as large as raw files and lack the advantages of raw files.)

Choosing preferences for Camera Raw

To choose preferences for the Camera Raw plug-in:

1. Do either of the following:

   In Bridge, choose Edit/Adobe Bridge CS4 > **Camera Raw Preferences**.

   If the Camera Raw dialog is open, click the **Open Preferences Dialog** button ☰ at the top of the dialog (Ctrl-K/Cmd-K).

2. In the **General** area of the Camera Raw Preferences dialog (**A**, next page), choose a **Save Image Settings In** option. We recommend choosing **Sidebar ".xmp" Files** (this won't increase the file size significantly). Leave the **Apply Sharpening To** setting as **All Images**, to allow Camera Raw to sharpen your photos.

3. In the **Default Image Settings** area, we recommend leaving Apply Auto Tone Adjustments unchecked, as this option would allow Camera Raw to apply Auto settings to your photos automatically. Also leave the two "Make Defaults" options unchecked unless you use more than one camera body of the same model or want the default settings to be used for a specific ISO setting. You can leave Apply Auto Grayscale Mix When Converting to Grayscale checked.

4. **Camera Raw Cache** specifies the cache size for thumbnail and preview data. Leave this on the default setting of 1.0 GB unless you're blessed with a lot of extra space on your hard disk.

5. For **DNG File Handling**, we recommend checking both options. The first one allows metadata to be written into your DNG files, and the second one allows the previews to update automatically when edits are made in Camera Raw.

6. For **JPEG and TIFF Handling**, choose options from the **JPEG** and **TIFF** menus to either allow files in those formats to open into Camera Raw or to have them bypass Camera Raw and open into Photoshop instead. ★ (For our suggestions on how to set these two preferences, see below.)

7. Click OK.

How we set our Camera Raw preferences for opening JPEG photos ★

Because we shoot only raw or JPEG (not TIFF) photos, we choose these JPEG Handling settings in the Camera Raw Preferences dialog:

➤ From the **JPEG** menu at the bottom of the dialog, we choose Automatically Open JPEGs with Settings (JPEG files "with settings" are those that have been previously opened into Camera Raw). With this option chosen (instead of Automatically Open All Supported JPEGs), JPEG files that haven't yet been opened into Camera Raw will open directly into Photoshop when double-clicked. To open JPEG files into Camera Raw, see step 1 in the left column on page 42.

➤ We don't capture photos in the TIFF format, so from the **TIFF** menu, we choose Disable TIFF Support. This way, our TIFF files open directly into Photoshop instead of into Camera Raw.

HOW TO KEEP CAMERA RAW CURRENT

Of the many proprietary raw "formats," some are unique to a particular manufacturer (such as Nikon or Canon) and some are unique to a particular camera model. To verify that you have all the latest interpreters for the raw formats that Camera Raw supports, periodically visit www.adobe.com and download any Camera Raw updates that are available for your camera model.

We prefer to have our raw and JPEG photos open into Camera Raw hosted by Bridge (instead of by Photoshop), whether they have been opened previously into Camera Raw or not. This way, after editing a file and then exiting Camera Raw, we're right back in Bridge.

To choose Bridge as the host for Camera Raw: ★

1. In Bridge, choose Edit/Adobe Bridge CS4 > Preferences (Ctrl-K/Cmd-K), then click General on the left side.

2. Check **Double-Click Edits Camera Raw Settings in Bridge**.

3. Click OK. Now if you double-click any thumbnail for a raw or JPEG photo in Bridge, it will open into Camera Raw, hosted by Bridge.

WHAT ABOUT USING LIGHTROOM?

The Camera Raw sliders and options are virtually identical to those in the Develop module in the Adobe Photoshop Lightroom application (and they have similar interfaces, too). Both the former and the latter preserve the original digital files when they apply corrections.

When deciding between the two, consider the volume and type of adjustments you typically apply to your photos. If you like to edit your photos in Photoshop, it makes sense to apply your initial corrections in Camera Raw. If you work with a large volume of photos and need the file management power of Lightroom, you could perform all of your file management and correction work in that program instead.

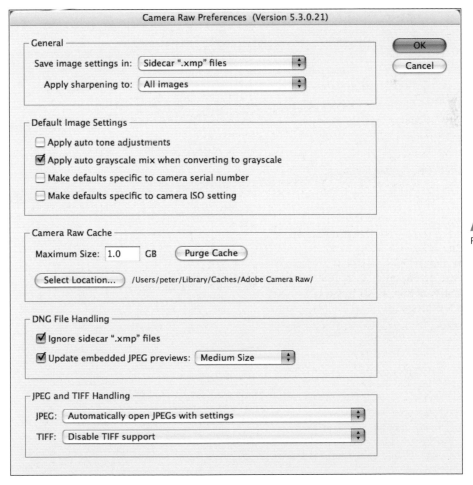

A The Camera Raw Preferences dialog

Opening files into Camera Raw

Next, you will open a file into the Camera Raw dialog (**A**, next page). Later in this chapter you'll apply corrections using basic and specialized adjustment tabs (shown in **B**, next page) and some of the Camera Raw tools (shown in **C**, next page).

Note: These steps for opening files into Camera Raw assume that you have set your Camera Raw preferences as we do (see the preceding two pages).

To open a digital photo into the Camera Raw plug-in: ★

1. In Bridge, locate a raw or JPEG photo. (Each digital camera manufacturer attaches a unique extension to its raw files, such as .nef for Nikon, .crw or .cr2 for Canon.) Do either of the following:

    Double-click the photo thumbnail.

    Click the photo thumbnail, then click the **Open in Camera Raw** button. Note: The button is available only for file formats that can be opened directly into Camera Raw.

    ➤ If a photo has been opened and edited previously in Camera Raw, a badge displays above its thumbnail.

2. The photo opens into Camera Raw. Information about the photo (which is taken from the metadata that the camera attached to it) is listed in the following locations in the Camera Raw dialog: the camera model in the title bar at the top of the dialog, the file name below the preview, and the camera settings that were used to take the photo (aperture, shutter speed, ISO sensitivity, and focal length) below the histogram in the upper right.

    The underlined link (color space, bit depth, dimensions, and resolution) below the preview gets you to the Workflow Options dialog.

    To correct the photo, you'll wend your way through some or all of the nine tabs: Basic, Tone Curve, Detail, HSL/Grayscale, Split Toning, Lens Corrections, Camera Calibration, Presets, and Snapshots. You will use most of the tabs in this chapter.

    Once you're satisfied with how the corrected photo looks, you'll click Open Image. Camera Raw will convert and open a copy of the image into Photoshop using your chosen settings, leaving the original data unchanged.

Now that you've opened a photo into Camera Raw, you can magnify it to get a closer look. And once it's magnified, you can shift it around in the preview window.

To use the zoom features in Camera Raw:

1. Do any of the following:

    Choose the **Zoom** tool (Z), then click the preview image to zoom in or Alt-click/ Option-click it to zoom out.

    Below the preview image, click the – or + zoom level button, or from the **Zoom Level** menu, choose a preset percentage.

    Press **Ctrl–/Cmd–**(hyphen) to zoom out or **Ctrl-+/Cmd-+** to zoom in.

    To change the zoom level to **100%**, double-click the **Zoom** tool.

    To change the zoom level to **Fit in View**, double-click the **Hand** tool.

2. If the image preview is magnified, you can use the **Hand** tool (H) to move it in the preview window. (With another tool chosen, hold down the Spacebar for a temporary Hand tool.)

OPENING MULTIPLE PHOTOS INTO CAMERA RAW

To open multiple files into Camera Raw for viewing and rating, or possibly to synchronize their settings, see pages 76–77.

The Camera Raw interface

A THE CAMERA RAW DIALOG

Camera model

Toggle between Full-Screen mode
and the previous dialog size

Indicates the
preview is still
rendering

Histogram

Camera
settings

Camera Raw
Settings menu

Zoom
controls

Link to the Workflow Options dialog (see page 44)

B THE CAMERA RAW TABS

Tone Curve   HSL/Grayscale   Lens Corrections   Presets   Snapshots ★

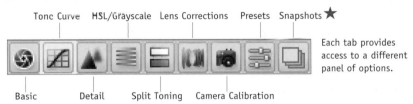

Each tab provides
access to a different
panel of options.

Basic   Detail   Split Toning   Camera Calibration

C THE CAMERA RAW TOOLS

Hand (H): Moves a
magnified preview
in the window

Color Sampler (S):
Places up to nine
RGB color sampler
points in the preview

Straighten (A):
Straightens the
photo along a
line you drag

Red Eye Removal
(E): Corrects
red-eye in
portrait photos

Graduated Filter
(G): ★ Applies
local edits
gradually across a
designated area

Rotate 90°
Counter-
clockwise (L):
Rotates
the image

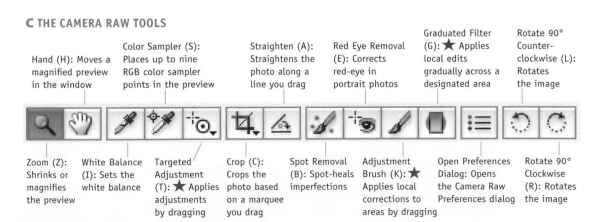

Zoom (Z):
Shrinks or
magnifies
the preview

White Balance
(I): Sets the
white balance

Targeted
Adjustment
(T): ★ Applies
adjustments
by dragging

Crop (C):
Crops the
photo based
on a marquee
you drag

Spot Removal
(B): Spot-heals
imperfections

Adjustment
Brush (K): ★
Applies local
corrections to
areas by dragging

Open Preferences
Dialog: Opens
the Camera Raw
Preferences dialog

Rotate 90°
Clockwise
(R): Rotates
the image

Choosing workflow options

Via the Workflow Options dialog, you can establish a default color space, and bit depth (number of bits per channel), size (width and height), and resolution settings for your photos before opening them into Photoshop—without altering the original files.

To choose default workflow options:

1. With a photo open in the Camera Raw dialog, click the underlined link below the preview that lists the color space, file dimensions, etc. The **Workflow Options** dialog opens.**A**

2. From the **Space** menu, choose the color profile to be used for converting the raw file to RGB: Adobe RGB (1998), ColorMatch RGB, ProPhoto RGB, or sRGB IEC61966-2.1 ("sRGB," for short). If you followed our instructions in Chapter 1, you assigned Adobe RGB (1998) as the default color space for color management, so we recommend choosing that option here, too.

3. From the **Depth** menu, choose a color depth of 8 Bits/Channel or 16 Bits/Channel (see page 90). Note: If you have a large hard drive and a fast system with a lot of RAM, you can more easily work with 16 Bits/Channel images. With the extra pixels, more of the original tonal levels will be preserved as you edit the photo in Photoshop.

4. If you want to resize the photo to a preset size (in megapixels, or MP), choose from the **Size** menu. If a crop marquee is present, the crop size will be listed as the default image size (the size without a – or +). If you choose a larger size than the original, the image will be resampled. To help prevent pixelization, avoid choosing the largest size.

➤ At the present time, experts disagree on whether Camera Raw or Photoshop does a better job of resampling. Until they reach a consensus, take your pick.

5. Enter a **Resolution** (e.g., for an image that is 2000 x 3000 pixels or larger and is to be printed on an inkjet printer or a commercial press, enter a resolution between 240 and 300). This value will affect only the print output size of the file.

6. *Optional:* From the Sharpen For menu, choose Screen, Glossy Paper, or Matte Paper to apply predefined output sharpening to your photo for the chosen medium. Also choose the desired amount of sharpening from the Amount menu.★ Note: For greater control over output sharpening, use the sliders in the Detail tab instead (see pages 56–58).

7. Click OK. The new workflow information will be listed below the preview and will be applied to the current photo and to future photos that you open into Camera Raw.

➤ If you want future photos to open from Camera Raw into Photoshop as Smart Objects when you click Open Object, check Open in Photoshop as Smart Objects in the Workflow Options dialog (see page 80). We keep this option off.

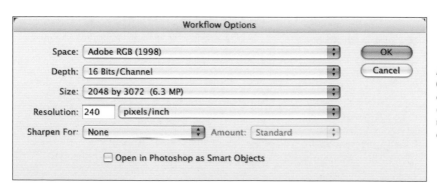

A Use the Workflow Options dialog to choose color space, bit depth, size (width and height), and resolution settings for the current and future photos.

Cropping and straightening photos

Qualities to look for in a great photo are a winning composition, intriguing subject matter, sharp focus in the key details, and proper exposure and lighting to create the right mood. If you didn't align your photo perfectly in the viewfinder, the steps on this page will enable you to improve the composition.

After opening a photo in Camera Raw, the first step (before applying any adjustments) is to decide whether it needs cropping and to straighten it if it's askew. By stripping away nonessential areas, you can eliminate distracting features, create an intimate close-up, or draw the viewer's attention to a key area. With the Crop tool in Camera Raw, you can control which part of a photo opens into Photoshop. (But fear not: Whether cropped or not, all the original raw pixels are preserved.)

To marquee a photo for cropping:

1. Choose the **Crop** tool (C). 🔲

2. Do either of the following:

   Drag a marquee in the preview window.

   To create a marquee based on a fixed proportion, from the Crop tool menu or the context menu, choose a preset (or choose Custom and enter values), then drag in the preview window. (To deactivate the preset, choose Normal.)

3. *Optional:* To move the crop marquee, drag inside it; to resize it, drag a handle.

4. Press Enter/Return to preview the result. Only the area within the marquee will import into Photoshop. (To redisplay the crop marquee at any time, choose the Crop tool.)

To remove a crop marquee:

1. Choose the **Crop** tool (C). 🔲

2. Press **Esc**, or choose **Clear Crop** from the Crop tool menu or from the context menu. You can undo the crop even after closing and reopening the dialog (you can't do the same in Photoshop).

To straighten a crooked photo:

1. Choose the **Straighten** tool (A). 🔺

2. Drag across the preview, along an edge in the image that you want to align to the horizontal or vertical axis.**A** A crop marquee will appear, aligned to the angle you drew.**B** Press Enter/Return. When you open the image in Photoshop, that edge will be aligned with the document window.**C**

A With the Straighten tool, drag along an edge to be aligned to the horizontal or vertical axis.

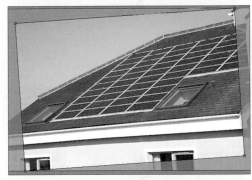

B A crop marquee appears, based on the angle we drew.

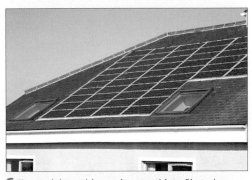

C The straightened image is opened into Photoshop.

TIPS FOR CROPPING PHOTOS

➤ To change a horizontal crop of a fixed size to a vertical crop of the same fixed size, drag a handle horizontally, until the marquee orientation changes.

➤ A preset choice of 2 to 3 for the Crop tool has the same proportions as a 4" x 6" image; 4 to 5 is the same as an 8" x 10", etc.

Correcting the white balance

With cropping out of the way (pun intended), it's time to study the photo, diagnose its weaknesses, and decide which Camera Raw options are best suited to fix them. Make any broad corrections that are called for before making local corrections. For example, with an exposure correction, you can compensate for under- or overexposure, enhance the details in both the shadow and highlight areas, and light up key features of the composition. A color cast, another broad (and common) problem, can be corrected via the temperature controls.

The Basic tab is the best place to begin making corrections (it's in the first slot for good reason). For the first round of adjustments, we recommend using the sliders in the order in which they appear.

To apply white balance adjustments:

1. Click the **Basic** tab ⬛ and double-click the Hand tool to change the zoom level to Fit in View.

2. To see the effect of one of the preset temperature settings, from the **White Balance** menu, choose a preset that best describes the lighting conditions under which the photo was taken. The presets are available only for raw files.

3. If the preset you chose successfully corrected the white balance, you're all set. If not, restore the original camera settings by choosing **As Shot** from the White Balance menu, and proceed to the next step.

4. Use the **Temperature** slider **A–B** to add blue or yellow (make the photo look cooler or warmer). This is a subjective adjustment. For outdoor shots, consider the time of day: Sunsets naturally have a warm tone, whereas midday shots usually have a neutral, blue-gray tone. An interior shot could be warm, cool, or neutral, depending on the light source. Portraits need the most careful adjustment, to ensure that the skin tones look natural.

   See also **A–C**, next page.

➤ Although the white balance can be adjusted based on a sampled area (by clicking the White Balance tool 🖊 on a grayish-white area that contains some details), deciding which area to click can be tricky, so we use the Temperature and Tint sliders instead.

A This photo has the default Temperature setting. It has a yellowish cast (looks too warm).

B We chose a lower Temperature setting to make the photo cooler and neutralize the color cast.

ADJUSTING THE WHITE BALANCE

A This photo is underexposed, and the clouds have a slightly greenish cast; the As Shot settings are shown above. We'll correct the white balance first and then the exposure. But rather than changing the Temperature, we'll let a white balance preset do the initial work for us, followed by a simple tweak of the Tint slider.

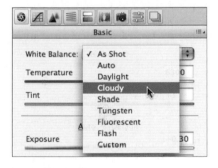

B Since the photo was shot on a cloudy day, we chose the Cloudy preset from the White Balance menu. The higher Temperature and Tint values in this preset successfully removed the greenish cast.

C The Cloudy preset added a slight reddish cast to the clouds, though, which we were able to correct by lowering the Tint value.

Correcting the exposure

To demonstrate how to correct common exposure problems via the Basic tab, we'll use two photos, one underexposed, the other overexposed.

To correct an underexposed photo:

1. Open an underexposed photo into Camera Raw, then click the **Basic** tab. 🔄 The sliders are set automatically to the default values for your camera model (the word "Default" is dimmed).

   ➤ To view which slider adjustments Camera Raw recommends, click Auto; then before proceeding, reset the sliders to their default settings by clicking Default.

2. Study the **histogram** to see how much the shadow pixels are being clipped (clustered at the left edge). Unless the subject matter itself is very dark or light, there should be a fairly uniform distribution of pixels from left to right in the histogram. The goal is to redistribute pixels to conform to the Adobe RGB (1998) color space, which you're using for color management.

3. Turn the clipping warnings on to view a representation of any shadow or highlight clipping in the preview:

   In the top left corner of the histogram, click the **Shadow Clipping Warning** button (U). Clipped shadows are represented by blue areas.**A**

   In the top right corner, click the **Highlight Clipping Warning** button (O). Clipped highlights are represented by red areas.

4. To reduce the clipping of shadow pixels, do the following:

   To lighten the photo and recover detail in the midtones, increase the **Exposure** value (**A–B**, next page). A value change of plus or minus 1 is equivalent to widening or reducing a camera aperture by one full f-stop.

   To recover shadow details, use the Fill Light and Blacks sliders as a pair. Move the **Fill Light** slider a quarter of the way to the right, and lower the **Blacks** value so only a trace remains of the blue shadow clipping color.

5. If you need to lighten and restore detail in the midtones, increase the **Brightness** and **Clarity** settings. To decrease the contrast and lighten the shadows, reduce the **Contrast** value slightly (**C**, next page). Note: The default Brightness and

---

Shadow Clipping Warning button   Highlight Clipping Warning button

A Turn on the clipping warnings via the buttons above the histogram (a white frame around a button indicates that the warning is on). This is the histogram for the original photo that is shown in **A** on the next page. Most of the pixels are clustered to the left side of the graph, signifying that the photo is underexposed.

Contrast settings for a raw photo are +50 and +25, respectively; for a JPEG photo, the default setting for these sliders is 0.

6. To boost the color saturation slightly, increase the **Vibrance** value by a moderate amount. This feature doesn't cause oversaturation. We've found it usually improves our photos.

CORRECTING UNDEREXPOSURE

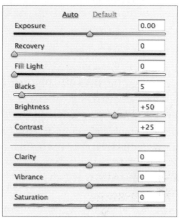

A To correct this underexposed photo, we'll use the controls in the Basic tab.

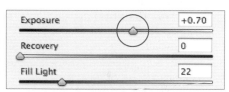

B A new Exposure setting (shown above) lightened the entire photo, and a new Fill Light setting lightened the shadows and darker midtones. The blue clipping warning disappeared, which confirms that our adjustments corrected the shadow clipping.

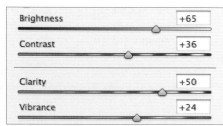

C Next we increased the Brightness value to lighten the midtones, increased the Contrast, and increased the Clarity to sharpen the shapes (by darkening the edges). Finally, we increased the Vibrance value to boost the color saturation. (To lighten the photo even more, we'll use the Tone Curve tab; see pages 52–53.)

To correct an overexposed photo:

1. Open an overexposed (bleached out) photo into Camera Raw, **A** then click the **Basic** tab.

2. The **histogram** shows that the highlight pixels are clustered at the right edge (are being clipped). **B**

3. Click the **Shadow Clipping Warning** (U) and **Highlight Clipping Warning** (O) buttons.

4. To reduce the clipping of highlight pixels, do either of the following:

   To darken the photo and recover details in the highlights, reduce the **Exposure** and increase the **Recovery** until you see none of the red highlight warning color.

   Alt-drag/Option-drag the **Exposure** and/or **Recovery** slider and release the mouse when only tiny areas of white (representing all three color channels) display on the black background **C** (and **A**, next page).

You can also Alt-drag/Option-drag the **Blacks** slider to display a clipping preview against a white background, and release the mouse when only tiny areas of black display. Color areas, if any, represent clipping in those channels.

5. If you need to darken and restore details in the lighter midtones, reduce the **Brightness** value slightly (**B**, next page).

6. Finally, to adjust the color intensity and contrast in the photo, work with the **Contrast**, **Clarity**, and **Vibrance** controls as a trio (**C**, next page). If you want to strengthen the contrast, increase the Contrast setting; and to darken the edges of shapes and restore contrast to the midtones, increase the Clarity setting slightly. You can also adjust the Vibrance setting to boost the color saturation.

A This photograph is overexposed (note the lack of detail in the highlights).

B In this Camera Raw histogram for the overexposed photo shown above, pixels are clustered at the right edge, which indicates that highlight areas are being clipped.

C In the Basic tab, we Alt/Option dragged the Recovery slider until only a few white highlight areas remained in the clipping preview.

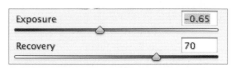

A We lowered the Exposure setting and readjusted the Recovery setting to darken the entire photo and recover details in the highlights. These corrections made the midtones too dark, however, so we'll need to remedy that next.

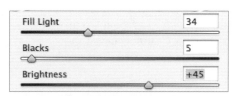

B Increasing the Fill Light setting lightened the shadows and darker midtones (note that the shadows in the trees and at the far side of the pool are now lighter). We also reduced the Brightness slightly to recover more detail in the highlights and lighter midtones.

C Finally, we reduced the Contrast to further lighten the midtones, increased the Clarity to sharpen the edges, and increased the Vibrance to restore some color saturation.

Using the Tone Curve tab

After using the Basic tab, **A** the next step is to tweak the adjustments in specific tonal ranges. In the Tone Curve tab (unlike in the Basic tab), you can adjust the exposure of such tonal ranges as the highlights or the lighter or darker midtones.

To adjust the curve, you could place points manually (as you would in the Curves dialog), but we prefer to use the Parametric sliders—one for each of the four tonal ranges. The sliders won't misshape the curve (which creates posterization).

To make targeted adjustments using the Parametric sliders:

1. Click the **Tone Curve** tab, ⊞ then click the nested **Parametric** tab. Behind the curve is a static image of the current histogram. **B**

2. Increase the value for the **Highlights**, **Lights**, **Darks**, or **Shadows** control to lighten that tonal range (and thereby raise the corresponding part of the curve above the diagonal line) **C** (and **A–B**, next page); or reduce the value to darken that tonal range (and thereby lower that part of the curve below the diagonal line).

3. *Optional:* Click and hold on the Targeted Adjustment tool, ⊹◎ then choose Parametric Curve from its menu. Drag up or down a short distance on a tonal range in the photo to move the slider that corresponds to that range. ★

4. *Optional:* To expand or contract the tonal range that a slider adjustment affects, move its corresponding region control, which is located

A This photo was adjusted by using the Basic tab (see pages 48–49).

C The Darks adjustment in the Tone Curve tab produced this change.

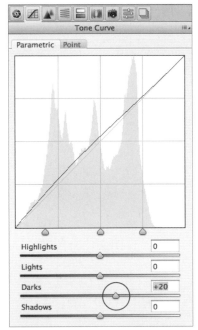

B By using the sliders in the Tone Curve tab (nested Parametric tab), you can fine-tune the exposure without throwing off the tonal balance that you achieved via the Basic tab. For our photo, we increased the Darks setting to lighten and restore detail in the lower midtones (the background behind the flowers).

below the graph. The left region control affects the Shadows slider, the middle control affects the Lights and Darks slider, and the right control affects the Highlights slider. **C–D** The more a control bends the curve away from the diagonal line, the more the adjacent tonal ranges are affected; the closer the curve gets to the diagonal, the less any of the adjacent ranges are affected.

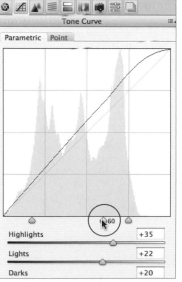

A Increasing the Lights and Highlights raised the upper part of the curve.

B Our Lights and Highlights adjustment lightened the flowers without diminishing the details in those areas. The contrast between the sunlit and darker areas was preserved as the tonal distribution was improved.

C Moving the middle region control to the right lowered the middle of the curve and narrowed the range and impact of the Lights slider.

D Moving the middle region control to the right darkened the midtones slightly and restored some detail.

Reviving color

If the contrast in your photo is pretty good but the colors are undersaturated and dull, make a few basic exposure corrections via the Basic tab and then try using the controls in the HSL/Grayscale tab to brighten it. By improving the color, you'll also improve the contrast. (If you were to use only the Basic tab sliders to correct the color, the photo would probably end up looking washed out.)

To increase color saturation and luminance:

1. Into Camera Raw, open a photo that is undersaturated but has good contrast.**A**

2. To brighten the midtones by lightening them, do either of the following:

   In the **Tone Curve** tab ▨ (nested **Parametric** tab), increase the **Lights** and/or **Darks** setting.**B**

   In the **Basic** tab, ⚙ increase the **Brightness** setting.

3. In the **Basic** tab, do any of the following:

   If it's hard to distinguish individual colors in the shadows or lower midtones, increase the **Fill Light** value.

   To make the colors richer, set the **Vibrance** to around +20.

4. In the **HSL/Grayscale** tab ▤ (nested **Saturation** tab), use the sliders to boost the saturation of individual colors (**A–B**, next page), and in the **Luminance** tab, use the sliders to increase their brightness (**C–D**, next page).

➤ Click and hold on the Targeted Adjustment tool, ⊕ then choose Hue, Saturation, or Luminance from its menu (depending on what needs correction). Drag a short distance to the left or right on a color in the photo to adjust the sliders that it corresponds to. ★

A The colors in this photo look dull and undersaturated.

B In the Tone Curve tab, we set the Lights value to +28 to lighten and brighten the colors in just the upper midtones, taking care not to overlighten the sky.

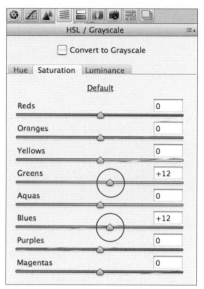

A In the HSL/Grayscale tab (nested Saturation tab), we increased the saturation of the greens and blues.

B The blue sky and the green foliage now look a bit brighter, but the colors still could use more oomph.

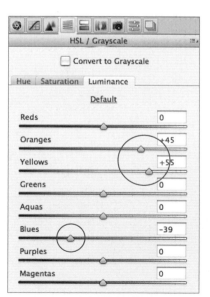

C In the nested Luminance tab, we increased the luminance (lightness) for the oranges and yellows but lowered it for the blues. (The effect of lowering the luminance for blues is like photographing a sky with a polarizing filter.)

D Now the darker blue sky is complemented by the richer colors in the lower half of the photo, and both provide a good contrast to the white clouds, white bark on the tree, and white trim on the houses.

Using the Detail tab

With the basic adjustments completed, you can now explore some of the more specialized features in Camera Raw, such as the Detail, Split Toning, and Lens Corrections tabs.

We're enthusiastic about the sharpening controls in the Detail tab of Camera Raw because they're very powerful yet easy to work with. And, of course, as with all Camera Raw adjustments, you can change the settings or undo the sharpening at any time without altering the original pixel data.

Note: The "capture" sharpening that you apply via Camera Raw shouldn't be your only round of sharpening. After editing and resizing your document in Photoshop—and before printing it — you should apply another round of sharpening by using the Smart Sharpen or Unsharp Mask filter.

To sharpen a photo via the Detail tab:

1. Double-click the Zoom tool to set the zoom level for the preview to 100%, so you will be able to gauge the effects of the sharpening.

2. Click the **Detail** tab. Note: If the words "Preview Only" display there, open the Camera Raw Preferences dialog and choose **Apply Sharpening To: All Images**.

3. With the **Hand** tool (press H or hold down the Spacebar), drag an area of detail to be monitored into view in the preview.

4. For subject matter that needs a lot of sharpening, such as hard objects or architecture, set the **Amount** value to 100;**A–B** if less sharpening is needed, try a value of around 50–60. For a portrait, keep the Amount at or below 70.

A We'll apply sharpening to enhance the detailed surfaces and clearly defined shapes in this photo of a vintage windmill.

B After setting the zoom level to 100%, our next step was to Alt-drag/Option-drag the Amount slider to 100 to set the strength for the sharpening.

➤ To judge a sharpening setting in a mono-chromatic grayscale preview without the distraction of color, Alt-drag/Option-drag a slider.

5. The **Radius** setting controls how many pixels surrounding the edges are modified; keep this setting between 1 and 1.4.

6. Alt-drag/Option-drag the **Detail** slider until the grayscale preview displays the amount of edge detail that you want to revive in moderate to high-contrast areas.**A** At a low setting (25–50),

only high-contrast areas will be affected; at a high setting (50 or higher), most areas will be affected.

7. To limit the sharpening to high-contrast edges, Alt-drag/Option-drag the **Masking** slider to the right until the black-and-white preview displays areas of black (low-contrast areas that won't be sharpened) and white lines along the edges of shapes (areas of high contrast).**B** As you drag the slider to the right, the areas of black will

Continued on the following page

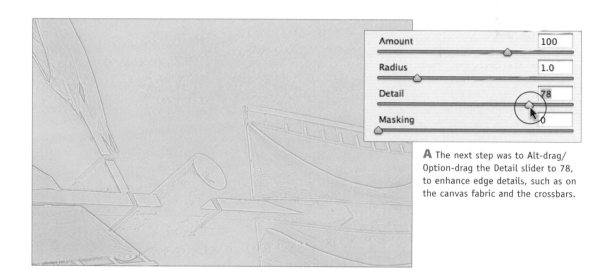

A The next step was to Alt-drag/Option-drag the Detail slider to 78, to enhance edge details, such as on the canvas fabric and the crossbars.

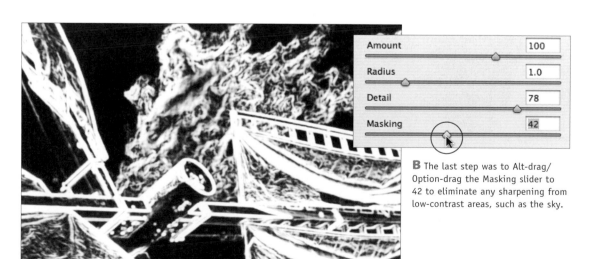

B The last step was to Alt-drag/Option-drag the Masking slider to 42 to eliminate any sharpening from low-contrast areas, such as the sky.

increase in the display and the areas of white will be limited to high-contrast edges.**A–B**

➤ Try not to oversharpen your photo. Sharpen it only to the point where crisp edges start to become evident at 100% view. Remember, this is just the first round of sharpening; you'll apply stronger sharpening, more selectively, in Photoshop.

➤ By using the Masking slider in Camera Raw and the visual feedback it provides, you can apply sharpening where needed without sharpening areas of low contrast or areas that contain artifacts or stray pixels (noise).

➤ To learn how to use the Luminance and Color sliders in the Detail tab to reduce color and luminance noise, see our *Photoshop CS4, volume 1: Visual QuickStart Guide.*

A This is the original photo before we applied sharpening.

B And this is the same photo after using the sharpening controls in the Detail tab.

Using the Split Toning tab

The Split Toning tab lets you reduce an image to grayscale and then apply one or more color tints ("tones") to make it look richer and more luminous, or to give it an aged quality. You can apply one tint to the highlight areas and a different one to the shadow areas. In our testing, this technique works well on photos of metallic objects or images that have subdued coloration.**A**

To convert a photo to grayscale and apply a color tint:

1. After correcting the exposure in the image, click the **HSL/Grayscale** tab, ≣ then check **Convert to Grayscale**.

2. Click the **Split Toning** tab. ▄

3. Move both **Saturation** sliders about halfway across the bar to make it easier to judge the colors you'll apply in the next step (this is just a temporary change).

4. Move the **Highlights Hue** slider to tint the highlights **B** and/or the **Shadows Hue** slider to tint the shadows.

5. Readjust the **Saturation** value for each hue. Avoid oversaturating the highlights, or the coloring effect will be too strong.

6. *Optional:* Reduce the **Balance** setting to apply more of the Shadows tint to the entire photo, or increase it to apply more of the Highlights tint to the entire photo.**C–D**

A To emphasize the elegant geometric shapes and linear details in this photo of an antique car, we'll apply a tint to the dark areas.

B Via the HSL/Grayscale tab, we tinted the highlights with blue.

C Next, we tinted the shadows with brown. Finally, an adjustment made to the Balance setting to favor the shadow color more lends the photo an antique feel.

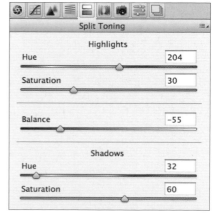

D These are the final Split Toning settings that we chose.

Using the Lens Corrections tab

The Lens Corrections tab provides controls for correcting two peculiarities of photography. Depending on the lens and aperture being used, sometimes a camera lens can't properly focus all the wavelengths of colored light to exactly the same spot. The result may be a color fringe around some of the shapes in the photo, most noticeably along the edges of high-contrast areas. To correct this problem in Camera Raw, you can resize the offending color channel by using one of the Chromatic Aberration sliders.

Another problem, over- or underexposure near the edges of a photograph, is usually created by a wide-angle or telephoto lens. This can be corrected by using the Lens Vignetting sliders. The same sliders can also be used to intentionally add a vignette, in order to focus the viewer's attention toward the center of a photo.

To fix chromatic aberrations:

1. Click the **Lens Corrections** tab  and zoom in to a high-contrast area in the photo.

2. Under **Chromatic Aberration**, do any of the following:

   Reduce the **Fix Red/Cyan Fringe** setting to remove a red fringe from high color-contrast edges,**A–C** or increase it to remove a cyan fringe. (The image may "jump" in the preview while the color channel is being scaled.)

   Reduce the **Fix Blue/Yellow Fringe** setting to remove a blue fringe from high color-contrast edges, or increase it to remove a yellow fringe.

3. From the **Defringe** menu, choose **All Edges**.

A Note the red fringe around the rock on the left, which is noticeable against the light color of the water.

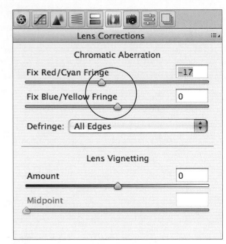

B We reduced the Fix Red/Cyan Fringe value in the Lens Corrections tab.

C The Chromatic Aberration adjustment reduced the red fringe.

To correct or apply lens vignetting:

1. Click the **Lens Corrections** tab.

2. Under **Lens Vignetting**:

   If your camera lens created a dark area (vignette) around the edges of the photo that you want to remove, increase the **Amount**. Or conversely, if you want to focus attention to the center of your photo by softly darkening the outer border, reduce the Amount.

   Reduce the **Midpoint** setting to widen the vignette toward the center of the photo, **A–B** or increase it to shrink the vignette outward toward the edges.

A Adding a dark vignette around the edges of this photo will help focus attention to the center, which is the area we want to showcase.

Lens Vignetting	
Amount	−100
Midpoint	8

B In the Lens Corrections tab, we moved the Amount slider all the way to the left to create a dark edge. Then, to widen the darkening vignette (expand it inward), we set the Midpoint value to 8.

APPLYING POST-CROP VIGNETTING ★

If you crop a photo that you previously applied lens vignetting to, parts of the vignette will be cropped out. Using the Post Crop Vignetting sliders in the Lens Corrections tab, you can readjust the vignette, as shown in **A–B** this page and **A–C**, next page.

A Using the Lens Vignetting sliders in the Lens Corrections tab, we applied a dark vignette to the outer edges of this photo.

B Then a crop that we applied to the photo eliminated the vignette along the top and right edges.

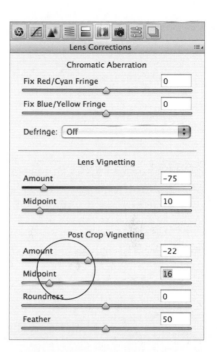

A Under Post Crop Vignetting, we lowered the Amount value to darken the edges, then lowered the Midpoint value to expand the vignette inward (see the values at right).

| Roundness | +77 |
| Feather | 8 |

B The Roundness setting controls the shapes of the vignette; the Feather setting controls the softness of the transition. The values shown above produced an obvious round vignette, with a relatively sharp transition area.

Post Crop Vignetting

Amount	−22
Midpoint	16
Roundness	−25
Feather	60

C We lowered the Roundness value and increased the Feather value, to produce a soft-edged oval vignette.

Using the Adjustment Brush tool ★

Unlike settings chosen in the Camera Raw tabs which apply to the overall photo, the Adjustment Brush tool lets you make local adjustments to specific areas. You can do this to apply corrections or to emphasize a particular detail in a composition. The sliders are similar to the ones in the Basic tab, except in this case, you apply a mask with the tool first to isolate areas for adjustment.

To use the Adjustment Brush tool:

1. After adjusting the photo via the Basic and Tone Curve tabs, click the **Adjustment Brush** tool ✐ (K). The sliders for the tool display.**A**

2. To "zero out" all the other sliders except one, click the + or – button for any one of the sliders.

3. Adjust the brush diameter by pressing [or], and choose a **Feather** value well above 0 to allow the adjustment to fade at the edges of your strokes. Set the **Flow** to 50 (for the smoothness of the stroke) and set the **Density** to 60 (for the strength of the adjustment).

4. Check **Show Mask** and **Show Pins**, then draw strokes over areas of the photo that you want to apply corrections to. You can release the mouse, then paint over any other noncontiguous areas that you want to add to the mask. A pin will mark the location of the mask.

5. Uncheck Show Mask, then adjust the masked areas by using the sliders (**A**, next page) and/or apply a tint via the Color swatch.

6. *Optional:* To apply local adjustments to other areas, click New, then repeat steps 2–5 (see **B–C**, next page and also pages 66–67).

7. *Optional:* To edit an adjustment, click a pin, then add to the mask and/or change the settings.

➤ To change the mask color, click the swatch next to Show Mask.

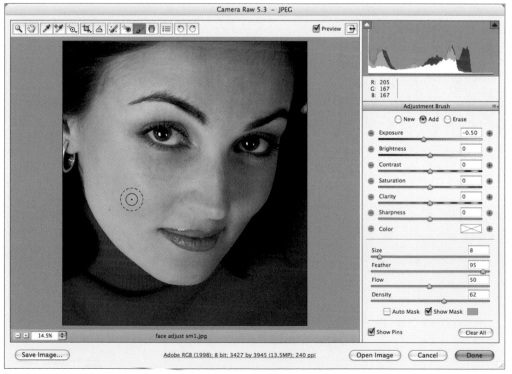

A In this photo, we want to smooth the model's skin, lighten her eyes, and sharpen her lips and eyelashes. We clicked the Adjustment Brush tool. On the right, we clicked the – button (next to Exposure) to zero out the sliders, checked Show Mask and Show Pins, then started dragging over the face to paint a mask.

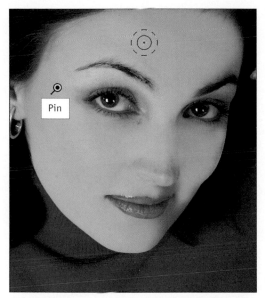

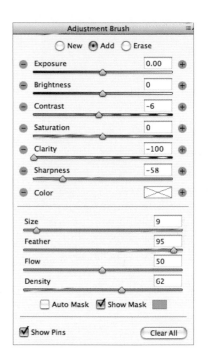

A A pin appeared when we finished creating the mask. We unchecked Show Mask, then lowered the Contrast, Clarity, and Sharpness values (shown at right) to smooth the skin.

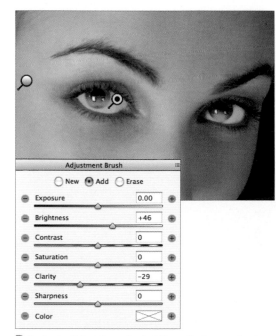

B Next, we clicked New, checked Show Mask, zeroed out the sliders, then painted a mask over the white areas of the eyes. We unchecked Show Mask, then chose the values shown above.

C Now the skin is smoother and the eyes are lighter. To hide the pins temporarily, we unchecked Show Pins (V), then rechecked it before proceeding with the next step.

See also the figures on the following page

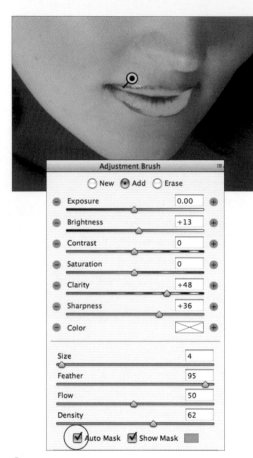

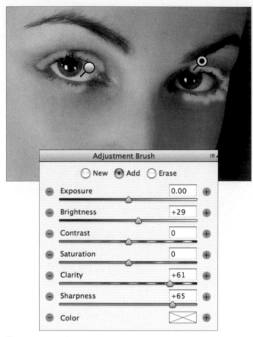

A To sharpen the lips, we clicked New and zeroed out the sliders. To help mask the specific color area of the lips, we checked Auto Mask, scaled the brush to an appropriate size, and applied brush strokes, each time starting with the pointer over the lip color. The mask covered only the areas that matched the initial color we clicked. We chose the values shown above.

B To sharpen the eyelashes, we clicked New, checked Show Mask, zeroed out the slider settings, then painted a mask over the eyelashes. We unchecked Show Mask, then chose the values shown above.

C Now the lips and eyelashes are sharper.

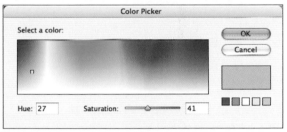

A To subdue the highlight above the eyebrow, we clicked New, checked Show Mask, zeroed out the slider settings, then painted a mask over the eyebrow. We unchecked Show Mask, then chose the values shown at left.

B To add a tint of "skin color" to the adjustment that we applied to the eyebrow area, we clicked the Color swatch on the panel, then chose a color from the Color Picker.

C The final results show the smoothing, sharpening, and tonal corrections that we applied to various areas with the Adjustment Brush tool.

REMOVING ADJUSTMENT BRUSH EDITS

➤ To remove a local adjustment, click an existing pin in the preview, click Erase on the panel, check Show Mask, then apply brush strokes where you want to erase the mask.

➤ To remove an entire mask and its adjustments, click a pin, then press Backspace/Delete.

Using the Graduated Filter tool ★

When shooting a landscape, sometimes setting the proper exposure for the foreground can result in an overexposed sky. To solve this problem on site, photographers reduce light on the upper part of the lens by using a graduated neutral-density filter. With the Graduated Filter tool in Camera Raw, you can simulate the effect of such a filter.

To adjust the exposure in part of a landscape with the Graduated Filter tool:

1. After adjusting the photo via the Basic and Tone Curve tabs, click the **Graduated Filter** tool ▢ (G). The sliders for the tool display.**A**

2. To "zero out" all the other sliders except one, click the + or – button for one of the sliders.

3. Shift-drag the tool over an area in the photo to isolate it for editing, starting from where you want the strongest adjustment to be applied.**B**

4. Use the sliders to adjust the exposure of the filtered area (**A–C**, next page) and/or apply a tint by clicking the Color swatch.

➤ At any time, you can decrease or increase the length of the filter overlay by Shift-dragging the green or red dot. To reposition the overlay, drag the line that connects the two dots.

➤ To apply a separate filter to another area of the photo, click New, then repeat steps 2–4.

➤ To hide the filter overlay, uncheck Show Overlay or press V. To remove the filter overlay, click it, then press Backspace/Delete.

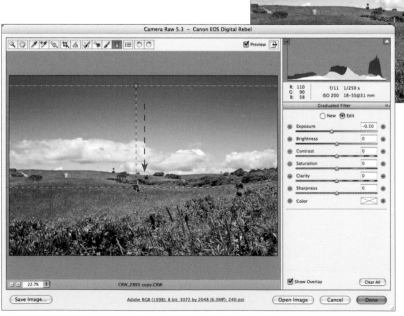

A The sky in this photo looks overexposed (washed out).

B We clicked the Graduated Filter tool, then clicked the – button (next to Exposure) to zero out the sliders. Next, we Shift-dragged the tool downward through the center of the sky.

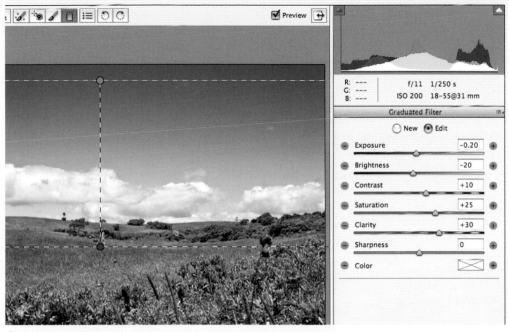

A The tool created an overlay, which defines the editable area. We chose the panel settings shown above to darken the exposure for the sky. The adjustment is applied fully at the green dashed edge of the overlay and gradually diminishes to no adjustment at the red dashed edge.

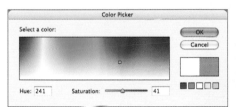

B To tint the upper part of the sky to enhance the color, we clicked the Color swatch on the panel, then clicked a deep blue in the Color Picker.

C In the final image, you can see that we were able to deepen the sky without changing the foreground.

Combining multiple exposures

You've probably had the experience of trying to shoot a subject against a bright sky or in front of a window. If you set the exposure properly for the figure or object in shadow, details will be lacking in the bright sunlit areas (and vice versa). To simulate what the human eye sees naturally, one solution is to shoot dual exposures and then combine them into one image. If you didn't bracket your shots, you can simulate two exposure versions for a single raw photo with Camera Raw. If you did bracket your shots, follow the instructions in the sidebar on the next page. In either case, the last task is to blend the best of the two exposures by using a layer mask.

To simulate two exposures with one photo:

1. Open a raw photo **A** into Camera Raw.*

2. In the **Basic** tab,  use the exposure sliders to create a proper exposure for the shadows and lower midtones, **B** then in the **Tone Curve** tab, use the Parametric sliders to refine the adjustment in the four tonal regions.

3. Hold down Shift (Open Image becomes Open Object) and click **Open Object.** ** The photo will open in a new document window in Photoshop, on a Smart Object layer.

JPEG photos are unlikely to contain enough pixel data for this technique to work successfully.

**If Open in Photoshop as Smart Objects is checked in the Workflow Options dialog, don't hold down Shift.*

A The range of lighting in this scene was too wide to be captured in this single exposure: The alley of trees is slightly underexposed, whereas the sky and background are slightly overexposed. We'll use Camera Raw to create a proper exposure for each area, then combine them to create the best of both worlds.

	Auto	Default	
Exposure			0.00
Recovery			0
Fill Light			22
Blacks			0
Brightness			+34
Contrast			−9
Clarity			+22
Vibrance			+18
Saturation			0

B We used the sliders in the Basic tab to recover shadow details (in the trees), then Shift-clicked Open Object to open the photo into Photoshop as a Smart Object layer.

4. Right-click/Control-click below the Smart Object layer name and choose **New Smart Object via Copy** from the context menu (don't use Ctrl-J/Cmd-J, the Duplicate Layer command).**A**

5. Double-click the thumbnail on the Smart Object copy to reopen the photo in Camera Raw. Because you used the New Smart Object via Copy command, this Smart Object isn't linked to the original one, and changes made in Camera Raw will affect only this copy. This time, use the **Basic** and **Tone Curve** tabs to create a proper exposure for the upper midtones and highlights,**B** then click OK. Upon your return to Photoshop, your edits will be applied to the copy of the Smart Object layer.

6. To blend the two layers, follow the steps on the next page.

A The New Smart Object via Copy command created an unlinked copy of the original Smart Object.

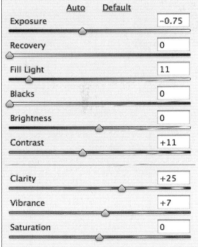

B We opened the copy of the Smart Object into Camera Raw, used sliders in the Basic tab to properly expose the upper midtones and highlights in the background and sky, then clicked OK to return to the Photoshop file.

COMBINING BRACKETED SHOTS

To combine bracketed shots, follow steps 1–3 on the preceding page to open the first photo as a Smart Object. In Bridge, select the next bracketed photo and choose File > Place > In Photoshop. It will open into Camera Raw. Apply any corrections, then click OK. The second photo will become a new Smart Object layer in the current Photoshop document. Finally, follow the steps on the next page.

To blend two exposures via a layer mask:

1. Continuing in Photoshop, select the upper of the two image layers. If more of the properly exposed areas are on the topmost layer, click the **Add Layer Mask** button  at the bottom of the Layers panel to create a white mask;**A** or if the lower layer contains more of the properly exposed areas, Alt-click/Option-click the **Add Layer Mask** button to create a black mask.

2. Choose the **Brush** tool (B or Shift-B), a Soft Round tip, Normal mode, and an Opacity of 70–80%. If you created a white mask, paint with black, or if you created a black mask, paint with white. Press [or] to change the brush diameter. Draw strokes to reveal some of the corrected areas.**B** If you need to remask any areas, press X and paint with the reverse color.

3. Make any other edits, then save your file.**C**

A In the layer mask thumbnail for the copy of the Smart Object layer, you can see the dark brush strokes that we applied to reveal areas from the underlying layer.

B We added a white mask to a copy of the Smart Object layer, then chose the Brush tool (70% Opacity) and black as the Foreground color, and painted to reveal some of the corrected midtone and shadow areas from the underlying layer.

C In the final image, the exposure information from the two Smart Object layers is combined (compare it with **A** on page 70). The sky looks richer now, and you can see more details in the trees. Note: As a last step, we applied a Hue/Saturation adjustment layer to tone down the acid green in the grassy field.

Retouching photos

Camera Raw has its own healing tool for zapping small imperfections: the Spot Removal tool (formerly called the Retouch tool). It's useful for removing spots caused by dust or debris on a camera lens or to heal blemishes in a portrait, but we recommend using the healing tools in Photoshop for more complex retouching tasks.

To remove spots with the Spot Removal tool:

1. Open a photo that has spots that need retouching. Choose the **Spot Removal** tool ✎ (B) and zoom to 100%.

2. Drag in the preview; a red and white **target** circle displays (don't release the mouse button).**A** Drag inward or outward to scale the circle and cover the spot or blemish. When you release the mouse, a green and white source circle will appear, linked to the target circle.

3. Drag the **source** circle over an area to copy those pixels to the target circle.**B**

4. From the **Type** menu, choose **Heal** (our preferred setting) to blend source pixels into the texture and tonal values of the target pixels, or **Clone** to produce an exact copy of the source pixels.

5. Do any of the following optional steps:

   Drag the edge of either circle to **scale** the pair, **reposition** a pair by dragging, or **add** more circle pairs to correct other blemishes. They'll remain available even after you exit the dialog, because the original raw pixels haven't been altered.

   To **hide** the circles, uncheck Show Overlay or click a different tool.

   To **remove** a pair of circles, click inside one circle, then press Backspace/Delete; or to remove all the pairs, click **Clear All**.

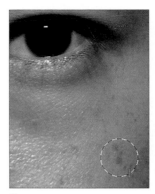 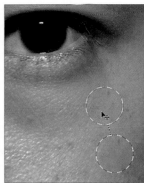

A With the Spot Removal tool, drag to create a target circle over a blemish…

B …then drag to position the source circle. Pixel data will copy automatically from the source circle to the target circle.

RETOUCHING ASSEMBLY-LINE STYLE

If you have a series of photos with the same dust spots in the same, er…spots, you can remove them all by retouching just one of the photos, and letting Camera Raw fix the rest. Open the photos into Camera Raw (see step 1 on page 76). Use the Spot Removal tool, but be careful not to reposition the green and white source circle. Keep the tool selected, click Select All, click Synchronize, choose Spot Removal from the Synchronize menu, then click OK. Camera Raw will position a source circle automatically in an appropriate spot in each of the other photos. Verify that Camera Raw has positioned them correctly, and reposition them, if needed.

We can use the Spot Removal tool to fix the dust spots in this photo, then synchronize the edit to correct the same dust spots in other photos of the same shoot and subject.

Red-eye (red eyes) in portrait photos results from light emitted by a camera-mounted or built-in electronic flash reflecting off the retina. If your camera doesn't have a built-in red-eye control (or you forgot to use it), a click of the Red Eye Removal tool in Camera Raw can fix it. It's even easier to use than the Red Eye tool in Photoshop.

To remove red-eye from a portrait:

1. Zoom in on the eye area in a portrait.

2. Choose the **Red Eye Removal** tool 🔴 (E).

3. Drag a marquee across the pupil of one of the eyes.**A–B** The tool will remove all traces of red.

4. Hide the overlay rectangle by unchecking Show Overlay or pressing V so you will be able to judge the slider adjustments. Adjust the **Pupil Size** for the recolored pupil. You don't want the pupil to be enlarged.

5. Adjust the **Darken** value to control the darkness of the pupil. Try a value of 30–50%. Light-colored eyes need a lower setting than dark ones.

6. Repeat steps 3–5 for the other eye.

➤ To resize the overlay rectangle in order to expand its effect, drag one of its edges with the Red Eye Removal tool.

➤ To remove one overlay rectangle, click it with the Red Eye Removal tool, then press Backspace/Delete. To remove all rectangles, click Clear All.

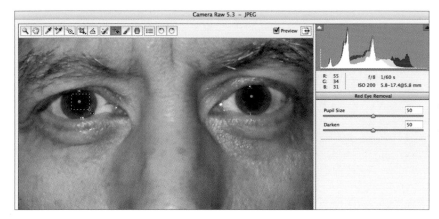

A With the Red Eye Removal tool, we dragged a marquee over one eye.

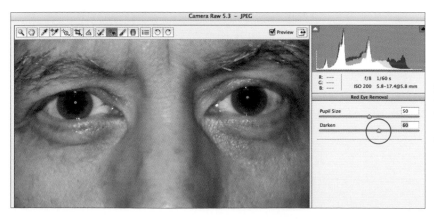

B The tool removed the red area (shown here with the overlay hidden). We used the Darken slider to darken the pupil.

Using Camera Raw presets

By saving your carefully chosen Camera Raw settings as a preset, you'll be able to reestablish those settings quickly when needed simply by choosing that preset. A saved preset can also be applied to a series of photos from the same shoot or that were taken under the same studio lighting conditions if they happen to need the same or similar corrections. Settings presets can be applied to a single photo or multiple selected photos in Camera Raw, or to multiple selected thumbnails in Bridge.

To save Camera Raw settings as a preset:

Method 1

1. Open a photo into Camera Raw that has been corrected with the settings that you want to save as a preset (or use Camera Raw to apply corrections to a photo now).

2. Choose **Save Settings** from the Settings menu. The Save Settings dialog opens. **A**

3. Check which settings you want saved in the settings file (if you want to display check marks for just one category of settings, choose that category from the Subset menu). Click Save. In the next Save Settings dialog, enter a Name (preferably one that describes the type of settings being saved). Keep the .xmp extension, and keep the location as the Settings folder, then click Save.

Method 2

1. Follow step 1 in Method 1, above.

2. Click the **Presets** tab, then click the **Add Preset** button at the bottom. The New Preset dialog opens.

3. Enter a Name for the preset, then check which settings you want saved in the settings file (if you want to display check marks for just one category of settings, choose that category from the Subset menu). Click OK.

You can apply a user-defined preset (a saved collection of settings) to any photo in Camera Raw.

To apply a Camera Raw preset:

With a photo open in Camera Raw, do either of the following:

Click the **Presets** tab, then click the desired preset.

From the **Apply Preset** submenu on the Camera Raw Settings menu, choose the desired preset.

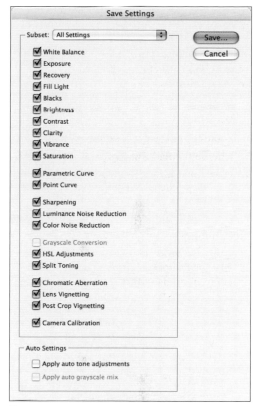

A In the Save Settings dialog, check which of your Camera Raw settings are to be saved in the preset.

TAKING SNAPSHOTS OF YOUR EDITS ★

You can periodically save the current editing stage of your photo (and the current Camera Raw settings) as a snapshot, then use the snapshots to compare, or restore the photo to, different editing stages. The snapshots will save with the file.

To create a snapshot of the current editing stage, click the Snapshots tab, then click the New Snapshot button. In the New Snapshot dialog, enter a name and click OK. You can continue editing the photo.

To restore the photo (and preview) to the snapshot version, click the snapshot name in the Snapshots tab. You can choose Custom Settings from the Camera Raw Settings menu to restore your latest settings, or save your latest settings as a new snapshot.

Want more options? Right-click/Ctrl-click a snapshot name and choose: Rename (to rename it), Update with Current Settings (to have your latest edits overwrite those in the snapshot), or Delete (to delete the snapshot).

Processing multiple photos via Camera Raw

In theory, you could open multiple files from the same photo shoot into Camera Raw, choose settings for one of the photos, then click Synchronize to apply those settings to all the photos. In actuality, it's unlikely that all the adjustments needed for one photo will work like a charm on the rest—even if they were taken during the same shoot. However, for applying some initial settings, such as basic white balance, exposure, and tone curve adjustments, the Synchronize option may prove to be a useful timesaver.

To synchronize the Camera Raw settings of multiple files:

1. In Bridge, select two or more photo thumbnails that were shot under the same lighting conditions and that require the same corrections, then double-click one of them. Note: The photos should be in the same format (e.g., all raw or all JPEG photos).

2. The photos will display on the filmstrip panel on the left side of the Camera Raw dialog (**A**, next page).

3. Click one of the thumbnails, and make the necessary adjustments to it—including cropping, if you want all the photos to be cropped the same way.

4. Click **Select All** at the top of the filmstrip panel or Ctrl-click/Cmd-click multiple thumbnails, then click **Synchronize** (**B**, next page). The Synchronize dialog opens. It has the same options as the Save Settings dialog, which is shown on the previous page.

5. Check the settings to be applied; or choose a category of settings from the Synchronize menu, then remove or add any check marks.

6. Click OK. The current settings in the category you chose will be applied to all the thumbnails that you selected.

USING THE RATING FEATURES

If you open multiple files into Camera Raw, before performing any adjustments, you can scroll through the images to get a closer look and, if you like, also select and rate them. When you do so, these shortcuts will come in handy:

TASK	SHORTCUT
Scroll through the images sequentially	Press the up or down arrow on the keyboard
Apply star ratings	Select one or more image thumbnails, then press Ctrl-./Cmd-. (period)
Remove stars one by one from selected thumbnails	Press Ctrl-,/Cmd-, (comma)
Select only the images that have star ratings	Alt-click/Option-click the Select Rated button (Select All becomes Select Rated)

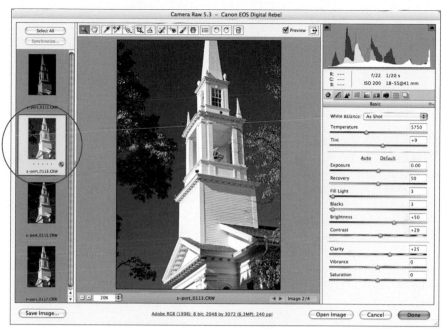

A If you open multiple raw photos into Camera Raw via Bridge, the image thumbnails will display in the filmstrip panel on the left side of the dialog. Click the thumbnail for one of the photos that you want to apply corrections to, then make the needed corrections.

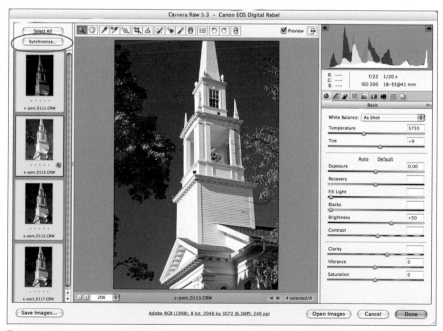

B Either Ctrl-click/Cmd-click the other thumbnails that you want to apply the same corrections to or click Select All, then click Synchronize.

The user-created settings presets that are listed in the Presets tab of the Camera Raw dialog are also accessible in Bridge and can be applied to multiple photos in one pass via batch processing. If you like, you can assign a series of preset settings to selected photos—with each one controlling a handful of adjustments—simply by choosing one preset after another.

To apply Camera Raw presets to multiple photos via Bridge:

1. In Bridge, do either of the following:

   Shift-click or Ctrl-click/Cmd-click multiple photo thumbnails, then from the Edit > **Develop Settings** submenu, choose the desired preset or presets. Those settings will be applied to the selected photos.

   Click the thumbnail for a photo that you know contains the desired settings, then choose Edit > Develop Settings > **Copy Camera Raw Settings** (Ctrl-Alt-C/Cmd-Option-C). Click one or more other thumbnails, then choose

   Edit > Develop Settings > **Paste Settings** (Ctrl-Alt-V/Cmd-Option-V).**A** The Paste Camera Raw Settings dialog opens. Check the settings to be pasted or choose a tab name from the Subset menu, remove or add any check marks, then click OK.

➤ To remove all Camera Raw settings from a selected photo thumbnail in Bridge, choose Edit > Develop Settings > Clear Settings or right-click/Control-click the thumbnail and choose that command from the Develop Settings submenu on the context menu.

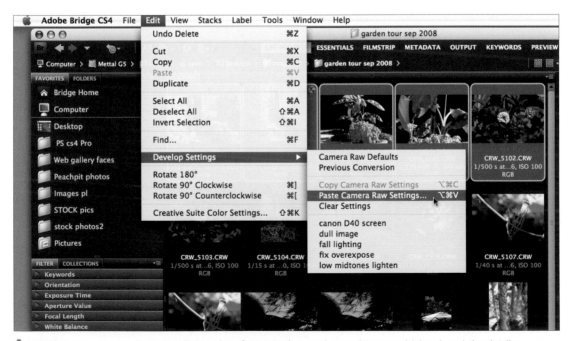

A In Bridge, you can copy the Camera Raw settings from one photo and paste them to multiple selected thumbnails.

Saving files via Camera Raw

Via the Save Options dialog in Camera Raw, you can rename your photos and convert them to the DNG (digital negative), JPEG, TIFF, or PSD (Photoshop) format without having to open them in Photoshop. DNG is an up-and-coming format that Adobe has developed for long-term archiving of raw photos (see the sidebar on page 13). Camera Raw lets you save files in this format, but Photoshop does not.

To save a copy of a photo via Camera Raw:

1. Open a raw file (not a digital JPEG or TIFF photo) into Camera Raw; or if you opened multiple photos into the Camera Raw dialog, select the ones to be converted.

2. Click **Save Image** in the lower left corner of the dialog. The Save Options dialog opens.**A**

3. Choose a **Destination** (location), and choose **File Naming** options, which can include the file name, current date, and sequential numbering.

4. Choose a file **Format**, then check the desired options for that format. If you want to archive the files, choose Digital Negative (DNG).

   ➤ Via the Embed Original Raw File option, you can embed the entire original raw file into the DNG file. We recommend doing this only if you also plan to edit your raw photos in the conversion software that was included with your camera.

5. Click Save.

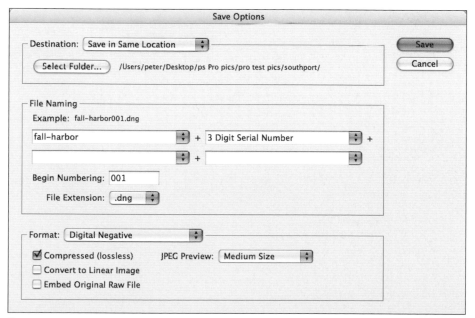

A One purpose of the Save Options dialog is for saving photos in a different format, such as Digital Negative (DNG).

Working with photos as Smart Objects

If you open or place a Camera Raw photo into Photoshop as a Smart Object, you'll be able to readjust its Camera Raw settings at any time.

To open a Camera Raw photo into a new Photoshop file as a Smart Object:

With a photo open in Camera Raw, hold down Shift (Open Image becomes Open Object) and click **Open Object.*** A new document window opens in Photoshop, with the image on a Smart Object layer.

To place a Camera Raw file into an existing Photoshop file as a Smart Object:

1. Open a Photoshop document.

2. In Bridge, click the thumbnail for a raw photo, or for a JPEG photo that was edited previously in Camera Raw.

3. Choose File > Place > **In Photoshop**. The Camera Raw dialog opens.

4. Make adjustments to the photo, then click OK. It will appear on its own layer in the Photoshop document, in a transform box.

5. Apply any scale or shape transformations, then either press Enter/Return or double-click in the transform box to accept the image. It is now a Smart Object layer.

To edit a Smart Object (Photoshop) layer in Camera Raw:

1. In Photoshop, double-click a **Smart Object** layer thumbnail to reopen an embedded copy of the photo into the Camera Raw dialog.

2. Make any desired adjustments, then click OK to apply your edits to the Smart Object layer. Like all Camera Raw edits, the original photo won't be altered.

   Note: When you scale a Smart Object layer, Photoshop uses the pixel data from the original photo, so the image quality isn't diminished—provided you don't enlarge it beyond the size at which it was originally captured.**A–C** To learn its original dimensions, click its thumbnail in Bridge, then look in the File Properties category of the Metadata panel.

If Open in Photoshop as Smart Objects is checked in the Workflow Options dialog, don't hold down Shift.

THE BEST WAY TO SCALE A PHOTO

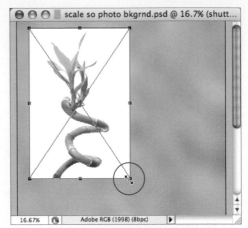

A To scale a Smart Object layer in Photoshop, Shift-drag a corner handle on the transform box (Move tool).

B This photo was opened in Photoshop as an ordinary layer. When we enlarged it, it lost definition.

C This time, the photo was enlarged after being placed as a Smart Object layer: The details remained crisp and the image quality remained high.

This chapter summarizes fundamental Photoshop features that you will use throughout the book. Topics include using the main application features; configuring the panel docks; choosing the correct image size and bit depth; cropping and rotating images; applying content-aware scaling; choosing and saving colors; using the Layers and History panels; creating and using adjustment and fill layers; and creating and managing presets.

Using the main application features

To display the Application frame (Mac OS): ★

Choose Window > **Application Frame**. (The Application frame always displays in Windows.)

To dock document windows as tabs: ★

To dock a floating document window **manually**, drag its title bar to the tab area (or to the bottom of the Application or Options bar) of the Application frame or just below the title bar of another floating document window, and release when the blue drop zone bar appears. (If this doesn't seem to work, make sure Enable Floating Document Window Docking is checked in Edit/Photoshop > Preference > Interface.)

If one or more documents are already docked as tabs and you want to dock all floating document windows into the Application frame or into the currently active document window, right-click/ Control-click a tab and choose **Consolidate All to Here** from the context menu.**A**

To set a preference so all future documents that you open will dock as tabs automatically, go to Edit/Photoshop > Preferences > Interface and check **Open Documents as Tabs**.

➤ To cycle among currently open documents, press Ctrl-Tab/Control-Tab.

A Three documents are docked in this Application frame.

USING PHOTOSHOP

4

IN THIS CHAPTER

To use the Application bar: ★

Use the controls on the **Application bar** to manage your document windows.**A** In Windows, the main Photoshop menus also display on the Application bar. In the Mac OS, the Application bar is docked in the Application frame. When the Application frame is hidden, the Application bar is docked below the main menu bar; if you don't see the bar, choose Window > Application Bar.

Using the Arrange Documents menu, you can quickly display multiple tabbed or floating documents in various layouts, such as two documents side by side or stacked vertically, or four or six documents in a grid.

To arrange multiple document windows: ★

Click the **Arrange Documents** menu icon ▦ on the Application bar to open the menu, release the mouse, then click one of the icons (the availability of the icons depends on how many documents are open).

You can just as effortlessly go back to displaying one document at a time.

To redisplay one document at a time: ★

On the **Arrange Documents** menu ▦ on the Application bar, click the **Consolidate All** icon ▦ (the first icon on the menu).

The screen modes control which Photoshop interface features are displayed.

To change the screen mode: ★

From the **Screen Mode** menu ▣ on the Application bar, choose **Standard Screen Mode, Full Screen Mode with Menu Bar,** or **Full Screen Mode;** or press **F** to cycle through the modes. Note: In Edit/Photoshop > Preferences > Interface, you can customize the background and border colors for each screen mode.

SHORTCUTS FOR ZOOMING

TASK	WINDOWS	MAC OS
Zoom in	Ctrl- + (plus), or Ctrl-Spacebar click or drag	Cmd- + (plus) or Cmd-Spacebar click or drag
Zoom out	Ctrl- – (minus) or Alt-Spacebar click	Cmd- – (minus) or Option-Spacebar click

CHOOSING ZOOM PREFERENCES

The following options are available in Edit/Photoshop > Preferences > General:

► Check Animated Zoom for smooth, continuous zooming when using the Zoom tool or zoom shortcuts (OpenGL is required*).★

► With Zoom Resizes Windows checked, a floating document window will resize if you change the zoom level via the Ctrl/Cmd- + (plus) or Ctrl/Cmd- – (minus) shortcut or the Zoom tool.

► If your mouse has a scroll wheel and you check Zoom with Scroll Wheel, you can change the zoom level by scrolling the wheel.

► Check Zoom Clicked Point to Center to center the zoom view at the location you click.★

► Check Enable Flick Panning to move a magnified image across the screen by dragging with the Hand tool a short distance and then releasing the mouse (OpenGL is required*).★

Check Enable OpenGL Drawing in Preferences > Performance.

View Extras menu for showing or hiding guides, grids, and rulers   Zoom tool   Arrange Documents menu   Screen Mode menu

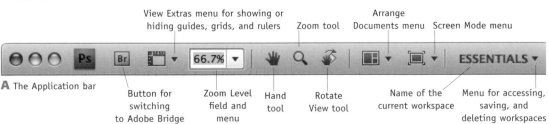

A The Application bar   Button for switching to Adobe Bridge   Zoom Level field and menu   Hand tool   Rotate View tool   Name of the current workspace   Menu for accessing, saving, and deleting workspaces

Using the panels

When you need to fully maximize your screen space, you can hide all the currently open panels, then make them reappear only when needed. If you hide the panels when your document is in Standard screen mode, the document window will resize dynamically to the maximum screen width; when you redisplay the panels, the document window resizes again.

To hide (or show) the panels:

Do any of the following:

Press **Tab** to hide (or show) all open panels, including the Tools panel.

Press **Shift-Tab** to hide (or show) all open panels except the Tools panel.

To make hidden panel docks reappear:

With the panels hidden as per the instructions in the preceding steps, move the pointer to the dark gray bar at the right edge of the Application frame. The panel docks (but not freestanding panels) will redisplay temporarily. Move the pointer away from the panels, and they'll disappear again. (If this doesn't seem to be working, go to Edit/Photoshop > Preferences > Interface, and check Auto-Show Hidden Panels.) ★

➤ If you want to conserve screen space, collapse the panels you use least frequently to icons **A** (see also the following page).

A Each panel in Photoshop has a unique icon, which displays when the panel is collapsed.

➤ Memorize the icons for the panels you use often, so you'll be able to identify them quickly as you work.

CHOOSING VALUES QUICKLY

➤ In many panels (e.g., Adjustments, Masks, Layers, Character, and Paragraph), in some dialogs, and on the Options bar, you can change numerical values quickly by using a scrubby slider: Drag slightly to the left or right over the option name or icon.

 A scrubby slider

➤ To access a pop-up slider (e.g., to choose an Opacity percentage) click the arrowhead. To close a slider, click anywhere outside it or press Enter/Return. If you click an arrowhead to open a slider, you can press Esc to close it and restore its last setting.

➤ To change a value incrementally, click in a field in a panel or dialog, then press the up or down arrow key.

Most edits made in Photoshop require the use of one or more panels. Photoshop has a clever system for storing and accessing panels so they're easily expandable and collapsible and don't intrude on the document window when they're not being used.

In the predefined workspaces (which are accessed from the Workspace menu on the Application bar), the panels are arranged in docks on the right side of your screen—except for the Tools panel, which is on the left side. Each dock can hold one or more panels or panel groups;**A** we'll show you how to reconfigure them.

To configure the panel groups and docks:

Show or hide an individual panel: Show a panel by choosing its name from the Window menu. The panel will display either in its default group and dock or in its last location. To bring a panel to the front of its group, click its tab (panel name). A few panels can also be shown or hidden via keyboard shortcuts, which are listed on the Window menu.

Show or hide an individual panel (icon): Click the icon or panel name. If Auto-Collapse Iconic Panels is checked in Edit/Photoshop > Preferences > Interface and you open a panel from an icon, it collapses back to the icon when you click elsewhere. With this preference unchecked, the panel stays expanded. To collapse a panel back to an icon, click the Collapse to Icons button ▶️ on the panel bar or click the panel icon.

Maximize or minimize a panel (non-icon) or group (to toggle the full panel to just a panel tab, or vice versa): Double-click the panel tab; or click the title bar (the gray bar next to the panel tabs).

Use a panel menu: Click the ▤ icon to open a menu for whichever panel is in front in its group.

Close a panel or group: ★ To close (but not collapse) a panel, right-click/Control-click the panel tab and choose Close from the same context menu. To close a whole panel group, choose Close Tab Group from the context menu. To close a group that's an icon, expand it first.

Collapse a whole dock to icons or to **icons with names:** Click the Collapse to Icons button ▶️ or the dark gray bar at the top of the dock.**B** To further collapse the dock to just icons (no names), drag the vertical edge of the dock inward horizontally; **C** to expand the dock, click the dark gray bar again.

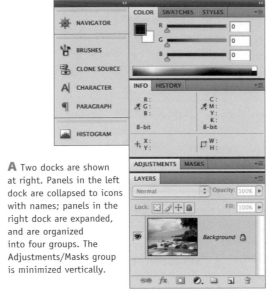

A Two docks are shown at right. Panels in the left dock are collapsed to icons with names; panels in the right dock are expanded, and are organized into four groups. The Adjustments/Masks group is minimized vertically.

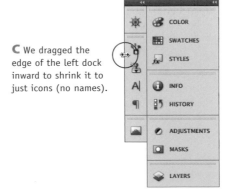

B When we clicked the Collapse to Icons button to collapse the whole right dock to icons, the panel groups were preserved.

C We dragged the edge of the left dock inward to shrink it to just icons (no names).

Widen or narrow a dock and panels: Position the pointer over the vertical edge of the dock (↔ cursor), then drag sideways.

Lengthen or shorten a panel or group (in the Mac OS, when the Application frame is hidden): Position the pointer over the bottom edge of the panel or group, and when you see this pointer,↕ drag upward or downward. Panels docked in the same group will scale accordingly.

Move a panel to a different slot, same group: Drag the panel tab (name) to the left or right.

Move a panel to a different group: Drag the panel tab over the title bar of the desired group, and release when the blue drop zone border appears.**A**

Move a panel group upward or downward in a dock: Drag the title bar, and release the mouse when the horizontal blue drop zone bar appears in the desired location.**B**

Create a new dock: Drag a panel tab or title bar sideways over the vertical edge of the dock,**C** and release the mouse when you see the blue vertical drop zone bar.

Make a panel or group free-floating: Drag the panel tab, icon, or title bar out of the dock. You can stack free-floating panels and groups together from top to bottom.

Reconfigure a dock (icons): Use methods similar to those for an expanded group. Drag the group "title" bar (double dotted line) ▦ to the edge of a dock to create a new dock; or drag the title bar between groups to restack it (look for a horizontal drop zone line); or drag the title bar into another group to add it to that group (look for a blue drop zone border).

➤ To redock floating panels into the Application frame, drag the dark gray bar at the top of the panel group to the right edge of the Application frame, and release when the pointer is at the edge and you see a vertical blue drop zone line.★

➤ To create a custom workspace that remembers panel locations and which panels are displayed, choose Save Workspace from the Workspace menu on the Options bar.

➤ To reset the panels to their default locations and visibility states, choose Essentials from the Workspace menu on the Application bar. ★

A A blue drop zone border appears as we drag a panel into a different group.

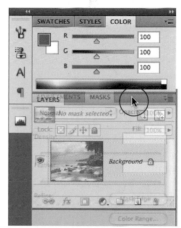

B A blue horizontal drop zone bar appears as we move a panel group upward within the same dock.

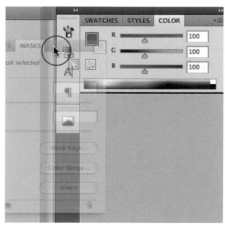

C A blue vertical drop zone bar appears as we drag a panel out of a dock to create a new dock for it.

Tools on the Tools panel

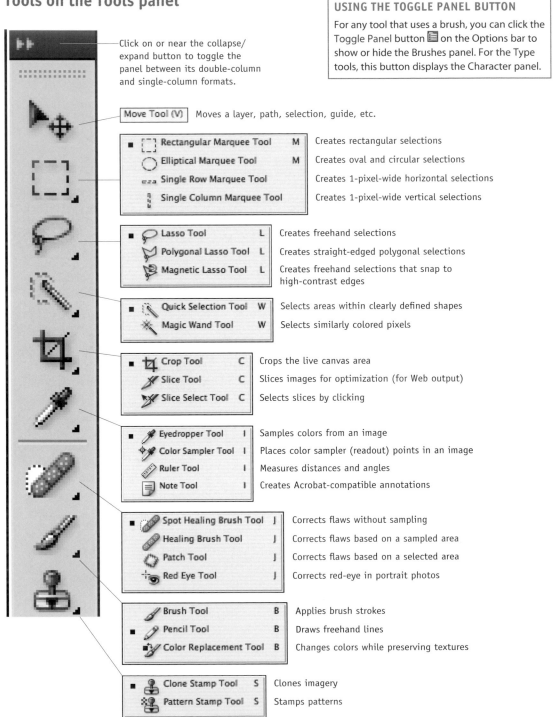

Click on or near the collapse/expand button to toggle the panel between its double-column and single-column formats.

| Move Tool (V) | Moves a layer, path, selection, guide, etc. |

■ Rectangular Marquee Tool — M — Creates rectangular selections
  Elliptical Marquee Tool — M — Creates oval and circular selections
  Single Row Marquee Tool — Creates 1-pixel-wide horizontal selections
  Single Column Marquee Tool — Creates 1-pixel-wide vertical selections

■ Lasso Tool — L — Creates freehand selections
  Polygonal Lasso Tool — L — Creates straight-edged polygonal selections
  Magnetic Lasso Tool — L — Creates freehand selections that snap to high-contrast edges

■ Quick Selection Tool — W — Selects areas within clearly defined shapes
  Magic Wand Tool — W — Selects similarly colored pixels

■ Crop Tool — C — Crops the live canvas area
  Slice Tool — C — Slices images for optimization (for Web output)
  Slice Select Tool — C — Selects slices by clicking

■ Eyedropper Tool — I — Samples colors from an image
  Color Sampler Tool — I — Places color sampler (readout) points in an image
  Ruler Tool — I — Measures distances and angles
  Note Tool — I — Creates Acrobat-compatible annotations

■ Spot Healing Brush Tool — J — Corrects flaws without sampling
  Healing Brush Tool — J — Corrects flaws based on a sampled area
  Patch Tool — J — Corrects flaws based on a selected area
  Red Eye Tool — J — Corrects red-eye in portrait photos

  Brush Tool — B — Applies brush strokes
■ Pencil Tool — B — Draws freehand lines
  Color Replacement Tool — B — Changes colors while preserving textures

■ Clone Stamp Tool — S — Clones imagery
  Pattern Stamp Tool — S — Stamps patterns

A The upper part of the Tools panel

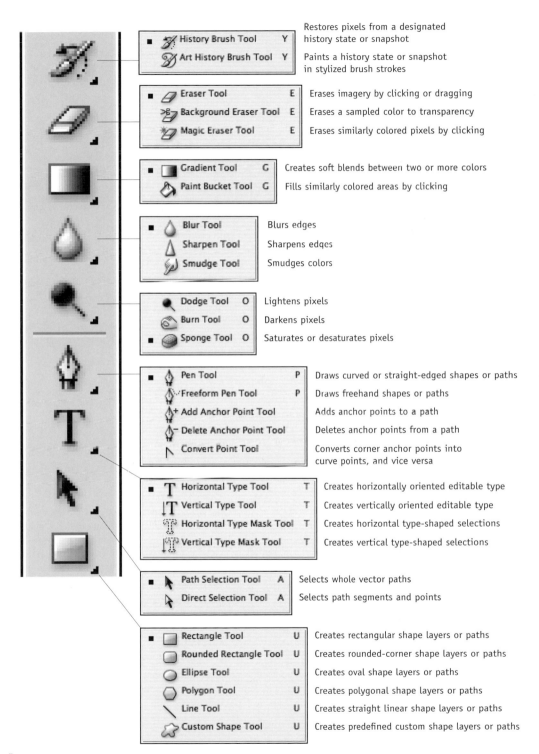

History Brush Tool	Y	Restores pixels from a designated history state or snapshot
Art History Brush Tool	Y	Paints a history state or snapshot in stylized brush strokes

Eraser Tool	E	Erases imagery by clicking or dragging
Background Eraser Tool	E	Erases a sampled color to transparency
Magic Eraser Tool	E	Erases similarly colored pixels by clicking

Gradient Tool	G	Creates soft blends between two or more colors
Paint Bucket Tool	G	Fills similarly colored areas by clicking

Blur Tool	Blurs edges
Sharpen Tool	Sharpens edges
Smudge Tool	Smudges colors

Dodge Tool	O	Lightens pixels
Burn Tool	O	Darkens pixels
Sponge Tool	O	Saturates or desaturates pixels

Pen Tool	P	Draws curved or straight-edged shapes or paths
Freeform Pen Tool	P	Draws freehand shapes or paths
Add Anchor Point Tool		Adds anchor points to a path
Delete Anchor Point Tool		Deletes anchor points from a path
Convert Point Tool		Converts corner anchor points into curve points, and vice versa

Horizontal Type Tool	T	Creates horizontally oriented editable type
Vertical Type Tool	T	Creates vertically oriented editable type
Horizontal Type Mask Tool	T	Creates horizontal type-shaped selections
Vertical Type Mask Tool	T	Creates vertical type-shaped selections

Path Selection Tool	A	Selects whole vector paths
Direct Selection Tool	A	Selects path segments and points

Rectangle Tool	U	Creates rectangular shape layers or paths
Rounded Rectangle Tool	U	Creates rounded-corner shape layers or paths
Ellipse Tool	U	Creates oval shape layers or paths
Polygon Tool	U	Creates polygonal shape layers or paths
Line Tool	U	Creates straight linear shape layers or paths
Custom Shape Tool	U	Creates predefined custom shape layers or paths

A The midsection of the Tools panel

Continued on the following page

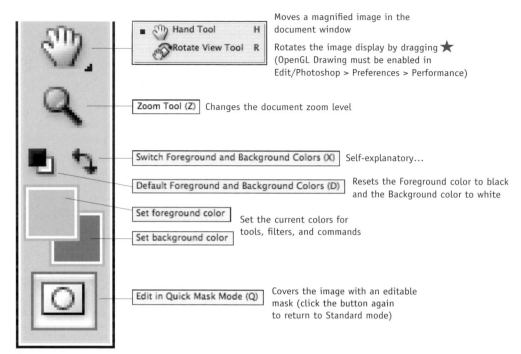

Moves a magnified image in the document window

Rotates the image display by dragging ★ (OpenGL Drawing must be enabled in Edit/Photoshop > Preferences > Performance)

Changes the document zoom level

Self-explanatory...

Resets the Foreground color to black and the Background color to white

Set the current colors for tools, filters, and commands

Covers the image with an editable mask (click the button again to return to Standard mode)

A The lower part of the Tools panel

SPRING-LOAD YOUR TOOLS ★

If you want to quickly access a tool and its Options bar settings temporarily without having to actually click the tool on the Tools panel, hold down the default letter that's assigned to it.

For example, say you happen to have the Brush tool selected but you want to move imagery on a layer, which requires using the Move tool. You would hold down the V key, drag in the document window, then release V. Or to access the Hand tool temporarily, you would hold down the H key. This process is a little less efficient if you want to access a tool that shares a slot with other tools (which most tools do). In this case, the letter shortcut accesses whichever tool happens to be visible on the Tools panel, so you would have to plan ahead and select the two tools that you want to switch back and forth between before using them.

USE THE AVAILABLE INFO

➤ Do you need to refresh your memory on the function of an icon or a panel or dialog option? If Show Tool Tips is checked in Edit/Photoshop > Preferences > Interface and you rest the pointer on a tool icon without clicking the mouse button, the tool name and shortcut pop up onscreen.

➤ Some dialogs (such as Select > Refine Edge) have a Description area containing information about the option your pointer is currently hovering over.

➤ Keep an eye on the Info panel for color breakdowns, document data (e.g., file size, color profile, dimensions, resolution), and tool hints (ways to use the currently selected tool).

➤ Use the Histogram panel to monitor changes to the tonal ranges in an image as you apply color and tonal adjustments.

Changing the image size

There are three ways to choose a file resolution:

➤ When opening a raw digital photo, set the output resolution in the Workflow Options dialog (see page 44).

➤ For a JPEG photo or other image that you need to change the resolution for, use the Image Size dialog after opening the file in Photoshop.

➤ When scanning, set the input resolution to control how many pixels the device is to capture.

Changing the image size without resampling

Via Image > **Image Size** (Ctrl-Alt-I/Cmd-Option-I), you can change the resolution of your file and/or its width and height. If you do so with the **Resample Image** option **unchecked A** (to prevent resampling), the image quality will remain at its current level. This method is recommended for digital photos and scanned images.

By default, JPEG photos from a digital camera have a low resolution (72–180 ppi) and very large width and height dimensions, with a sufficient number of pixels for high-quality output (prints as large as 8" x 10")—provided you increase the resolution to the proper value. When you increase the resolution to suit your output device, the pixel dimensions remain constant and the print dimensions are reduced.

Unlike photos from a digital camera, scanned images usually have small document size dimensions, yet contain a high resolution and sufficient pixel dimensions to produce large, high-quality prints. For a scanned image, change the Width or Height (under Document Size) with Resample Image unchecked; the Resolution and Pixel Dimensions values will remain constant.

Changing the image size with resampling

If your file contains too few pixels to meet the resolution requirement of your target output device, you'll have to increase the resolution with **Resample Image** checked. **B** Pixels will be added to the file (its pixel dimensions will increase) and its storage size will increase. Increase the resolution only to a level that is sufficient for achieving the desired output quality.

When you downsample a file (decrease its resolution with Resample Image checked), pixels are discarded permanently. For a Web graphic, downsampling isn't an issue, as users will view it on a computer display, which is a low-resolution device. For print output, on the other hand, try to avoid resampling, because it reduces the image sharpness (although you can use a sharpening filter to remedy blurring from a minor degree of resampling).

A With Resample Image unchecked in the Image Size dialog, the Document Size values can be changed, but not the Pixel Dimensions.

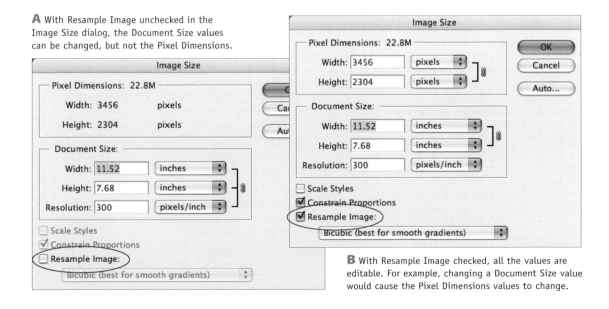

B With Resample Image checked, all the values are editable. For example, changing a Document Size value would cause the Pixel Dimensions values to change.

Choosing a bits per channel mode

To get good-quality output from any device, you must capture or input a wide range of tonal values. One of the challenges in photography is capturing detail in the shadow areas of a scene. The wider the dynamic color range of the camera, the more subtleties of color and tone it is capable of capturing. Most advanced amateur and professional digital SLR cameras capture from 12 to 16 bits of accurate data per channel, and the resulting photos contain abundant pixels in all levels of the tonal spectrum.

Consumer-level scanners capture 10 bits of accurate data per channel, whereas high-end professional scanners can capture up to 16 bits of accurate data per channel. Like photos from the better digital cameras, scans from a high-resolution device contain an abundance of pixels in all the tonal ranges.

Three bit depths are available on the Image > **Mode** submenu in Photoshop: 8, 16, and 32 Bits/Channel mode. At the present time, 16 Bits/Channel mode offers the most advantages. 32 Bits/Channel mode may be the mode of choice for high-end photographic work in the future, but at the moment Photoshop doesn't support it sufficiently to make it a practical choice.

Another requirement for getting good-quality output is the ability to preserve the full tonal range of your images as you edit them in Photoshop. Because they contain more pixels, 16-bit images are better able to withstand the wear and tear of editing and resampling. Levels and Curves adjustments, for example, remove pixel data and alter the distribution of pixels across the tonal spectrum. After editing, the reduction in image quality will be visible on high-end print output of an 8-bit image, but not of a 16-bit image, because the latter contains more pixels in all parts of the tonal spectrum.

To summarize, the following are some basic facts about 16-bit files that you should know:

➤ Photoshop can open 16-bit CMYK and RGB files.

➤ 16-bit files can be saved in the following widely used formats: Photoshop (.psd), Large Document (.psb), PDF (.pdf), PNG (.png), TIFF (.tif), and JPEG2000 (.jpf).

➤ 16-bit images can be successfully edited and adjusted in Photoshop, with merely a few restrictions. Most of the filters on the Blur, Noise, Render, Sharpen, and Other submenus on the Filter menu are available, as is the Distort > Lens Correction filter, whereas filters on the other submenus are not.

➤ When you print your file, you will need to convert your 16-bit images to 8-bit (Image > Mode > 8 Bits/Channel).

If system or storage limitations prevent you from working in 16 Bits/Channel mode, consider taking this two-stage approach: Perform your initial tonal corrections (such as Levels and Curves adjustments) on the original 16 Bits/Channel version, then convert it to 8 Bits/Channel for further editing.

KEEP YOUR FILES IN RGB COLOR MODE

There are many reasons to keep your files in RGB Color mode (the mode in which digital photos are captured):

➤ Editing is faster in RGB Color mode.

➤ RGB Color is the only Photoshop mode in which all the tool options and filters are accessible.

➤ RGB is the mode of choice for online output, for export to video and multimedia applications, and for desktop inkjet printing.

Your files should be converted to CMYK Color mode only for commercial printing. If and when you do so, convert a copy of the file — not the original!

Cropping and rotating images

You can crop your photos in Camera Raw (see page 45) or by using the Crop tool in Photoshop.

To crop an image using a marquee:

1. Choose the **Crop** tool (C). ⛏

2. Drag a marquee over the part of the image you want to keep.**A**

3. On the Options bar, do the following:

   If you're cropping a layer (not the Background), you can click **Cropped Area: Delete** to delete the cropped-out areas, or click **Hide** to save those areas with the file (they'll extend beyond the visible canvas area but can be moved back into view with the Move tool).

   Check **Shield** to cover the area outside the crop marquee with a dark shield to help you see which part will remain after cropping. You can change the shield color by clicking the **Color** swatch, or change its **Opacity** value.

   For the Perspective option, see Photoshop Help. We prefer to use the Lens Correction filter to correct perspective problems (see our *Photoshop CS4, volume 1: Visual QuickStart Guide*).

4. Perform any of these optional steps:

   To **resize** the marquee, drag any handle (double-arrow pointer). Shift-drag a corner handle to preserve the proportions of the marquee; Alt-drag/Option-drag a handle to resize the marquee from its center; hold down Shift and Alt/Option to do both.

   To **reposition** the marquee, drag inside it.

   To **rotate** the marquee, position the cursor just outside it (curved arrow pointer), then drag in a circular direction. To change the axis point around which the marquee rotates, drag the center point away from the center of the marquee before rotating. The image orientation will change after the next step. (For another way to straighten a crooked photo, see page 93.)

5. Do one of the following:

   Press Enter/Return.**B**

   Double-click inside the marquee.

   Right-click/Control-click the image and choose Crop from the context menu.

➤ To cancel a crop marquee, press Esc.

➤ To create presets for the Crop tool, see page 111.

CROPPING TO A SPECIFIC SIZE

To crop an image to a specific size (say, a standard photo size of 4" x 6"), before using the Crop tool, enter the desired Width and Height values on the Options bar. (You can click the Swap Width and Height button ⇄ to swap the two current values.) For Web output, lower the image Resolution value to 72 ppi; for print output, enter the current image Resolution value to prevent it from changing when the image is cropped. Finally, drag a crop marquee on the image.

A With the Crop tool, drag a marquee across part of an image, and resize or reposition the marquee if needed.

B The image is cropped.

By using a temporary shape layer, you can crop an existing image based on the rule of thirds.

To crop an image using the rule of thirds: ★

1. Open an image, and choose a Foreground color for the temporary grid shape.

2. Choose the **Custom Shape** tool. On the Options bar, click the **Shape Layers** button and choose the **Grid** preset from the Custom Shape preset picker. (If you don't see that preset, choose Reset Shapes from the picker menu, then click Append or OK.)

3. Click the **Geometry Options** arrowhead on the Options bar. Click **Fixed Size**, enter values, and check **From Center.A**

4. Click in the center of the image to make the shape appear. Press V, then reposition the shape so one of the points where the interior lines intersect is over a key feature of the composition.

5. With the **Crop** tool (C), drag a marquee around the outer edges of the grid shape,**B** then to accept the crop, either press Enter/Return or double-click inside the marquee.

6. Delete the selected shape layer by pressing Backspace/Delete).**C**

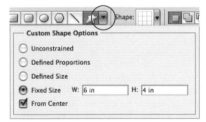

A Choose Custom Shape options via the Options bar.

B With the Grid preset chosen, we clicked the image with the Custom Shape tool, then dragged the Crop tool across the grid.

PLAYING BY THE RULE OF THIRDS

The rule of thirds is a guideline for composition that visual artists use: You imagine that a scene is segmented horizontally and vertically into thirds, and try to position the key features of the scene where the imaginary lines intersect. Aligning a subject at these points creates more visual tension and interest in a composition than simply centering the subject would.

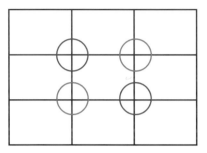

If the center of interest is positioned at one of the imaginary intersections, you can create balance in the picture by positioning a secondary object at the opposing intersection (see the pairs of red circles and blue circles above).

Remember that the rule of thirds is not hard and fast—you can produce a good composition without adhering to it. The important thing is to be conscious of where you position objects in your images and why, and to consider their visual impact.

C The focal points of the improved composition land roughly at the intersections of the former grid.

The Image Rotation commands rotate all the layers in an image. (To rotate just one layer at a time, use a rotate command on the Edit > Transform submenu instead.)

To rotate an image by an exact amount:

Do either of the following:

Choose Image > Image Rotation > **180°, 90° CW** (clockwise), or **90° CCW** (counterclockwise).

Choose Image > Image Rotation > **Arbitrary**. The Rotate Canvas dialog opens. Enter an **Angle** value, click **°CW** (clockwise) or **°CCW** (counterclockwise), then click OK.

You didn't have a tripod handy for that unforgettable moment? Did a sloppy job of scanning? You can straighten out your photo with the Ruler tool.

To straighten a crooked image:

1. Choose the **Ruler** tool ✐ (I or Shift-I).

2. Drag along a feature of the image that you want to orient horizontally or vertically,**A** noting the angle (A) value on the Options bar as you do so.

3. Choose Image > Image Rotation > **Arbitrary**. The angle you dragged will appear in the **Angle** field in the dialog automatically. Click OK.**B**

4. With the **Crop** tool (C), ◫ remove any background color areas that resulted from the rotation.**C**

A We dragged the Ruler tool from left to right along the horizon.

B The Image > Image Rotation > Arbitrary command rotated the image along the angle we drew with the Ruler tool.

C We used the Crop tool to remove the resulting white areas. Now the image looks level.

QUICK SUMMARY: CHOOSING COLORS

The current Foreground color is applied when you create type and when you use some tools and commands, such the Brush or Pencil tool. The current Background color is applied by other edits, such as when you apply a transform command to, or move a selection on, the Background, or rotate the image. The two colors are displayed in the Foreground and Background color squares on the Tools panel **A** and Color panel.

There are many ways to choose a Foreground or Background color:

➤ Enter values or click a color in the **Color Picker.B**

➤ Sample a color in the image with the **Eyedropper** tool.

➤ Click a preset or user-saved swatch on the **Swatches** panel.

➤ Enter values or move sliders on the **Color** panel.**C**

➤ Choose a premixed color from a matching system via the **Color Libraries** dialog (click Color Libraries in the Color Picker to make the dialog appear).

The Default Foreground and Background Colors button (D) makes the Foreground color black and the Background color white.

The Switch Colors button (X) swaps the current Foreground and Background colors.

Foreground color square

Background color square

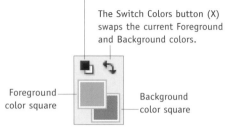

A These are the color controls on the Tools panel.

New color   Current color

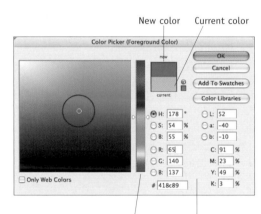

Click a hue on the color slider, then click a variation of that hue in the large square.

Or enter exact values in the HSB, RGB, Lab, or CMYK fields.

B To open the Color Picker, click the Foreground or Background color square on the Tools panel.

Start by clicking the square that you want to mix a color for, if it's not already selected.

Foreground color square

Background color square (selected)

Choose a model for the sliders.

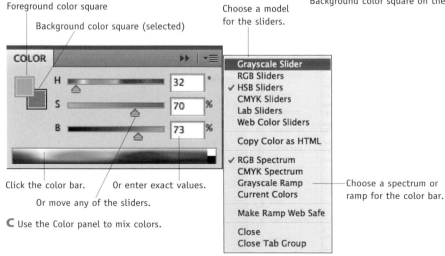

Click the color bar.   Or enter exact values.

Or move any of the sliders.

Choose a spectrum or ramp for the color bar.

C Use the Color panel to mix colors.

QUICK SUMMARY: USING THE SWATCHES PANEL

TASK	METHOD
Choose a color from the Swatches panel	To choose a color for the currently selected color square (Foreground or Background), click a color swatch; to choose a color for the unselected color square, Ctrl-click/Cmd-click a swatch.
Add a color to the Swatches panel (colors on the panel are available for all documents)	Mix or choose a Foreground color by using the Color panel, Color Picker, or Eyedropper tool, then click the New Swatch of Foreground Color button ⬛ on the panel. (Or to name the swatch as you create it, click the blank area below the swatches on the Swatches panel or right-click/Control-click any swatch and choose New Swatch; enter a name, then click OK.)
Delete a swatch from the Swatches panel	Alt-click/Option-click the swatch to be deleted (scissors pointer), **A** or right-click/Control-click a swatch and choose Delete Swatch. This can't be undone.
Save the current swatches on the panel as a library	Choose Save Swatches from the panel menu (keep the .aco extension when you enter a name in the dialog). Relaunch Photoshop to make the library appear on the panel menu.
Save changes to an existing user-created library	Follow the instructions above, except click the existing library name. When the alert dialog appears, click Replace.
Load a user-created or preset swatch library	From the Swatches panel menu, choose a library name, then either click Append to append the new swatches while keeping the existing ones on the panel or click OK to replace the current swatches with the new ones (an alert may appear, giving you the option to save the current swatches).
Restore the default swatches	Choose Reset Swatches from the Swatches panel menu, then click OK. An alert may appear, giving you the option to save the current swatches.
Save the current swatches for use in another Adobe Creative Suite program	On the Swatches panel menu, choose Save Swatches for Exchange.

CHOOSING COLORS FOR WEB OR PRINT

► To mix a specific process color for print output, enter C, M, Y, and K percentages in the Color Picker or Color panel from a printed color swatch book for a matching system, such as the PANTONE® Formula Guide.

► For Web output, enter R, G, and B values (0–255) . White (the presence of all colors) is produced when all the sliders are positioned at the far right, black (the absence of all colors) is produced when all the sliders are at the far left, and gray is produced when all the sliders are aligned vertically with one another at any other location.

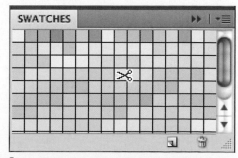

A Alt-click/Option-click a swatch to delete it from the panel.

Using the Layers panel

Every new image contains either a Background or a transparent layer, on top of which you can add layers of many kinds, such as:

➤ **Image** layers, which can contain all opaque pixels or a combination of opaque, transparent, and semitransparent pixels.

➤ **Adjustment** layers and **fill** layers, which apply editable tonal or color adjustments to underlying layers.

➤ **Editable type** layers, which are created with the Horizontal Type or Vertical Type tool.

➤ **Smart Object** layers, which are created when you bring an Illustrator vector file, another Photoshop file, or a raw file into a Photoshop

document via File > Place, or when you convert a standard layer. Double-click a Smart Object layer and the object reopens in its original application for editing; save and close it and the object updates in Photoshop. Apply a filter to a Smart Object layer and it becomes an editable and removable Smart Filter.

➤ **Shape** layers, which contain vector shapes.

You will use the **Layers** panel **A** in most or all of your Photoshop sessions. It lets you create, select, show and hide, duplicate, group, restack, link, merge, flatten, and delete layers; change the layer blending mode, opacity, and fill opacity; apply editable effects; attach layer and vector masks; move layer content; and copy layers between files.

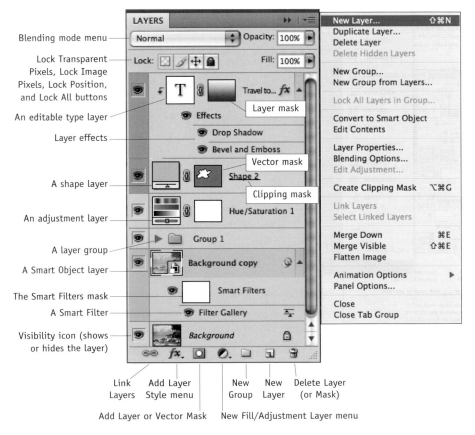

A This figure shows almost every conceivable Layers panel feature. As you work, your panel list may become as long as this one, but it won't look as complex because you'll probably use fewer types of layers and masks at a given time.

QUICK SUMMARY: USING THE LAYERS PANEL

TASK	METHOD
Create a new layer, 100% opacity and fill	Click the New Layer button.
Choose options (name, identifying color, etc.) for a layer as you create it	Alt-click/Option-click the New Layer button or press Ctrl-Shift-N/Cmd-Shift-N.
Copy selected pixels to a new layer	Press Ctrl-J/Cmd-J; or right-click/Control-click in the document window and choose Layer via Copy.
Duplicate the Background, a layer, or a layer group	Click the Background, a layer, or a layer group, then press Ctrl-J/Cmd-J; or drag it onto the New Layer button.
Select multiple layers	Shift-click or Ctrl-click/Cmd-click to the right of the layer names.
Select all layers (not the Background)	Press Ctrl-Alt-A/Cmd-Option-A.
Select all layers of a similar kind (e.g., all image layers or all adjustment layers)	Right-click/Control-click a layer and choose Select Similar Layers.
Select a layer or layer group below the pointer that contains visible pixels	Choose the Move tool (V), check Auto-Select and choose Group or Layer on the Options bar, then click visible pixels.
Open the Layer Style dialog	Double-click next to or below a layer name.
Convert the Background to a layer	Alt-double-click/Option-double-click the Background (or double-click it with no modifier key to choose options).
Create a Background if there is none	Click a layer, then choose Layer > New > Background from Layer.
Create a layer group from existing layers	Select multiple layers, then press Ctrl-G/Cmd-G.
Ungroup a group and keep the layers	Click the layer group, then press Ctrl-Shift-G/Cmd-Shift-G.
Delete a group and its contents	Right-click/Control-click a layer group and choose Delete Group, then click Group and Contents.
Delete a layer or group	Click the layer to be deleted, then press Backspace/Delete. ★
Hide or show all layers except one	Alt-click/Option-click one visibility icon; or right-click/Control-click in the visibility column and choose Show or Hide All Other Layers.
Reposition a layer group in the document	Choose the Move tool (V), check Auto-Select and choose Group on the Options bar, then drag in the document window (or to move just one layer in a group, choose Layer instead).
Choose panel options	Right-click/Control-click a layer thumbnail; choose from the menu.
Change the color behind the visibility icon	Right-click/Control-click the visibility column and choose a color (for color coding layers or layer groups).
Merge layers	Click the upper of two layers (the bottom one must be an image layer) or select multiple layers, then right-click/Control-click and choose Merge Down or Merge Layers (Ctrl-E/Cmd-E). Merge Visible (Ctrl-Shift-E/Cmd-Shift-E) merges all visible layers.
Flatten layers (and discard hidden layers)	Right-click/Control-click any layer and choose Flatten Image.
Copy and merge layers	Select multiple layers, then hold down Alt/Option and choose Merge Visible from the panel menu.

Creating adjustment layers

Unlike the commands applied via the Image > Adjustments submenu, which cause permanent changes to the current layer, adjustment layers are temporary and flexible. You can change their settings; restack, hide, show, or delete them at any time; and even drag-copy them between files—and they don't increase the file size. The adjustment becomes permanent only when you merge the layer downward into the underlying one or flatten the document. Note: The last six commands on the Image > Adjustments submenu can be applied only via their respective dialogs, not via an adjustment layer.

The Adjustments panel makes it super easy to create and edit adjustment layers. In addition to providing quick access to most adjustment controls, the panel also provides added features, such as adjustment presets and preview and resetting options. When creating an adjustment layer, you can choose a settings preset (if available) or custom settings. By using the presets, you can quickly apply basic adjustments, such as increasing the image contrast using three progressively stronger settings via Levels, or increasing the saturation using progressively stronger settings via Hue/Saturation. You can also customize the settings from any preset.

To create an adjustment layer: ★

1. Click the image layer above which you want the adjustment layer to appear.

2. *Optional:* To restrict the effect of the adjustment to a specific area, create a selection.

3. Display the **Adjustments** panel.🖉 The **Add an Adjustment** buttons and scroll list display.**A**

   ▶ To redisplay the Add an Adjustment list when controls for an adjustment layer are displaying, click the Return to Adjustment List button ◁ at the bottom of the panel.

4. Do either of the following:

   Click the **button** for the desired adjustment type. They are arranged as follows: tonal adjustments in the top row, color adjustments in the middle row, and miscellaneous adjustments in the bottom row.

   Click an arrowhead on the scroll list to expand a category of **presets**, then click a preset (not all of the adjustment types have Adobe presets).

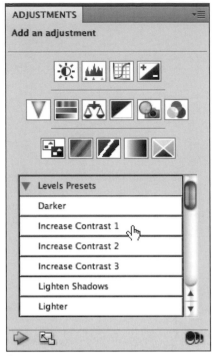

A On the Add an Adjustment list of the Adjustments panel, click a button to display controls for that adjustment type; or click a preset, if available on the scroll list, to display its predefined settings.

5. Controls for the adjustment layer will display on the panel. A new adjustment layer will appear on the Layers panel, containing a thumbnail icon for that particular adjustment type and an editable mask (**A**, next page). If you clicked a preset, the controls are set for you already.

6. Choose the desired settings (if you chose a preset, you can customize the settings or leave them as is).

   ▶ To enlarge the Adjustments panel, click the Switch Panel to Expand View button 🖼 at the bottom of the panel; click the button again to restore it to Standard view.

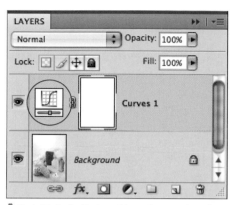

A Each kind of adjustment layer has a unique icon, which displays in the layer thumbnail (and in its button on the Adjustments panel).

Editing adjustment layers

To change the settings for an adjustment layer: ★

1. On the Layers panel, double-click an adjustment layer **thumbnail** to display its settings on the Adjustments panel (or click an adjustment layer and show the Adjustments panel).**B**

2. Do either or both of the following:

   Edit the settings.**C**

   For the Levels, Curves, Exposure, Hue/Saturation, Black & White, or Channel Mixer adjustment type, choose a **preset** from the menu at the top of the panel.

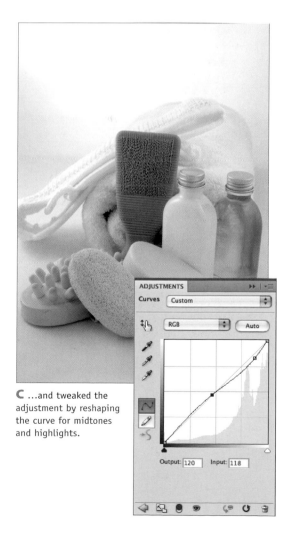

B First, we used a Curves adjustment to darken the midtones in this photo. Later, we double-clicked the Curves layer thumbnail to display our initial settings...

C ...and tweaked the adjustment by reshaping the curve for midtones and highlights.

By holding down the View Previous State button, you can temporarily display the image without any new settings you have chosen for the currently selected adjustment layer.

To view the image without the current adjustments: ★

1. On the Layers panel, double-click an adjustment layer **thumbnail** to display its settings on the Adjustments panel, then edit the settings.**A**

2. To toggle the latest edits off and on, press and hold the **View Previous State** button 🔄 or the \ key, then release.**B**

To hide the effect of an adjustment layer: ★

Click the visibility icon 👁 on the Adjustments panel or Layers panel; click it again to redisplay.

The Reset button either undoes the most recent changes made to an adjustment layer (if any) since the document was opened or restores the default settings. The button icon changes depending on whether you have changed the adjustment layer settings.

To reset an adjustment layer: ★

1. On the Layers panel, double-click an adjustment layer **thumbnail** to select the layer and show the Adjustments panel.

2. Edit the settings.

3. Click the **Reset to Previous State** button 🔄 to cancel the current changes (restore the last settings).

4. Click the **Reset to Adjustment Defaults** button 🔄 to restore the default settings.

➤ To undo the last individual slider, check box, or other adjustment edit, press Ctrl-Z/Cmd-Z.

A We used a Vibrance adjustment layer to reduce the color intensity in this photo.

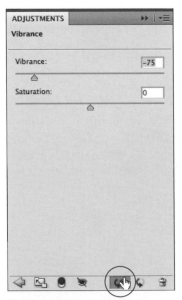

B We pressed the View Previous State button to temporarily remove the current Vibrance adjustment.

Limiting the effect of an adjustment layer

Normally, an adjustment layer affects all the layers below it, but you can clip (restrict) its effect to just the layer directly below it.

To restrict the effect of an adjustment layer to just the layer directly below it: ★

1. On the **Layers** panel, click an adjustment layer.
2. On the **Adjustments** panel, click the **Clip to Layer** button. (Click the button again to "unclip" the adjustment effect.) **A–C**

➤ Another way to limit the effect of an adjustment layer is by lowering the adjustment layer opacity.

By default, all new adjustment layers have a layer mask. To limit which area of the image an adjustment layer affects, edit its mask by creating and filling a selection or by applying brush strokes.

To edit an adjustment layer mask manually:

1. Click an adjustment layer.
2. Press D to choose the default colors (black as the Foreground color).
3. Do either or both of the following:

   Create a **selection** with any selection tool (e.g., the Rectangular Marquee or Lasso), choose Edit > Fill (Shift-Backspace/Shift-Delete), choose Use: Black, then click OK. Deselect.

   Choose the **Brush** tool ✐ (B or Shift-B). On the Options bar, choose a brush tip, Mode: Normal, and Opacity 100%, then paint on the image.

4. *Optional:* To remove black areas from the mask, apply strokes with white chosen as the Foreground color.

   Note: To see illustrations of this technique, see pages 124–127 and 182–183. To edit the mask further via the Masks panel, see pages 152 and 154.

➤ To remove all the black areas from the mask, deselect, click the adjustment layer, then apply Edit > Fill (choose Use: White).

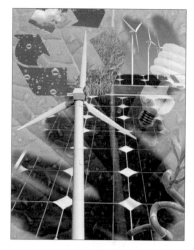

A In the original image, the wind turbine has a yellowish cast.

B A Hue/ Saturation adjustment layer is correcting the cast of the wind turbine, but is also affecting all the underlying layers in the image.

C We clipped the effect of the adjustment layer to just the wind turbine layer directly below it.

Saving adjustment presets

Regardless of how you arrive at custom settings (whether by choosing a preset first or not), you can save your settings as a preset for future use.

To save custom adjustment settings as a preset: ★

1. Create and choose settings for an adjustment layer.

2. From the Adjustments panel menu, choose **Save** [adjustment type] **Preset**. In the Save dialog, enter a name, keep the default location, then click Save. Your user preset is now available for any document via the Add an Adjustment list on the Adjustments panel, and also via the preset menu at the top of the panel when the controls for that adjustment type are displaying.

➤ To delete a user preset, choose that preset, then choose Delete Current Preset from the panel menu.

Merging and deleting adjustment layers

When an adjustment layer is merged downward, the adjustments are applied permanently to the underlying image layer. If you change your mind, either choose Edit > Undo right away or click the prior state on the History panel.

To merge an adjustment layer downward:

Do either of the following:

Click the adjustment layer to be merged downward, then press **Ctrl-E/Cmd-E**.

Right-click/Control-click near the adjustment layer name and choose **Merge Down**.

To delete an adjustment layer: ★

Do either of the following:

Click an adjustment layer on the **Layers** panel, then press **Backspace/Delete**.

Click an adjustment layer on the **Layers** panel (not the mask thumbnail), then click the **Delete Layer** button on the same panel, or on the **Adjustments** panel, click the **Delete Adjustment Layer** button. Click Yes if an alert appears. *Optional:* Click Don't Show Again to prevent the alert from reappearing.

Working with layer groups

During the course of correcting an image, you may use multiple adjustment layers to address different tonal and color problems. If you nest all the adjustment layers in a group, the Layers panel will be better organized, plus you'll have the option to add a layer mask that applies to all the layers in the group.

To create a layer group:

On the Layers panel for an image that contains two or more consecutive adjustment layers, click the topmost adjustment layer, Shift-click the bottommost one,**A** then press **Ctrl-G/Cmd-G** (or from the Layers panel menu, choose New Group from Layers, then click OK).**B** The layers are now nested in a group. Click the triangle to expand or collapse the group listing.

➤ To quickly hide or show all the adjustment layers in a group, click its visibility icon.

As we showed you on page 101, you can limit which areas of the image an individual fill or adjustment layer affects by editing its mask. Now that you have created a layer group of adjustment layers, you can create (and edit) a layer mask specifically for that group.

To create a layer mask for a layer group:

1. Do either of the following:

   Create a **selection** on an image layer.

   To load a selection that you've already saved, Ctrl-click/Cmd-click the alpha channel on the **Channels** panel.

2. On the **Layers** panel, click the adjustment group, then click the **Add Layer Mask** button.🔲 A mask thumbnail will appear on the group layer.

3. *Optional:* Edit the layer mask, such as by applying a gradient or by applying strokes with the Brush tool.**C**

➤ Although each adjustment layer in a group has its own layer mask, the mask effect may be limited by any dark areas that are added to the group mask.

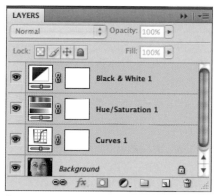

A We selected three adjustment layers on the Layers panel...

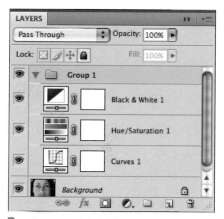

B ...then pressed Ctrl-G/Cmd-G to put the selected layers in a group.

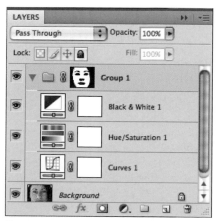

C A mask that we added to the group is controlling the visibility of all the adjustments in the group.

Applying content-aware scaling

The Content-Aware Scale feature is smart enough to resize parts of a photo that it deems to be neutral, or of lesser importance, without distorting key areas, such as figures, buildings, or prominent objects. It comes in handy if you want to change the proportions of a photo to fit a specific layout or to improve the overall composition.

To apply content-aware scaling: ★

1. Open a photo.**A** Press Ctrl-J/Cmd-J to duplicate the Background. Leave the duplicate layer selected and hide the Background.

2. Choose Edit > **Content-Aware Scale** (Ctrl-Alt-Shift-C/Cmd-Option-Shift-C).

3. Drag a center handle on the bounding border. Nonessential areas are scaled first.**B** If you keep dragging, eventually more essential areas are also scaled; if this occurs, drag back in the opposite direction.

4. To accept the scaling, double-click the image or press Enter/Return (**A–C**, next page). Or to cancel it, press Esc.

➤ To protect an area from scaling, select it, choose Select > Save Selection, click OK, then deselect. Choose Edit > Content-Aware Scale, then choose Alpha 1 from the Protect menu on the Options bar.

A In the original photo, the horizon is located smack at the vertical center, which is boring. To reposition the horizon, we will shorten the sky and enlarge the foreground.

B To shrink the sky area, we dragged the top center handle on the Content-Aware Scale border downward. Note that the smart command scaled the sky but not the clouds or the details near the horizon! We will double-click the image to accept the scaling change.

A We moved the imagery upward on its layer. To limit our next round of content-aware scaling to the foreground shapes at the bottom of the image, we created a selection with the Rectangular Marquee tool.

B When we chose Content-Aware Scale, the bounding border surrounded only the selected area. We dragged the bottom center handle downward. This time, the scaling primarily affected the grasses in the midground, and produced the result at left. (Had we not created a selection first, the neutral sky area would also have been scaled.)

C As an additional option, before accepting the Content-Aware Scale edit, we lowered the Amount value (Options bar) to 51%. This changed the result to a blend of content-aware scaling and normal Free Transform scaling. Specifically, the scaling is now affecting the foreground more than the midground. Satisfied with the result, we accepted the edit by double-clicking the image.

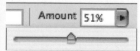

Choosing a mode for the History panel

Whenever you work on a document, your edits are automatically listed as states on the **History** panel 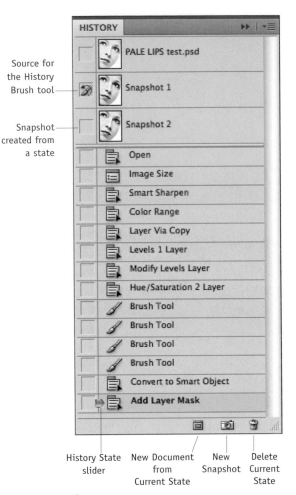 (whether the panel is displayed or not).**A** Via the History & Cache: History States setting in Edit/Photoshop > Preferences > Performance, you can specify the maximum number of states that the panel may list. If this number is exceeded, prior states are deleted to make room for the new ones. Each open document has its own list of states, but they will remain on the panel only until the document is closed.

A fast way to undo multiple edits is by clicking a prior state on the History panel. You can work with the panel in either of two modes. To change modes, choose History Options from the panel menu, then check or uncheck Allow Non-Linear History. With the panel in **linear** mode (Allow Non-Linear History unchecked), if you click an earlier state and resume editing from or delete that state, all subsequent (dimmed) states are discarded. Simple.

In **nonlinear mode**, if you click (or delete) an earlier state, subsequent states aren't deleted or dimmed. In this mode, if you resume image editing with an earlier state selected, your next edit will show up as the latest state on the panel. This latest state will incorporate the earlier stage of the image plus your newest edit, and all the states in between will be preserved. If you change your mind, you can click any in-between state whenever you like and resume editing from there. To learn more about this mode, see pages 108–110.

► The Make Layer Visibility Changes Undoable option in the History Options dialog causes the clicking on or off of a visibility icon on the Layers panel to register as a history state. If you want to prevent this from happening (so those states don't take up needed space on the panel), keep this option off.

► To undo an unintentional file save, click a pre-Save state on the History panel.

Source for the History Brush tool

Snapshot created from a state

History State slider / New Document from Current State / New Snapshot / Delete Current State

A The History panel lists edits made to a document (the most recent edit is listed at the bottom), lets you create snapshots of various editing stages, and lets you undo multiple steps.

Making snapshots of history states

A snapshot is like a copy of a history state, with one major difference: Unlike a state, a snapshot remains on the panel for the current editing session, even if you delete the state from which it was created. You can click a snapshot thumbnail at any time to restore your document to that stage of editing. Take note: All snapshots (and states) are deleted when you close your document.

You should get in the habit of creating snapshots periodically as you work, and certainly before running any actions on your document. To create snapshots manually, follow one of the methods below. In Method 2, you'll be able to choose whether the snapshot will be made from the full document, from merged layers, or from just the current layer.

To create a snapshot of a state:

Method 1 (without choosing options)

1. On the History panel, click the state that you want to create a snapshot of.

2. If the Show New Snapshot Dialog by Default option is off in the History Options dialog, click the **New Snapshot** button at the bottom of the History panel. If the aforementioned dialog option is on, Alt-click/Option-click the New Snapshot button. A new snapshot thumbnail will appear below the last snapshot in the upper section of the panel.**A** Click the last state on the panel to resume editing.

Method 2 (choosing options)

1. *Optional:* To create a snapshot of a layer, click that layer on the Layers panel.

2. Right-click/Control-click a history state and choose **New Snapshot**. The New Snapshot dialog opens.

3. Type a **Name** for the snapshot.

4. Choose a **From** option:

   Full Document creates a snapshot from all the layers on the Layers panel and is useful if you want to preserve all the edits at a particular stage of your document.

   Merged Layers merges all the visible layers on the Layers panel at that state into the snapshot.

   Current Layer makes a snapshot from only the currently selected layer in its current editing state.

5. Click OK.

To make a snapshot become the current state:

Click a snapshot thumbnail. If the Allow Non-Linear History option is off and you edited the document after taking that snapshot, the document will revert to the snapshot stage of editing and all the states will be dimmed; when you resume editing, all dimmed states will be discarded. If Allow Non-Linear History is on and you resume editing, subsequent states remain on the panel.

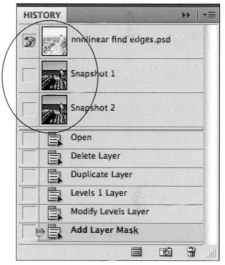

A Create snapshots to preserve editing states that you can potentially revert the document to for the current work session.

CHOOSING SNAPSHOT OPTIONS

Choose History Options from the History panel menu. In the History Options dialog, check or uncheck any of the following options:

► Automatically Create First Snapshot to have Photoshop create a snapshot each time you open a file (this useful option is checked by default).

► Automatically Create New Snapshot When Saving to have Photoshop create a snapshot each time a file is saved. The time of day that a snapshot is created is listed next to the snapshot thumbnail.

► Show New Snapshot Dialog by Default to have the New Snapshot dialog appear whenever you click the New Snapshot button, allowing you to choose options.

Working with nonlinear histories

The History panel's nonlinear mode gives you the flexibility to go back to prior edit states without losing any of the recent edit states. In this exercise, you'll set the History panel to nonlinear mode, create three different edit states, and then go back and compare the three states. This way, you won't have to create a lot of duplicate or merged layers in order to compare your edits.

To compare history edits in nonlinear mode:

1. Choose **History Options** from the **History** panel menu, check **Allow Non-Linear History**, then click OK.

2. Perform an edit in your document, then click the state prior to that edit.**A–D**

3. Create a new edit or a variation of the first one. Again, click the state prior to the first edit to restore the document to its preedited state (**A–D**, next page, and **A–B**, page 110).

4. Create a third edit. All three edits will be listed on the History panel. Click each edit state to compare them, click the one you prefer, and continue working on your document.

A We'll try out three different ways to create a "find edges" version of this photo and use the nonlinear mode of the History panel to compare the results.

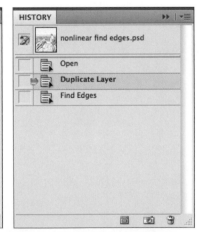

B When we applied the Find Edges filter to a duplicate layer...

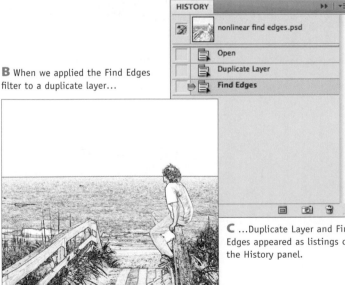

C ...Duplicate Layer and Find Edges appeared as listings on the History panel.

D Because the panel is in nonlinear mode, when we clicked the Duplicate Layer state to restore the photo to its prefilter stage, the more recent state didn't become dimmed.

A We created a Black & White adjustment layer (right), merged it downward, changed its blending mode, and applied Find Edges a second time.

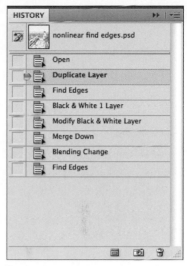

B Next, we clicked on "Duplicate Layer" to restore the image to its prefilter state.

C We applied a Levels adjustment layer to the photo (right), merged that adjustment layer down, then applied Find Edges once more.

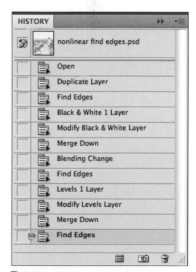

D This is the History panel after our third application of Find Edges.

See also the figures on the following page

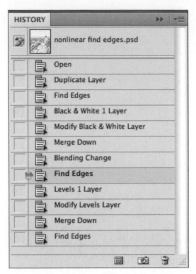

A We clicked the second Find Edges state to display and compare it with the third Find Edges state...

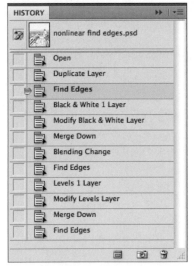

B ...and then we clicked the first Find Edges state to compare it with the second one. This is the History panel in action.

MEMORY USAGE AND THE HISTORY PANEL

► The History panel uses some system memory, which you can free up periodically by choosing Edit > Purge > Histories.

► To clear all states (but not the snapshots) from the History panel for just the current document, right-click/Control-click any state (it doesn't matter which one) and choose Clear History. This command can be undone.

Using presets

For any tool, you can save a collection of the current Options bar settings as a tool preset. Thereafter, when you use that tool, you can choose your preset from either the Tool preset picker on the Options bar or the Tool Presets panel. Having a variety of tool presets at your disposal saves you setup time when you use specific tools, even if the differences among the presets are minor.

If you check Current Tool Only on the Tool Presets panel or on the Tool preset picker, only those tool presets that pertain to the current tool will display on the panel and picker, and you'll have fewer presets to wade through. With Current Tool Only unchecked, the tool presets for all tools will display. Regardless of this setting, when you click a tool preset, the tool that the preset is used with becomes selected automatically.

To create a tool preset:

1. Customize a tool, such as the Brush, Crop, or Type tool.**A** Choose a preset from the appropriate picker (such as a brush tip for the Brush tool or a gradient for the Gradient tool), choose settings from the Options bar (such as dimensions and a resolution for the Crop tool), and choose a Foreground color, if applicable, to be saved with the preset.

2. Do either of the following:

   On the Options bar, click the Tool preset picker thumbnail or arrowhead to display a temporary Tool Presets panel.**B**

   Display the Tool Presets panel.✂

3. Click the **New Tool Preset** button ▣ on the picker or panel. The New Tool Preset dialog opens.**C**

4. If the default **Name** doesn't describe the preset adequately, change it. Also, if the dialog displays an Include Color option (such as for the Brush or Pencil tool), you can check it to save the current Foreground color with the preset.

5. Click OK. The new tool preset will appear on, and can be chosen from, both the picker and the panel.**D**

6. To preserve your tool presets for future use in any document, save them to a tool presets library by choosing **Save Tool Presets** from the picker or panel menu. You can also load any previously saved preset library via either menu.

A Choose options for a tool.

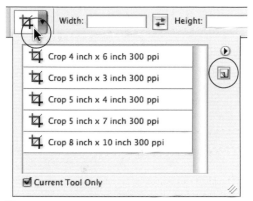

B Click the thumbnail or arrowhead to open the Tool preset picker (a temporary Tool Presets panel), then click the New Tool Preset button (on the right).

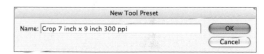

C Be sure to give the new tool preset a descriptive name.

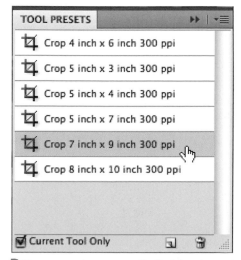

D The new preset appears on the Tool Presets panel.

As an evolving pro user, you're probably already familiar with many of the preset pickers in Photoshop, such as the Brush and Gradient preset pickers that can be accessed via the Options bar. The Swatches and Brushes panels are preset pickers, too. Each item on a picker is called a preset, and each collection of presets that can be loaded onto a picker or panel is called a library.

To create a preset:

Each kind of preset—such as a pattern, color swatch, gradient, custom brush, custom shape, contour (for layer effects), or graphic style—is created in a particular way. The following are a few examples:

➤ Customize a brush via the Brushes panel or Brush preset picker, then click the **New Preset** button ▣ on the panel or picker.

➤ Add a swatch to the Swatches panel by clicking the **New Swatch of Foreground Color** button. ▣

➤ Create a gradient by clicking **New** in the Gradient Editor dialog.

➤ Create a style by clicking the **New Style** button ▣ on the Styles panel or by clicking **New Style** in the Layer Style dialog.

➤ Create a pattern via Edit > **Define Pattern**.

If you've created some presets that you want to preserve for future use, save them in a library.

To save all the presets currently on a picker as a new library:

1. From the panel or picker menu, choose **Save** [preset type].

2. Enter a name, keep the default extension and location, then click **Save**.

3. To make the new library appear on the panel or preset picker menu and on the menu in the Preset Manager, you must relaunch Photoshop.

Preset and user-saved libraries can be loaded as needed from the lower portion of the appropriate panel or picker menu.

To load a library of presets:

1. From the lower portion of the panel or the picker menu, choose the desired library name.

2. When the alert dialog appears, click **Append** to add the additional presets to the panel or picker, or click **OK** to replace the current presets on the panel or picker with those in the library.

Note: If you made changes to the current panel, another alert dialog will appear. Click Save if you want your changes saved.

The Preset Manager is a central dialog in which you can organize, append, replace, and reset your preset libraries and control which libraries load onto individual panels and pickers at startup. Changes made to an individual preset picker are reflected in the Preset Manager, and vice versa.

To use the Preset Manager:

1. Do either of the following:

   Choose Edit > **Preset Manager**.

   From the menu on any panel or picker that contains presets, such as the Brush Preset picker or the Brushes panel, choose **Preset Manager**.

2. In the Preset Manager (**A**, next page), choose from the **Preset Type** menu.

3. Do any of the following:

   To add presets to the current library, from the menu ◉, choose a **library name** (**B**, next page), then in the alert dialog, click Append (**C**, next page), or click OK to have them replace the current library.

   To append (to the current presets) a library that isn't currently listed on the menu, click **Load**, locate the library, then click Load again.

   To restore the default library for the chosen type, from the menu ◉, choose **Reset** [preset type], then click Append to append the default presets to the current library, or click OK to replace the current library with the default presets.

4. Respond to any alert prompt that appears regarding saving changes to the current presets.

5. Click **Done**.

➤ To change how the presets are displayed, choose a thumbnail or list view from the Preset Manager menu.

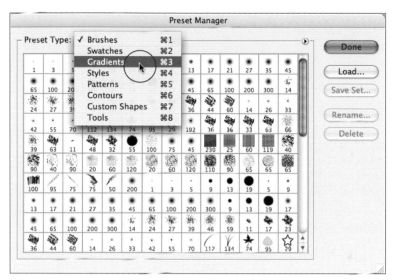

A In the Preset Manager dialog, choose the Preset Type that you want to work with.

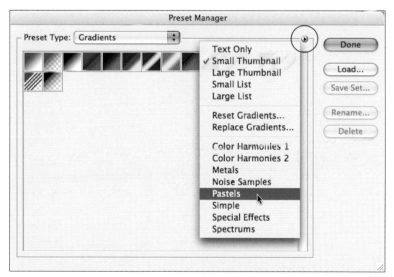

B From the menu in the dialog, choose a library, then in the alert dialog, click Append to add the presets to the existing ones on the picker or click OK to replace them.

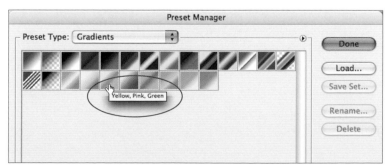

C The library will appear in the Preset Manager dialog and on the respective picker or panel when you exit the dialog.

Streamlining your workflow

This page lists some Photoshop features that you can incorporate into your workflow to add flexibility to your editing and boost your productivity.

Keep your edits flexible

➤ Copy imagery to duplicate or separate **layers;** use **adjustment layers** to try out tonal and color adjustments; use **fill layers** to try out colors, gradients, or patterns; apply editable and removable **layer styles;** and use **layer comps** to show variations of a document to your clients without having to open and close separate files.

➤ Place Camera Raw images or vector objects from Illustrator into Photoshop as **Smart Objects** for easy round-trip edits and updates.

➤ If you can afford the processing lag, apply filters as editable and removable **Smart Filters** to layers that you've converted to Smart Objects.

➤ Use **layer masks** and **vector masks** to conceal or reveal areas of a layer.

Save, reuse, recycle

➤ Save your Camera Raw and adjustment settings as **presets**.

➤ Create and save **presets** for brushes, swatches, gradients, type, patterns, shapes, contours, styles, and tools. Save your presets in **libraries** for safekeeping and easy access.

➤ Save collections of layer effect, opacity, and blending mode settings as **styles** in the Styles panel for use in any Photoshop file.

➤ Store selections as **alpha** (grayscale) **channels,** then load them as selections when needed.

➤ Save repetitive sequences of editing or processing steps as **actions**.

➤ Create and save theme-oriented **workspaces** for Photoshop (choose Save Workspace from the Workspace menu on the Application bar ★).

Get there fast

➤ To open a context-sensitive menu for quick access to related commands, **right-click/Control-click** the image, or on an interface feature, such as the Layers panel.**A**

➤ Memorize the **panel icons,** so you can identify and display them quickly.

➤ Practice **keyboard shortcuts** and gradually add them to your repertoire.

Keep a spare

➤ **Duplicate** a **layer** (or a file, for that matter) and edit the copy.

➤ Create snapshots on the History panel as you work, or save snapshots of your files as separate documents via the **Create Document from Current State** button on the History panel.

Work out your ideas on paper

➤ Get a notebook and use it to **take notes** (we're not kidding!). Jot down command sequences—even specific settings—for future reference. Draw new design concepts, make quick sketches of images that inspire you as you go about your daily life, paste in clippings from magazines, or write down ideas for streamlining your workflow. There's something about working ideas out on paper....

A This is the context menu for a selection.

GET PROGRAM UPDATES PERIODICALLY

To find out if there's an update available for Photoshop, Bridge, or any other Adobe product, choose Help > Updates. If updates are available, you can click Show Details to see a listing of them (and of the software components that are presently installed on your system), then click Download and Install Updates. Click Preferences to specify whether you want downloads to happen automatically or would rather be notified via an alert (and how often), and for which programs.

To edit, adjust, copy, or move only part of a layer, you must select that area first to isolate it.**A** To hide or reveal part of a layer, you can use a mask. Creating selections and masks is prep work—and the more careful the prep, the better the results. Like house painting, some Photoshop work sessions can involve doing quite a bit of prep work before you get to the actual job of "painting."

It's not easy to distinguish among the many selection and masking controls in Photoshop, let alone decide which tasks they're best suited for. Without this knowledge, you could spend hours trying one selection technique after another and get nowhere; with the right tool in hand, you'll be better equipped to reach your goal. For techniques that will help you strategize at the beginning of your work sessions and make informed choices instead of guesses, see the summary of selection and masking methods that begins on the following page.

Following that summary, you'll learn how to use the Quick Selection and Magnetic Lasso tools, then tackle some challenging selection and masking tasks, such as selecting a complex object in a landscape, using adjustment layer masks, selecting feathery edges and hair, and creating a selection based on a color range. Hopefully, you'll exit this chapter with some useful new techniques up your sleeve.

Creating selections and masks, though exacting work, is far from an exact science. Even more variables are thrown in when you consider that every image—not to mention Photoshop user—is unique. As you work with increasingly complex assignments, adopt a pro mindset, which means taking the liberty to veer from "standard" practice. If it works, it works.

SELECTING & MASKING

5

IN THIS CHAPTER

A The coins are selected in this image, as shown by the dashed outline.

Choosing a selection method

SELECT IRREGULARLY SHAPED AREAS BASED ON COLOR OR TONAL VALUES

Magic Wand tool ✎ **A** *(see pages 124, 129, 132, 224)*
Click to select color areas based on Options bar settings: a Tolerance range (the number of shades or colors the tool may select) and whether you want to select Contiguous areas and/or Sample All Layers. This tool is useful for selecting a background in a photo, such as sky or water, or a solid-colored area.

Quick Selection tool ✎ **B** *(see pages 121, 132, 168)*
Click or drag to select a well-defined but irregular area, such as a figure on a plain background. The tool detects color boundaries automatically.

Magnetic Lasso tool ✎ **C–D** *(see pages 122–123)*
Click, then move the pointer along the border of a shape (mouse button up), and the tool will create fastening points where it detects a high-contrast edge. (Click if you need to create fastening points.) Use this tool to select objects or figures that are clearly delineated from their background in tonality or color; it's more precise than the Lasso tool.

Color Range command *(see pages 119, 134, 152–155)*
For selecting areas by color, this dialog is more powerful than the Magic Wand tool. Hide any layers you don't want to sample from, then choose Select > Color Range. With Sampled Colors chosen on the Select menu (the default option), click or drag with the eyedropper in the preview or document window. Add Shift to add to the selection or Alt/Option to subtract from it, or move the Fuzziness slider. Via the Select menu, you can limit the selection to a specific color family or tonal range, such as Reds or Highlights.

SELECT STRAIGHT-EDGED OR GEOMETRIC AREAS

Rectangular Marquee tool ⬚
Elliptical Marquee tool ○
Drag to create a rectangular or elliptical selection. To specify a specific width-to-height ratio or dimensions, choose from the Style menu on the Options bar and enter Width and Height values before dragging. To draw from the center of the selection, start dragging, then hold down Alt/Option and continue dragging; or use Shift to constrain the selection to a square or circle.

A We selected the tabletop by clicking once with the Magic Wand tool.

B We selected the egg yolk with one quick drag of the Quick Selection tool.

C We selected the cookie cutter by moving the Magnetic Lasso tool over its edges.

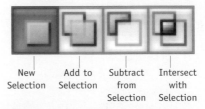

New Selection   Add to Selection   Subtract from Selection   Intersect with Selection

D Before using your selection tool, click one of these options on the Options bar (New Selection is the default setting).

Polygonal Lasso tool 📐 *(see pages 204, 296)*
Click to create corners in a straight-edged selection.
To reverse your steps, press Delete.

SELECT IRREGULAR AREAS

Lasso tool 📐 **A** *(see pages 120, 184, 296)*
Drag to create an irregularly shaped nonmagnetic
selection. You can use this tool to create a new
selection, such as a loosely defined, feathered area
for an adjustment, or to modify an existing selection that you created with another tool (see the
next page). While using the Lasso tool, you can
hold down Alt/Option to toggle to a temporary
Polygonal Lasso tool, and vice versa.

CREATE A SELECTION BY PAINTING A MASK

Quick Mask mode B *(see pages 170, 174, 180)*
Click the Edit in Quick Mask Mode button 🔲 on
the Tools panel, with or without creating a selection first. Choose the Brush tool, then with black as
the Foreground color, paint a mask on the image.
Protected areas are covered with a light red, non-
printing "rubylith" shield. To remove unwanted
areas of the mask, press X to switch the Foreground
color to white, then paint out your strokes. When
you're done painting the mask, click the Edit in
Standard Mode button; the mask will convert automatically to a selection.

CREATE A VERY PRECISE SELECTION

Pen tool ✒ **C**
When you need the most precise and smooth selection possible, such as for a high-resolution image,
click the Paths button 🔲 on the Options bar for the
Pen tool, then trace some shapes. To convert the
path to a selection, Ctrl-click/Cmd-click the path
listing on the Paths panel. Or to convert a path to
a vector mask, select the path, create a new layer,
then choose Layer > Vector Mask > Current Path.
Note that a path (vector) will become less precise
when converted to a selection (pixels).

A We selected the cookie on the left by dragging with the Lasso tool.

B We put the image in Quick Mask mode,
then with the Brush tool, painted a mask on
the cookie.

C A path, in the shape of the
cookie cutter, is being stored
on the Paths panel. A path can
be converted to a selection at
any time.

*Note: For more page references to specific tools, see the
index. Our Photoshop CS4, volume 1: Visual QuickStart
Guide also includes instructions for many Photoshop
selection tools and techniques.*

CLEAN UP OR MODIFY A SELECTION

Refine Edge dialog **A** *(see pages 120, 168)*

With a selection active and a selection tool chosen, click Refine Edge on the Options bar; or press Ctrl-Alt-R/Cmd-Option-R; ★ or choose Refine Edge from the context menu. This versatile dialog lets you refine the smoothness, sharpness, and precision of a selection edge; expand or contract a selection; eliminate a fringe; and apply feathering, while allowing you to preview the refinements on a choice of backgrounds.

Lasso tool* ⟋ *(see page 120)*

This tool is useful for enlarging selection areas or for removing stray selection areas after using the Magic Wand tool. Hold down Shift while dragging to add areas to a selection, or Alt/Option to remove areas from it.

Quick Mask mode *(see pages 170, 174, 180)*

To subtract from a selection, click the Edit in Quick Mask Mode button ▢ on the Tools panel, choose black as the Foreground color, then apply strokes with the Brush tool; or to add to the selection, paint with white.* This method can also be used to eliminate stray selection areas left from using the Magic Wand tool.

Grow, Similar commands *(see pages 124, 129, 224)*

Based on the current Tolerance setting for the Magic Wand tool, the Grow command selects additional contiguous areas, and the Similar command selects additional noncontiguous areas.

Invert a selection *(see pages 170, 174, 180)*

To swap the currently selected and unselected areas, press Ctrl-Shift-I/Cmd-Shift-I (Select > Inverse).

Transform a selection marquee

To transform a selection marquee, choose Select > Transform Selection, then manipulate the handles on the transform box to scale (Shift-drag for proportional scaling), skew (Ctrl-drag/Cmd-drag a side handle), distort (Ctrl-drag/Cmd-drag a corner handle), or apply perspective (Ctrl-Alt-Shift/Cmd-Option-Shift drag a corner handle). To accept the edits, double-click inside the marquee.

Use a stylus and graphics tablet, if available.

MOVING AND COPYING SELECTIONS

TASK	METHOD
Move just the selection marquee	Drag within it with a selection tool
Move the selection contents**	Drag within the marquee with the Move tool (V) ▶⊕
Copy the selection contents on the same layer	Alt-drag/Option-drag within the marquee with the Move tool
Copy the selection contents to a new layer	Press Ctrl-J/Cmd-J

**If you move selection contents on a layer, the exposed area is replaced with transparency. If you move a selection on the Background, the exposed area is filled with the current Background color.*

MIND YER LAYERS!

Before or after creating a selection, click a layer or the Background to let Photoshop know which pixel areas are to be edited.

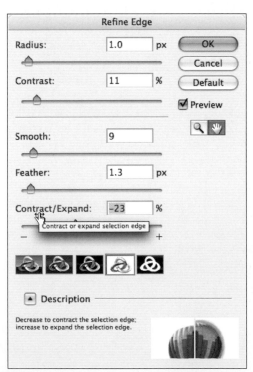

A The Refine Edge dialog lets you modify the edge of an active selection in many different ways.

SAVE SELECTIONS

Alpha channels

To store an active selection as an alpha channel, click the Save Selection as Channel button ▢ on the Channels panel. To display an alpha channel onscreen in grayscale, click the alpha channel name; or to display it as a rubylith shield, click the topmost channel, then click the visibility icon for the alpha channel.

An alpha channel can store up to 256 shades of gray in an 8-bit image, and up to 32,000 shades in a 16-bit image. You can distort, blur, or sharpen the shapes in an alpha channel by various means, such as with the Brush tool or filters. To load an alpha channel onto your image as a selection, Ctrl-click/Cmd-click the channel thumbnail (see the sidebar at right).

CREATE LAYER MASKS

Layer masks *(see pages 72, 162–164, 182, 194–198)*
Vector masks *(see pages 303–306)*
Filter effects masks *(see page 302)*

The purpose of a mask is to hide or reveal parts of a layer, such as to limit adjustments to a specific area or to soften the seams between image layers. Black areas in a mask hide pixels fully, white areas reveal pixels fully, and gray areas create a partial mask. A mask won't become permanent unless it's applied, and it can be hidden or discarded at any time. Layer masks are used extensively throughout this book.

You can attach a mask to an image, adjustment, Smart Object, or type layer, but not to the Background. Adjustment, fill, and shape layers automatically have their own mask, as do Smart Object layers that contain Smart Filters. If you add a layer (pixel) mask while a selection is active, the selection shapes become either white or black areas in the mask, depending on whether you click or Alt/Option-click the Add Pixel Mask button ▣ on the Masks panel.★ To copy a mask to another layer, Alt-drag/Option-drag the mask thumbnail.

EDIT LAYER MASKS *(see pages 101, 126–127, 132–133, 150, 152–155, 224–225)*

If created when no selection is active, a mask will be blank, but black or white areas can be added to it (e.g., with the Brush or Gradient tool). The Masks panel provides convenient, flexible controls for editing masks.**A ★** You can also edit a mask by using a filter (such as a blur filter) or an adjustment command (such as Levels or the Refine Mask dialog).

LOADING AS A SELECTION

To load a layer mask, a channel, or the nontransparent areas of a layer as a selection, use these modifier keys as you click the thumbnail on the panel:

TASK	WINDOWS	MAC OS
Load it as a selection	Ctrl-click	Cmd-click
Combine it with an existing selection	Ctrl-Shift-click	Cmd-Shift-click
Subtract it from an existing selection	Ctrl-Alt-click	Cmd-Option-click
Select the intersection of the existing and new	Ctrl-Alt-Shift-click	Cmd-Option-Shift-click

Add (or select) a Pixel Mask   Add a Vector Mask

Load Selection from Mask   Disable/Enable Mask   Delete Mask

Apply Mask

A Via the Masks panel, you can add a pixel, vector, or filter mask to a layer; adjust the mask settings at any time; load the mask as a selection; disable or enable it; and finally apply or delete it. The Density control changes the mask opacity, the Feather control softens the transition between the white and black areas, Mask Edge gets you to the Refine Mask dialog (which is like the Refine Edge dialog), Color Range gets you to the Color Range dialog, and Invert swaps the black and white areas in the mask.

Next, we'll review two selection tools that you probably use often: Lasso and Quick Selection. They both select irregular areas via dragging, but in distinctly different ways.

Using the Lasso tool

We use the Lasso tool to select nongeometric areas; to create loose selections for limiting adjustments or other edits; and to clean up selections made with another tool, such as the Quick Selection or Magic Wand tool (e.g., to eliminate stray areas remaining from a Magic Wand selection).

To create a free-form selection:

1. Choose the **Lasso** tool ⌾ (L or Shift-L).

2. Click a layer, then drag to select an area.**A** Don't worry if your initial selection isn't perfect; you can refine it later. When you release the mouse, the open ends of the selection will join automatically with a straight edge.

3. Do any of the following:

   To **add** to the selection, Shift-drag around the area to be added.

   To **subtract** from the selection, starting with the pointer outside the selection, Alt-drag/ Option-drag around the area to be removed.

   To refine the selection, click **Refine Edge** on the Options bar, then adjust the settings.**B–D**

▶ To create a straight side with the Lasso tool, keep the mouse button down and Alt-click/ Option-click to create corners. To resume drawing the free-form selection, release Alt/Option and continue dragging.

C Using a Hue/Saturation adjustment layer, we increased the Saturation for the Blues. (Our selection became the white area in the adjustment layer mask.)

USING A FEATHERED LASSO SELECTION FOR A SATURATION ADJUSTMENT

A With the Lasso tool, we selected an area of water that we will brighten.

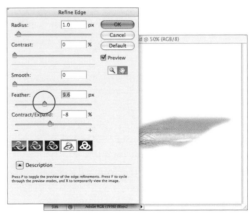

B Using the Refine Edge dialog, we raised the Feather value of the selection.

D The water is now a brighter blue. Because the edge of the selection was feathered, the adjustment is fading gradually into adjacent (unadjusted) areas.

Using the Quick Selection tool

The Quick Selection tool creates a selection more quickly and with less effort than the Lasso tool (all you have to do is drag across a shape), and the results are very precise when used on shapes that have distinct borders. You can enlarge the resulting selection to include adjacent shapes, or push back into the selection to contract it.

To use the Quick Selection tool:

1. Click a layer, then choose the **Quick Selection** tool ⬩ (W or Shift-W).

2. On the Options bar, make sure the **New Selection** button ⬩ is active and check **Auto-Enhance** for improved edge detection.

3. To choose a diameter for the tool that's appropriate for the area to be selected, press] or [, then drag within that area.**A** The selection will expand to the first distinct shape boundary that the tool detects. It will preview as you drag, then become more precise when you release the mouse.

4. Zoom in, then do the following:

   To **enlarge** the selection, click or drag in an adjacent area; the selection will expand to include it.

   ➤ You can use another tool to add or subtract from the selection, such as the Lasso tool.**B**

   To **subtract** from the selection, Alt-drag/Option-drag across the area to be subtracted.**C–D**

   To **contract** the selection inward, Alt-drag/Option-drag along the edge of the selection.

   ➤ To block an adjacent area from becoming selected as you enlarge a selection, Alt-click/Option-click that area, release Alt/Option, then drag to enlarge the selection area. The block will remain in effect only until you click that area again with the Quick Selection tool.

   ➤ To undo the last click or drag of the Quick Selection tool, press Ctrl-Z/Cmd-Z.

USING A QUICK SELECTION TO ISOLATE PART OF A LAYER

A We want to move the buckets and table in this image to a different background. Our first step was to select most of the background with the Quick Selection tool.

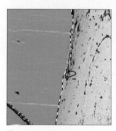

B We cleaned up some selection edges with the Lasso tool.

C With the Quick Selection tool and Alt/Option down, we dragged carefully on the handles of the pails to deselect them.

D We inverted the selection (Ctrl-Shift-I/Cmd-Shift-I), then with the Move tool, drag-and-dropped it into a different document.

Using the Magnetic Lasso tool

The Magnetic Lasso tool is well suited for selecting shapes that have clearly defined edges. Drag or move the tool along a shape, and a selection line snaps to where the tool detects a change in contrast. The stronger the contrast between the shape and the surrounding areas, the more precise the selection. You can set up parameters for the tool to control its accuracy (plus, it requires less dexterity than the Lasso).

To use the Magnetic Lasso tool:

1. Choose the **Magnetic Lasso tool** (L or Shift-L).

2. Choose Options bar settings:

   Feather (0–250 pixels) to soften the edge of the selection (the effect won't be visible until you edit the selected area). The higher the file resolution, the larger the feather value needed. For example, on a 300 ppi image, a Feather value of 5–7 would soften the edge slightly, whereas a Feather of 20–25 would soften a noticeably wider area. (If you prefer to feather the selection after creating it, use the Refine Edge dialog.)

   Width (1–256 pixels) for the size of the area below the pointer that the tool considers when it places a selection line.**A–B** Try a wide Width (20 pixels or wider) for a high-contrast image that has clearly delineated edges, or a narrow Width (2–6 pixels) for an image that has small shapes in close proximity or is low in contrast.

   Contrast (1–100%) for the degree of contrast needed between shapes in order for the tool to read it as an edge. For a low-contrast image, use a low Contrast value (less than 10%).

   ➤ If you choose a low or high Width, do the same for the Contrast.

   Frequency (0–100) to control how often fastening points are placed as the selection is made (**A–C**, next page). The higher the Frequency, the more points are placed. We usually use a Frequency value of 50. To select a highly irregular contour, try using a high Frequency (70 or higher).

   To use tablet pressure to control the Width, click the ✎ button.

3. Click in the image to establish the first fastening point. Move the mouse—with the button up—along the edge of the shape to be selected.

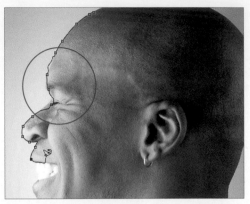

A At a Width setting of 10 pixels, the Magnetic Lasso tool correctly detected some parts of the man's profile but missed his forehead and brow.

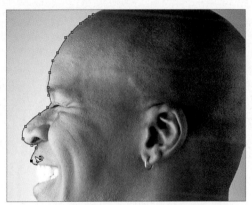

B At a Width setting of 4 pixels, the tool correctly detected the edge of the man's forehead and brow.

FRIENDS AND RELATIONS

While using the Magnetic Lasso tool, you can do either of the following:

➤ Click, then Alt-click/Option-click to use a temporary Polygonal Lasso tool (to draw a straight edge). To resume using the Magnetic Lasso, release Alt/Option and click.

➤ Alt-drag/Option-drag to use a temporary Lasso tool (to draw an irregular edge manually). To resume using the Magnetic Lasso, release Alt/Option, then continue moving the mouse (with the button up).

A selection line will snap to the edge of the shape, and temporary points will appear (they'll disappear after step 4).

If the selection line starts to follow adjacent shapes that you don't want to select, click the edge of the shape that you do want to select to add a fastening point manually, then continue to move or drag the mouse. (To delete the last fastening point, press Backspace/Delete.)

Note: If you move or drag the mouse quickly on a large image, the selection border may not keep pace with you. Pause to let it catch up.

4. To close the selection, do one of the following:

Double-click anywhere over the shape.

Click the starting point (a small circle will appear next to the Magnetic Lasso tool pointer).

Press Enter/Return.

Alt-double-click/Option-double-click to create a new fastening point and close the selection with a straight segment.

➤ To change the Width value by 1 pixel at a time while creating a selection, press [or].

➤ To cancel (remove) an incomplete Magnetic Lasso selection, press Esc.

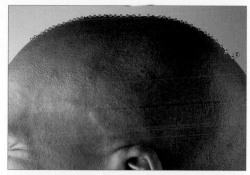

A The Magnetic Lasso tool used with a Frequency setting of 75 produced too many fastening points.

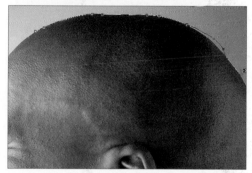

B The same tool used with a Frequency setting of 20 produced too few fastening points to accurately define the head shape.

MAKING THE MAGNETIC LASSO STRONGER

To temporarily heighten the contrast in an image to enable the Magnetic Lasso tool to work "smarter," create a Levels adjustment layer. Move the black Input Levels slider to the right (and also move the gray Input Levels slider, if needed). When you're done using the Magnetic Lasso, delete the adjustment layer.

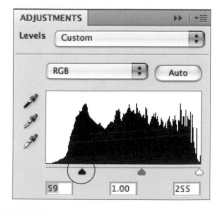

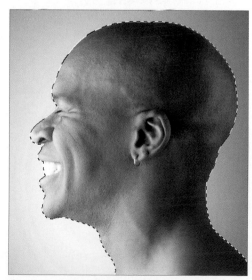

C We selected the head successfully using a Width setting of 4 and a Frequency setting of 50.

Selecting leaves on a tree

Small, finely detailed shapes, such as leaves on trees in a landscape, are extremely tedious to select manually with just a selection tool. We've devised an easier method in which you use adjustment layers and other features to differentiate and isolate delicate shapes from surrounding areas. We'll step you through three demanding tasks in which this method is used: selecting leaves on a tree, fur on an animal, and hair in a portrait.

In this first task, we will select leaves on a tree by using Black & White and Levels adjustment layers, the Similar command, and the Magic Wand and Lasso tools. Subsequent adjustments or edits can be limited to just the selected areas or unselected areas.

To select leaves on a tree: ★

1. Open an RGB image of a leafy tree (**A**, next page).

2. To simplify the selection process, you will heighten the contrast between the leaves and sky by using an adjustment layer. On the Adjustments panel, click the **Black & White** button. Using the Black & White controls, do the following: (**B**, next page)

   To darken the leaves, move the **Yellows** slider almost all the way to the left. If the leaves contain green, also move the **Greens** slider to the left by the same amount.

   To lighten the sky, move the **Cyans** and **Blues** sliders almost all the way to the right.

   Note: A different image may require different adjustments.

3. To pump up the contrast even more, click the **Return to Adjustment List** button on the Adjustments panel, then click the **Levels** button. Move the white Input Levels slider to the left to lighten the background (**C**, next page).

> **ANOTHER TECHNIQUE**
>
> To differentiate shapes from one another, we believe the method described on this page is more flexible and yields better results than the "traditional" approach in which you view each separate channel to see which offers the most contrast between the shapes to be selected and the surrounding areas, increase the contrast on the chosen channel, select the newly differentiated shapes and then, finally, save the selection as an alpha channel.

➤ Click the Black & White or Levels adjustment layer if you need to change the settings for it.

4. Now you're ready to create the selection. Choose the **Magic Wand** tool (W or Shift-W). On the Options bar, set the Tolerance to around 40 and check Contiguous.

5. With the Levels adjustment layer still selected, click a dark area of leaves in the image. To add to the selection, Shift-click more areas of leaves and branches, then right-click/Control-click and choose **Similar**.

6. If your selection includes shapes that aren't part of the tree, choose the **Lasso** tool (L or Shift-L), then Alt-drag/Option-drag around those areas to deselect them.

7. On the Layers panel, hide both adjustment layers by clicking their visibility icons, and click the Background.

Instructions continue on page 126

A We want to lighten and increase the saturation of just the leaves in this photo.

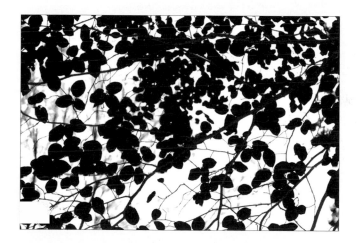

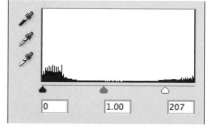

B For the Black & White adjustment layer, we moved the Yellows slider to −180 to darken the leaves and moved the Cyans and Blues sliders to +300 to lighten the sky.

C Next, we used a Levels adjustment layer to further lighten the sky, to make it contrast even more with the leaves.

8. Next, you will save the selection to an adjustment layer mask, then fine-tune the edge of the mask. On the Adjustments panel, click the **Curves** button. Note that the selection shapes are now white areas in the adjustment layer mask.**A** Keep the mask thumbnail selected.

9. On the Masks panel, click **Mask Edge** to open the Refine Mask dialog, then click **Default**. As you make the following adjustments, click the **On Black** preview button to gauge how much of the light background color appears in the selection, or **On White** to gauge the crispness of the selection edges: **B**

To include soft-edged pixels while preserving the edge contrast, set the **Radius** to around 10–35 px and set the **Contrast** percentage to around 15–40%.

To preserve the jagged edges on the leaves, set the **Smooth** value to 1 and the **Feather** value to 0 px.

To ensure that the fine edges of the leaves and branches stay visible, but not so much that any sky areas are included, set the **Contract/ Expand** value to +7.

Click OK, and save your document.

To use the Curves adjustment layer and mask to modify the image, follow the instructions on the next page.

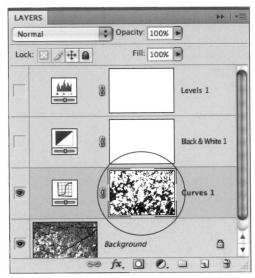

A The former selection shapes are now white areas in the Curves adjustment layer mask. Also listed on the panel are the adjustment layers (hidden) that were used to heighten the contrast.

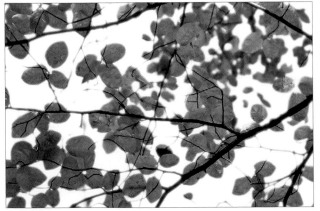

B As shown in this closeup of the preview in the Refine Mask dialog, the settings at right produced a cleaner and more clearly defined selection.

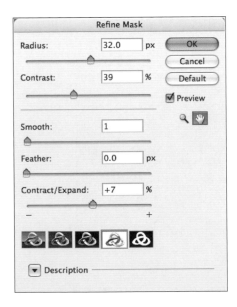

With the selection shapes from the preceding task stored as white areas in the adjustment layer mask, the adjustment will affect only those areas, while the rest of the image will remain protected.

To limit a tonal adjustment by using a mask: ★

Double-click the Curves adjustment layer thumbnail. On the Adjustments panel, tweak the curve to improve the tonality of the former selection areas (the leaves, in our image).**A**

To restrict edits to the former unselected areas, simply invert the adjustment layer mask.

To invert an adjustment layer mask for further edits: ★

1. Click the Curves adjustment layer, then press Ctrl-J/Cmd-J to duplicate it. Keep the duplicate layer selected, and click its mask thumbnail.

2. On the Masks panel, click **Invert** to swap the black and white areas in the mask.**B** (In our image, the duplicate Curves adjustment layer is now affecting just the sky.)

3. Double-click the Curves thumbnail on the duplicate adjustment layer. On the Adjustments panel, click the **Reset to Adjustments Default** button ↺ to zero out the settings, then reshape the curve.**C–D**

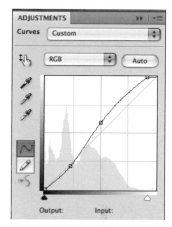

A The white areas in the mask for the original Curves adjustment layer are revealing the leaves, which we lightened by reshaping the curve.

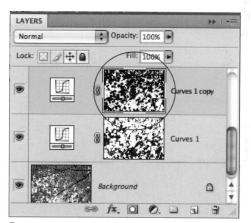

B We duplicated the Curves adjustment layer, then inverted its mask so the next adjustments will affect just the sky.

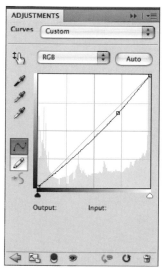

C The white areas in the mask for our second Curves adjustment layer are revealing the sky areas, which we darkened by choosing these settings.

D Compare this final image with **A** on page 125.

Selecting furry or feathered critters

Next, we'll show you how to select the fine edges of fur or feathers on an animal (or other fuzzy-edged object), using steps similar to those in the previous exercise.

To select furry or feathered critters: ★

1. Open an RGB image of a fuzzy-edged subject, such as a furry or feathered beast.**A** Press Ctrl-J/ Cmd-J to duplicate the Background.

2. On the Adjustments panel,◑ click the **Black & White** button.◥ Use the sliders to increase the contrast between the fur and background (the image is temporarily in grayscale). The goal is to heighten the contrast, not to create a pleasing image.**B** Keep the adjustment layer selected.

3. To heighten the contrast further, click the **Return to Adjustment List** button ◁ in the lower left corner of the Adjustments panel, then click the **Levels** button.▦

   Move the **black Input Levels** slider to the right and the **white Input Levels** slider to the left.**C**

A We want to put the tiger on a different background, so the first step is to select him (or her?).

B For the Black & White adjustment, we moved the Reds slider to 300 to lighten the fur, moved both the Greens and Blues sliders to –150 to darken the background, and moved the Yellows slider to –44 to boost the contrast between the fur and background.

C For the Levels adjustment, we moved the black Input Levels slider to the right to darken the background and the white Input Levels slider to the left to shift lighter shades to white, for better contrast.

Move the **gray Input Levels** slider to the left to increase the contrast, or to the right to decrease it.**A**

4. The shape to be selected should now stand out distinctly from its background. To create the selection, choose the **Magic Wand** tool (W or Shift-W). On the Options bar, set the Tolerance to around 30–40 and check Anti-alias and Contiguous. Click the background area.

5. If necessary, choose Select > **Grow** to expand the selection.

6. Shift-click with the Magic Wand tool again, if necessary, to select the rest of the background. To clean up the selection, choose the **Lasso** tool (L or Shift-L), then Shift-drag around any unselected areas of the background that you want to add to the selection.

7. When the cleanup is finished, hide the two adjustment layers, then click the duplicate image layer. On the Masks panel, click the **Add Pixel Mask** button, then click **Invert** to reverse the black and white areas in the mask.

8. Click **Mask Edge**. In the dialog, click **Default**, adjust the settings to refine the mask edge (to delineate the fur),**B** then click OK.

9. Save your document. To put the masked imagery on a new background, continue with the steps on the next page.

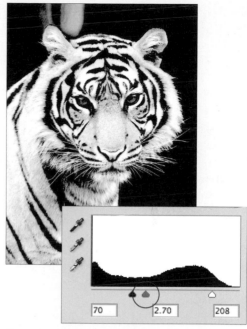

A For the last Levels adjustment, we moved the gray Input Levels slider to the left, to increase the contrast and thereby preserve the finely detailed fur.

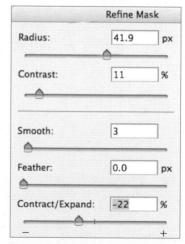

B In the Refine Mask dialog, we set Contrast, Smooth, and Feather to the values shown above to preserve the sharp edge, increased the Radius until we saw enough fine details on the edges of the fur, and reduced the Contract/Expand value to eliminate most of the remaining background pixels.

Putting masked imagery on a new background

Next, we'll show you how to place the soft-edged masked imagery (e.g., the tiger) on a new background. The black areas in the layer mask will reveal areas from the new Background.

To place masked imagery on a new background: ★

1. Open (or keep open) the document that contains masked imagery.

2. Open an RGB image to be used as a background for the masked layer, and make sure it has the same document resolution as, but a larger document size than, the masked image.

3. On the **Arrange Documents** menu ▦ on the Application bar, click a 2 Up button. Click the masked layer, then drag it from the Layers panel into the new background image. On the Arrange Documents menu, click the Consolidate All button.

4. With the **Move** tool (V), position the masked layer.

5. Zoom in to 100% view to examine the edge of the fur or feathers.**A**

6. If there's still some original background color showing along the edge, with the layer mask thumbnail still selected, choose Image > Adjustments > **Levels** (Ctrl-L/Cmd-L) (don't create an adjustment layer).

   ▶ If the original background color is visible only in a specific area of the masked imagery, drag a loose selection around that area with the Lasso tool before opening the Levels dialog.

   In the Levels dialog, move the gray **Input Levels** slider to the right until you see less of the original background along the edge,**B** but not so far that details start disappearing. Click OK. This adjustment contracts the white area of the mask, so fewer pixels along the edge of the masked layer will now be visible.

   ▶ If the masked imagery has a different color temperature than the background image, click the masked image layer and create a Photo Filter 🌑 adjustment layer. Choose a suitable Filter to make the layer warmer or cooler, and use the Density slider to control the degree of adjustment. Also click the Clip to Layer button 🌑 to limit the adjustment to the masked image layer.

A The tiger layer is revealed through its mask, and the Background is visible underneath. However, in this closeup, you can see that some of the tiger's original background is still visible on the edges of the fur.

B We loosely selected the right side of the tiger with the Lasso tool, then in the Levels dialog, moved the gray Input Levels slider to .80 to shrink the white area of the mask and hide a bit more of the tiger's background.

Selecting hair in a portrait ★

In this task, we'll select the hair on a model in preparation for adding subtle color "highlighting." The challenge will be to select all of her hair, including the delicate strands. As in the previous two exercises, we'll heighten the contrast by using a Black & White adjustment layer, increase the contrast further by using a Levels adjustment layer, and tweak the edge of the layer mask by using the Refine Mask dialog. To keep the hair from being converted to grayscale, Lighter Color blending mode will be chosen for the Black & White adjustment layer.

Note: You may follow the trail of figures and captions on this page and the next two pages, using the image file that we have provided.

See also the figures on the next two pages

A Selecting the hair in a portrait like this is a challenge because some of the background colors are close in hue and value to the hair color.

B We clicked the Black & White button on the Adjustments panel, then on the Layers panel, we set the blending mode for the new adjustment layer to Lighter Color. To increase the contrast between the hair and the background, on the Adjustments panel, we set the Reds value to −200 and the Yellows value to +300.

C To distinguish the hair even more from its background, we created a Levels adjustment layer and chose the Input Levels slider settings shown above. Our goal was to darken the edges of the individual hair strands slightly without making them disappear.

A We chose the Magic Wand tool and, on the Options bar, set the Tolerance to 60 and checked Contiguous. We clicked the hair, lowered the Tolerance to 30, then Shift-clicked to select the edges of her hair, including the small strands at the bottom.

B With the Quick Selection tool (small brush diameter), we dragged to add unselected areas of hair to the selection, then dragged with an even smaller brush diameter to select small strands on the edge. Where the tool pushed the selection into the background, we clicked or dragged with Alt/Option held down to shrink it back to just the hair.

C With the selection active, we clicked the Background, then on the Masks panel, clicked the Add Pixel Mask button. Next, we clicked Mask Edge on the same panel. In the Refine Mask dialog, we set Smooth, Feather, and Contract/Expand to the values shown at right to keep the fine hair strands selected, while minimizing the selection of background pixels. (Keep the Refine Mask dialog open.)

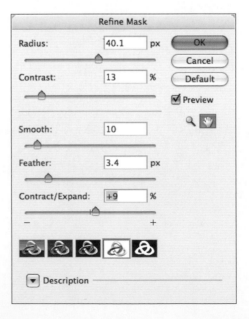

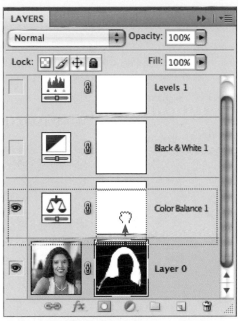

A Continuing with the Refine Mask dialog, we moved the Radius slider until individual hair strands looked soft but well defined (we settled on a value of 40), set the Contrast to 13 to sharpen the edge of the selection, then clicked OK.

B We hid the Black & White and Levels adjustment layers. Next, we created a Color Balance adjustment layer above what had become Layer 0, then dragged the layer mask from Layer 0 over the layer mask of the Color Balance layer, clicking Yes in the alert dialog.

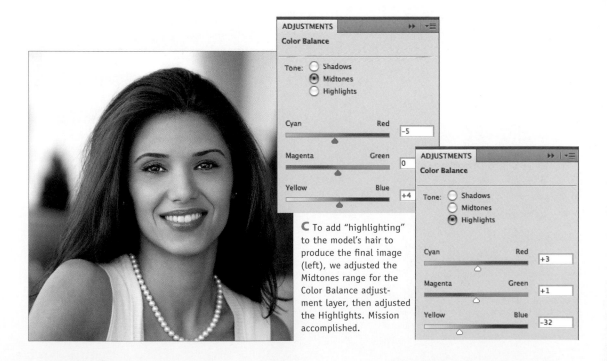

C To add "highlighting" to the model's hair to produce the final image (left), we adjusted the Midtones range for the Color Balance adjustment layer, then adjusted the Highlights. Mission accomplished.

Using the Color Range command

Via the Color Range dialog, you can select areas of an image by clicking in the preview or, as in these instructions, simply by choosing a tonal range from the menu. See, not everything is complicated.

To select a tonal range in an image:

1. Open an image,**A** then choose Select > **Color Range**.

2. From the **Select** menu in the Color Range dialog,**B** choose a color or tonal range. If desired, you can choose a Selection Preview option, such as Black Matte, for the preview in the document window. Click OK. The selection displays in the document window.

3. *Optional:* With the selection active, apply a correction, such as via an adjustment layer.**C** For further corrections, you could use the Color Range dialog to select a different tonal range, such as Midtones, and create another adjustment layer.

➤ The Color Range dialog can also be opened from the Masks panel (see pages 119 and 152).

SELECTING HIGHLIGHT AREAS FOR A LEVELS ADJUSTMENT

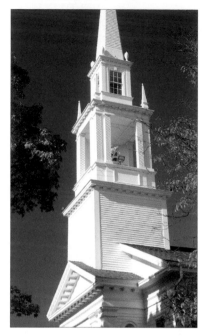

A In this image, the highlight areas look overexposed.

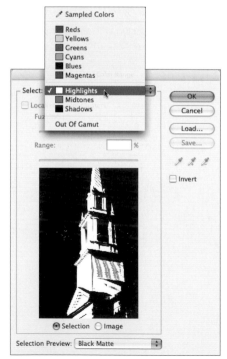

B We chose Highlights from the Select menu in the Color Range dialog.

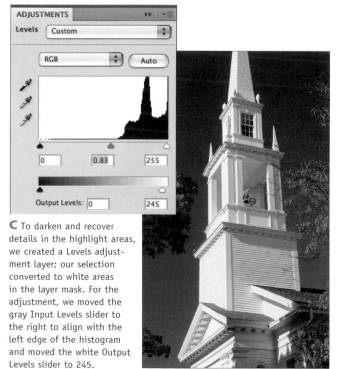

C To darken and recover details in the highlight areas, we created a Levels adjustment layer; our selection converted to white areas in the layer mask. For the adjustment, we moved the gray Input Levels slider to the right to align with the left edge of the histogram and moved the white Output Levels slider to 245.

In this chapter, you'll use various Photoshop features to remove noise, correct for under- and overexposure, enhance or correct contrast, simulate a neutral density filter, add glowing highlights, and neutralize a color cast.

If you shoot digital photos, as a first step we recommend performing as many color and tonal corrections in Camera Raw as possible (see Chapter 3). Camera Raw offers an impressive range of controls, its tab and slider interface is easy to use, and its corrections are nondestructive. Then, for digital photos that have been processed through Camera Raw but need further refinement, as well as for scanned images, Photoshop has plenty of excellent color and tonal correction features to choose from. The challenge is to learn which command or tool can best solve a specific problem you're faced with, and to use it effectively.

We'll introduce you to color samplers and the Info panel first so you can monitor how the colors in your image change as you perform corrections. Then you'll learn how to correct exposure problems by using the Shadows/Highlights command, which, like Camera Raw, preserves all the tonal levels in an image. We'll also show you how to remove noise by using a filter, use the Curves command to increase contrast and neutralize a color cast, use the Masks panel to accentuate shadows and highlights, and apply brush strokes to a neutral gray layer to enhance contrast.

The tasks in this chapter are presented in a logical progression, from broad corrections to subtle tweaks. If you're going to work with the photos we've supplied, plunge in. If you prefer to work with your own photos, study them and try to diagnose their weaknesses. You can pick and choose among the many methods we offer, depending on the nature of the problems you need to correct.

Note! Remember to calibrate your monitor on a regular basis, and especially before using this chapter.

➤ Related topics in other chapters include combining dual exposures on pages 70–72 and retouching portraits in Chapter 7.

COLOR & TONAL CORRECTION

IN THIS CHAPTER

Note: Settings listed in the captions in this chapter were chosen for photos that are approximately 3000 x 2000 pixels.

Using color samplers

Instead of relying on the single color readout that a click of the Eyedropper tool provides, you can get multiple readouts by placing up to four color samplers in your image with the Color Sampler tool. As you perform color and tonal corrections, pre- and postadjustment color breakdowns from the sampler locations display as instant readouts on the Info panel. The color samplers will save with your file and can be displayed or hidden as needed.

To place color samplers in a document:

1. Choose the **Color Sampler** tool 🎯 (I or Shift-I).

2. Click in up to four locations in the document window. A color sampler appears in each spot, and the color readout for each sampler appears on the Info panel.**A** If you want to include a broad spectrum of tonal values, place one sampler each in a highlight area, a midtone area, and a shadow area, and perhaps place the fourth one on a specific color that you want to monitor closely.

➤ To add color samplers while an adjustment dialog (such as Shadows/Highlights) is open, Shift-click in the document window.

➤ If you flip or rotate the whole canvas, your samplers will shift positions for the new orientation.

To move a color sampler:

Do either of the following:

Choose the **Color Sampler** tool 🎯 (I or Shift-I), then drag a color sampler.

Choose the **Eyedropper** tool 🖋 (I or Shift-I), then Ctrl-drag/Cmd-drag a color sampler.

When you remove a color sampler from a document, its readout, logically, disappears from the Info panel.

To remove a color sampler:

Do either of the following:

Choose the **Color Sampler** tool, then Alt-click/Option-click a sampler (the pointer becomes a scissors icon).**B**

Choose the **Eyedropper** tool, then Alt-Shift-click/Option-Shift-click a sampler.

A Click in the document window with the Color Sampler tool to create up to four samplers.

B A color sampler is deleted.

MAKING COLOR SAMPLERS REAPPEAR

Color samplers that you've placed in your document will display when a painting or editing tool is selected, but will disappear temporarily when other tools are selected (e.g., Move tool, type tool, selection tool). To redisplay the samplers, choose a tool for which they display.

The Info panel displays color breakdowns of the pixel(s) currently under the pointer and at the location of up to four color samplers. You can use the panel to get instant feedback, such as while changing the settings for an adjustment layer.

To view color readouts on the Info panel:

1 Display the **Info** panel.❶

2. To change the **color mode** for any readout on the panel, click the dropper icon and choose from the menu.**A** (Actual Color displays data in the current document color mode.)

3. While settings are being changed for an adjustment layer, the panel displays preadjustment data to the left of the slashes, followed by the postadjustment data, as in "45/34%." **B**

   When used with the default Sample Size setting of **Point Sample**, the Eyedropper and Color Sampler tools sample data only from the single pixel directly below the pointer. For color correction work, we recommend sampling from a slightly larger area. Choose the Color Sampler

tool,✐ then from the **Sample Size** menu on the Options bar,**C** either choose **3 by 3 Average** (the setting we use) to sample an average color from an area three pixels square or, if you're working on a very high resolution image, choose one of the other Average options.

➤ The Sample Size chosen for the Color Sampler tool also applies to the Eyedropper tool, and vice versa.

➤ When correcting an image on dual computer displays, choose the same sample size in both displays (different sample sizes would yield different sampler data).

➤ If you hide a layer that a sampler is reading information from, the Info panel will read data from the next visible layer.

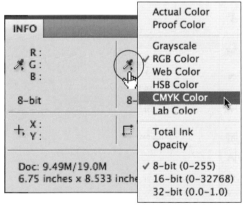

A To change the color mode for a readout, click its dropper icon and choose from the menu.

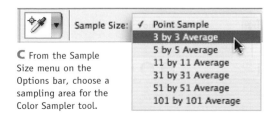

C From the Sample Size menu on the Options bar, choose a sampling area for the Color Sampler tool.

INFO			
R :	84/ 117	C :	62/ 54%
G :	89/ 122	M :	47/ 38%
B :	56/ 85	Y :	86/ 75%
		K :	37/ 16%
8-bit		8-bit	
X :	4.433	W :	
Y :	2.133	H :	
#1 R :	26/ 48	#2 R :	64/ 95
G :	35/ 60	G :	75/ 107
B :	16/ 32	B :	49/ 77
#3 R :	196/ 224	#4 R :	187/ 216
G :	195/ 223	G :	189/ 218
B :	199/ 227	B :	191/ 219

Doc: 9.49M/19.0M
6.75 inches x 8.533 inches (240 ppi)

B When an adjustment dialog is open, the Info panel displays pre- and postadjustment values for the pixels under the pointer and for any color samplers (#1–#4) that you've placed in your document.

Using the Shadows/Highlights command

One good use for the Shadows/Highlights command is to illuminate shadow areas that result from strong side or back lighting. The Shadows and Highlights sliders are similar to two sliders in Camera Raw: The Shadows sliders recover shadow detail, as the Fill Light slider in Camera Raw does, and the Highlights sliders recover highlight detail, as the Recovery slider in Camera Raw does. Best of all, the Shadows/Highlights command produces minimal data loss while preserving the full range of tonal values in the image.

To use the Shadows/Highlights command:

1. Click the Background, press Ctrl-J/Cmd-J to duplicate it, and keep the duplicate layer selected.**A**

2. *Optional:* Right-click/Control-click the duplicate layer and choose Convert to Smart Object. If you do this, the Shadows/Highlights command will be applied in the next step as a Smart Filter, which you can change the settings for at any time. Editing a Smart Filter will take more processing time, though, so be patient.

3. Choose Image > Adjustments > **Shadows/Highlights**. The Shadows/Highlights dialog opens, and it adjusts the image automatically, using the default settings.

4. Check **Show More Options.B**

A Because of the low position of the sun at the time this image was shot, the shadow and midtone areas are underexposed.

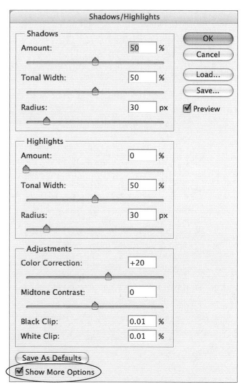

B In the Shadows/Highlights dialog, check Show More Options.

5. For the **Shadows**, you can increase the **Amount** slightly to lighten and recover details in the shadow areas. To keep the light from looking artificial, keep this value below 60%.

> You can use the scrubby sliders in this dialog.

6. To control which tonal levels will be adjusted, do the following:

Choose a **Tonal Width** value for the **Shadows** to control which part of the tonal range the command affects. **A–D** To limit the adjustment to just the darkest shadows, keep this value between 5 and 10%; or to allow the adjustment to affect the midtones, keep the value between 40 and 60%.

Continued on the following page

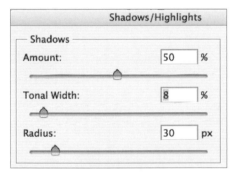

A This low Tonal Width setting is limiting the Shadows adjustment to the dark shadows.

B The shadows and dark midtones are still too dark, despite the fact that the Shadows slider is near the middle of its range.

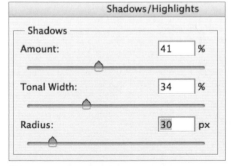

C This time, we reduced the Amount for the Shadows and increased the Tonal Width.

D The higher Tonal Width settings shown at left successfully corrected the exposure in both the shadows and the midtones.

Change the **Radius** value to expand or reduce the number of neighboring pixels that are affected by the adjustment.**A**

7. For the **Highlights**, increase the **Amount** to darken the highlights and recover some detail (at 0%, the slider has no effect). Also adjust the **Tonal Width** and **Radius** to control whether just the highlights, or both the highlights and midtone levels, are adjusted.**B**

8. If an increased Amount for the Shadows caused oversaturation, correct it by reducing the **Color Correction** value in the **Adjustments**

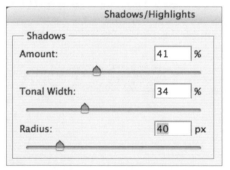

A In the Shadows area of the Shadows/Highlights dialog, a Radius setting of 40 spread the Shadows correction into just the right number of surrounding pixels. (A low Radius setting would have flattened the lighting, whereas a high Radius value—over 100 px, for our file—would have created too much contrast by allowing too many pixels to be compared.)

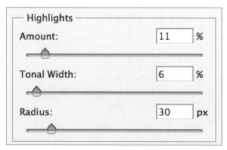

B In the Highlights area, we reduced the Tonal Width to restrict the adjustment to just the highlights (not the midtones) and raised the Amount to darken and recover details in the highlights. This also had a positive effect of subduing the yellow in the buildings in the foreground.

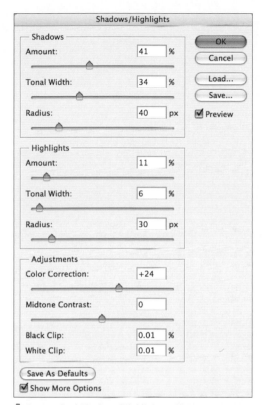

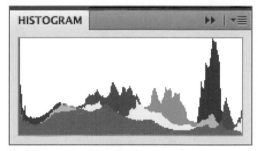

area (or to boost the saturation, raise the Color Correction value).**A**

You can also use the **Midtone Contrast** control to intensify or reduce the contrast in the midtones (this slider has the same effect as the gray Input Levels slider for a Levels adjustment layer).

9. Uncheck then recheck **Preview** to view the image without and with the adjustment, change any of the settings, then click OK.**B–C**

➤ If you created a Smart Filter layer and you want to change the filter settings, double-click the Shadows/Highlights listing. To change the visibility or opacity of the adjustment, use the controls for the Smart Object layer, which will take less processing time than using the visibility or opacity control for the individual Smart Filter.

A For our final Shadows/Highlights adjustment, we set the Color Correction value to +24 to boost the color saturation, but left the Midtone Contrast value at 0.

B There are no gaps or spikes in the histogram for the final image, which confirms that the Shadows/Highlights command preserved the full tonal spectrum.

C The Shadows/Highlights command improved the detail in the shadow areas in this image.

Reducing noise

Digital noise (graininess or speckling) may result from using a high ISO setting in a camera or may be the unintended result of corrections made to recover details in underexposed shadow areas. The Reduce Noise filter removes both luminance noise (a grainy texture) and color noise (randomly colored dots). The filter also includes an option that removes artifacts (caused by the JPEG compression methods) from JPEG photos.

To reduce noise in shadow areas:

1. Zoom to 200%. With the **Hand** tool 🖐 (H), move the image around in the window and inspect the shadow areas for stray red, green, or blue speckles or graininess.**A**

2. Choose Filter > Noise > **Reduce Noise.**

3. In the Reduce Noise dialog,**B** check Preview.

   ► If you click in the document window, that area will appear in the preview window.

4. As you choose settings, try to strike a balance between removing noise, which will soften the image slightly, and keeping the edges adequately sharp. Click **Basic** and examine the result in the preview as you do the following (you can use the scrubby sliders):

   Choose a **Strength** value (try 6–8).

   Choose a low value (around 5–10%) for **Preserve Details** to reduce luminance noise and to avoid introducing more noise.

   Choose a **Reduce Color Noise** value (try 60–70%).

   Keep the **Sharpen Details** value low (10%) to avoid introducing artifacts.

5. Click **Advanced**, then click the **Per Channel** tab (**A**, next page).

6. From the **Channel** menu, choose **Blue** (the most noise is usually in this channel), then choose a Strength value of around 4–6 and a Preserve Details value of 50–60%. Next choose the **Red** channel and a Strength value of 1–2.

   ► For a portrait, try these Strength settings for the channels: Red 4, Green 2, and Blue 2. For a photo shot outdoors at twilight, try a Strength setting for the Blue channel of 6–8.

7. *Optional:* To save the current settings, click the Save a Copy of the Current Settings button,

A In this closeup of a photograph shot at twilight, you can see some noise (tiny red, green, and blue dots).

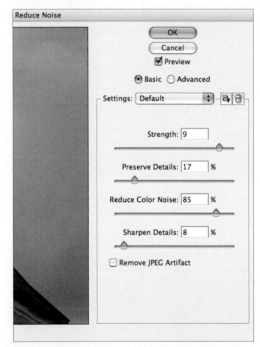

B In the Reduce Noise filter dialog, we clicked Basic, then chose these initial settings.

type a name, then click OK. You can choose a saved settings preset from the Settings menu for any file.

8. To compare the image without and with the adjustment, click and hold on the preview and then release. Change the settings if needed, then click OK.**B**

9. We recommend that you resharpen the image via the Smart Sharpen filter to restore some lost definition (use a low Amount setting).

➤ To reduce the visibility of artifacts created by compression in a JPEG file, check Remove JPEG Artifact in the Basic options panel of the Reduce Noise dialog.

Applying Curves adjustments

To adjust the tonal values, contrast, and white balance in a digital photo, we recommend using the nondestructive Basic and Tone Curve controls in Camera Raw first, whenever possible. If you then need to apply tonal and color corrections in Photoshop, use the adjustment control that the pros reach for: Curves. Curves is useful in many scenarios, such as:

➤ When you need to correct a file that for some reason can't be processed through Camera Raw.

➤ When you want to correct an imbalance in a specific tonal or color range of an image with more precision than the Camera Raw sliders allow.

➤ When you want to limit the adjustment to just the color or luminosity values of an image (you would do this by choosing a layer blending mode for the Curves adjustment layer).

We'll show you how to use a Curves adjustment layer to correct the color in a still life, a landscape, and a portrait. In each case, you'll use the controls in this order: make tonal adjustments to enhance the contrast via the Curves sliders first; neutralize a color cast by using the gray eyedropper next; then finally tweak the color correction by subtly reshaping the curves for one or more of the individual color channels.

Continued on the following page

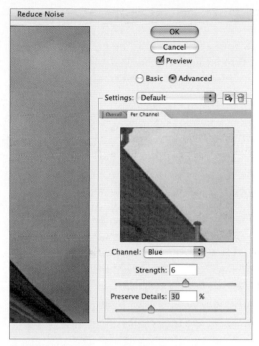

A Next, we clicked Advanced and chose settings for the Blue channel (and then the Red channel).

B The Reduce Noise filter successfully smoothed out the grainy texture.

In these instructions, you'll apply basic tonal corrections to the shadow, highlight, and midtone areas of an image by using a Curves adjustment layer.

To increase contrast by using a Curves adjustment layer: ★

1. Open an RGB image.**A**

2. On the **Adjustments** panel,⬤ click the **Curves** button.▦ Choose the **Curves Display Options** from the panel menu, check all four of the **Show** options, then click OK.

Adjust the shadows and highlights

3. Examine the static histogram behind the curve, then do either of the following:

   To increase the contrast in a dull image, drag the black and white **Input** sliders inward to align with the edges of the histogram.**B**

   To adjust the highlight and shadow clipping in high-contrast **Threshold** mode, Alt-drag/ Option-drag the black slider until a few areas of black appear,**C** then Alt-drag/Option-drag the white slider until a few areas of white appear.

Adjust the midtones

4. Do either of the following:

   To lighten the **midtones**, drag the middle of the curve upward; or to darken the midtones, drag the middle of the curve downward. A new point appears each time you move part of the curve.

   To boost the **contrast**, drag the part of the curve that represents the dark midtones downward slightly, and drag the part that represents the light midtones upward (**A–C**, next page).

Adjust a specific area of the image

5. Click the **On-Image Adjustment** tool ⤒⬚ on the panel, then move the pointer over an area of the image that needs adjusting. Drag upward to lighten that area, or downward to darken it. A point corresponding to that tonal area will appear on the curve (**D–E**, next page).

➤ Increasing contrast via a Curves adjustment may also have the unintended effect of boosting the color saturation. To limit the adjustment to just tonal values (not colors), set the blending mode of the adjustment layer to Luminosity.

A This image could use a boost in tonal contrast.

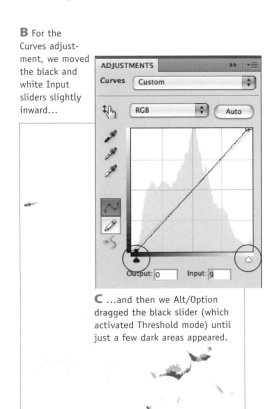

B For the Curves adjustment, we moved the black and white Input sliders slightly inward...

C ...and then we Alt/Option dragged the black slider (which activated Threshold mode) until just a few dark areas appeared.

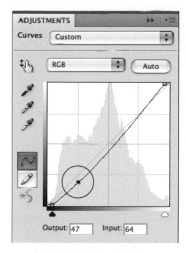

A We dragged the part of the curve that represents the dark midtones downward.

B The shadows and dark midtones are even darker now, especially in the foreground.

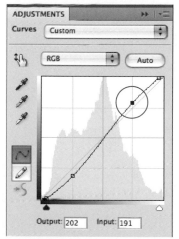

C We dragged the part of the curve that represents the light midtones upward; this raised the middle of the curve.

➤ To heighten the contrast in an image, replicate the S shape that you see on the curve at left.

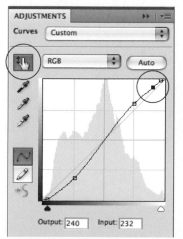

D With the On-Image Adjustment tool, we dragged downward on a light area of the image. A point appeared and the corresponding tonal region of the curve was lowered.

E Lightening the midtones and highlights improved the contrast; dragging downward on a light area of the image (as shown above) restored the needed details.

Neutralizing a color cast

Suppose, after adjusting the tonal balance in an image, you notice it still has a slight color cast. To remove it, the first step is to locate a 50% midtone gray area in the image that's neutral (has equal R-G-B values) or almost neutral. If you can easily pinpoint such a gray, skip this task and go directly to the instructions on the next page; if you can't, follow the instructions on this page first.

To pinpoint a neutral gray in an image:

1. Open an RGB image **A** and display the **Info** panel.❶ Choose **Actual Color** for the first readout on the panel (click the dropper icon to access the menu) and **Grayscale** for the second readout.

2. Choose the **Color Sampler** tool ✎ (I or Shift-I).

3. On the Layers panel, click the Background, then press Ctrl-J/Cmd-J to duplicate it.

4. Press Ctrl-I/Cmd-I to **invert** the colors in the duplicate layer.

5. To help you locate a neutral gray, choose **Difference** as the layer blending mode. Any colors in the duplicate layer that match colors in the Background will display as black. In other words, any inverted grays that are close to 50% neutral will still match the same grays in the background and will display as black.**B**

6. Move the pointer over black areas, noting the K readout on the Info panel. When you locate an area where the K value is at or near 99% (a neutral gray), click there to place a color sampler.**C**

7. Just as an added option, if you're able to spot another black area in the image that's close to 99%, click to create a second color sampler.

8. Hide the duplicate layer, then follow the steps on the next page.

A This image has a yellowish color cast.

B We inverted the duplicate layer and changed its blending mode to Difference.

C With the Color Sampler tool, we placed samplers on two areas that read as 98% K on the Info panel.

In this exercise, a gray area in an image is neutralized by using a Curves adjustment layer.

To neutralize a gray and remove a color cast with one click: ★

1. Open either an image that has an identifiable neutral gray or the image that you used for the instructions on the preceding page.

2. Show the **Info** panel.❶

3. On the **Adjustments** panel,⊘ click the **Curves** button.▣

4. Click the gray (middle) eyedropper,✎ then do either of the following:

   Click the identifiable neutral gray area, then view the RGB readouts on the Info panel.

Click the #1 sampler point in the image, then the #2 sampler point, viewing the readout for each on the Info panel to decide which one is removing the color cast more effectively.**A–B**

Verify that the readouts to the right of the slashes are close in value to one another, indicating the presence of a neutral gray.**C–D** If you think the color needs still more tweaking, see the following two pages.

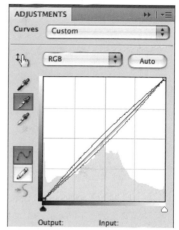

A With the gray eyedropper chosen for Curves, we clicked a sampler point in the document.

B Clicking with the gray eyedropper caused the curve for each color to be modified automatically and produced a neutral gray.

C Converting gray areas to a neutral gray successfully removed the yellow cast from the image. How simple was that?

NAVIGATOR	HISTOGRAM	INFO	▸▸ ▾≡
R :	133/ 122	K :	59/ 61%
✎ G :	125/ 122	✎	
B :	110/ 123		
8-bit		8-bit	
✛ X :	4.940	⊡ W :	
Y :	1.120	H :	
#1 R :	131/ 120	#2 R :	134/ 123
✎ G :	126/ 123	✎ G :	126/ 123
B :	111/ 124	B :	110/ 123

D On the Info panel, the RGB values from our Curves adjustment (to the right of the slashes) are nearly equal, which confirms that the color samplers are now reading neutral grays.

FINE-TUNING A COLOR CORRECTION USING INDIVIDUAL CHANNELS IN CURVES ★

If you were able to neutralize the midtone grays in your image by following the instructions on the preceding page, but the colors still don't look quite as well balanced as they should, try using a Curves adjustment layer again, except this time modify the curve for one or more of the individual color channels (**A–C** this page and **A–D**, next page).

A This image has a greenish cast. We used the technique described on page 146 to locate a neutral gray, then clicked to place a sampler point on the girl's sleeve (shown in the circle above).

B Clicking with the gray Curves eyedropper neutralized the midtones but left the girl's face with a reddish cast.

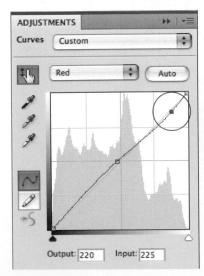

C On the Adjustments panel for Curves, we displayed the Red curve (Alt-3/Option-3), then dragged downward with the On-Image Adjustment tool on the girl's forehead to reduce reds in the highlights.

DON'T TOUCH THAT DIAL!

► When you click in an image with the gray eyedropper, a midtone point is placed on the curve for the individual Red, Green, and Blue channels automatically. To avoid throwing off the neutralizing effect, don't move those points.

► When adjusting the color channels via Curves, keep the blending mode for the adjustment layer on the default setting of Normal.

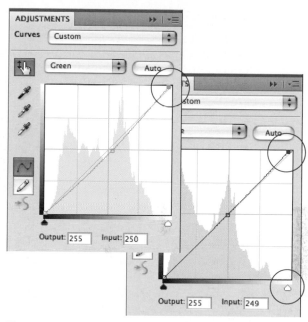

A Now the face is less red. So far, so good. To balance the Green and Blue channels, we pressed I (to reselect the eyedropper), then clicked to place another sampler point on a bright white area of the sleeve.

B While noting the sampler point #2 data on the Info panel (see **C** on this page), we displayed the Green curve (Alt-4/Option-4), then moved the white slider slightly inward, then did the same for the Blue curve (Alt-5/Option-5), making sure the G and B readouts closely matched the R readout.

NAVIGATOI	HISTOGRAN	INFO	▶▶	▼≡
R: G: B:		K:		
8-bit		8-bit		
X: Y:		W: H:		
#1 R: G: B:	126 127 126	#2 R: G: B:	217 213 213	

C This is the Info panel readout from sampler point #2 before we adjusted the Green and Blue curves...

NAVIGATOI	HISTOGRAN	INFO	▶▶	▼≡
R: G: B:		K:		
8-bit		8-bit		
X: Y:		W: H:		
#1 R: G: B:	126 127 126	#2 R: G: B:	217 217 217	

...and this is the readout after we adjusted the Green and Blue curves.

D In the final image, the face looks less red and the shirt sleeve is a brighter white.

Simulating a neutral density filter

When shooting a landscape scene, sometimes the proper exposure setting for a sky can leave the foreground area underexposed, or vice versa. To resolve this conflict on site, photographers reduce light on the upper part of the lens by using a graduated neutral density filter. We'll show you how to simulate the effect of such a filter for a landscape photo using Photoshop.

To simulate a graduated neutral density filter: ★

1. Open a landscape photo that contains a properly exposed ground and an overexposed sky. **A**

2. On the **Adjustments** panel, ⦿ click the **Curves** button.

3. If the sky lacks strong highlights, align the **white Input** slider with the edge of the histogram to brighten the highlights.

4. Click the **On-Image Adjustment** tool on the panel, then drag a short distance downward in the image to darken the sky and make it more saturated. **B–C** Don't worry that the foreground is too dark; you'll correct that next.

5. Keep the adjustment layer selected, and choose the **Gradient** tool ▭ (G or Shift-G). On the Options bar, click the **Black, White** preset on the Gradient preset picker, click the **Linear** style button (**A**, next page), choose Mode: Normal, choose Opacity 100%, and uncheck Reverse.

6. Starting from where the sky meets the ground, drag a short distance upward. You want the gradient in the layer mask to block the Curves effect from the lower part of the image (**B–C**, next page).

7. To control where the black part of the gradient mask ends, choose the **Move** tool ⊹ (V), and check **Show Transform Controls** on the Options bar. On the transform box for the gradient, drag the top center handle upward or downward until you're satisfied with where the Curves effect ends, then double-click inside the box to accept the edit (**D**, next page).

8. If any shapes from the foreground extend into the sky, choose the **Brush** tool, ⟋ a Soft Round tip, and an Opacity of 75%. With Black as the Foreground color, carefully draw strokes over those shapes. They will be added to the

A The sky in this photo is too light relative to the foreground.

B We created a Curves adjustment layer, moved the white Input slider inward, clicked the On-Image Adjustment tool on the panel, then dragged a short distance downward in the image to darken the sky.

C The Curves adjustment darkened the whole image.

mask, as you'll see in the updated layer mask thumbnail.**E–F**

➤ To learn about the Graduated Filter tool in Camera Raw, see pages 68–69.

A On the Options bar for the Gradient tool, we chose the Black, White preset on the Gradient preset picker and clicked the Linear style button.

B We dragged the Gradient tool upward a short distance, starting from where the sky meets the ground.

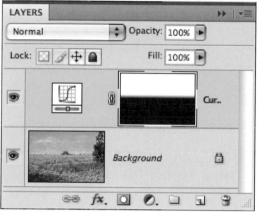

C The gradient appeared in the layer mask for the Curves adjustment layer.

D We dragged the top handle of the transform box for the gradient downward to change where the black part of the gradient mask ends.

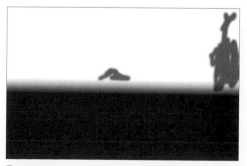

E Finally, we painted with the Brush tool to mask out shapes from the foreground (the tractor and tree) that extend into the sky area.

F In the final image, the sky looks as rich and saturated as the rest of the photo. Mission accomplished.

Creating dramatic lights and darks

Using the Masks panel, you can quickly add shadows and highlights to a photo without having to touch a brush or choose adjustment settings (take a break from using Curves!).

To create dramatic lights and darks by using the Masks panel: ★

1. Open an RGB photo that is evenly lit yet contains noticeable highlights.**A**

2. From the **New Fill/Adjustment Layer** menu,⬭ choose **Solid Color**. In the HSB area of the Color Picker dialog, enter 0 in the H and S fields and 10 in the B field, then click OK. Change the blending mode of the fill layer to Multiply.

3. Duplicate the Background (Ctrl-J/Cmd-J), then drag the duplicate layer above the Fill Color layer.**B**

4. On the Masks panel, click the **Add Pixel Mask** button,⬚ then click **Color Range**.

5. In the Color Range dialog, uncheck **Localized Color Clusters**. Choose **Black Matte** from the Selection Preview menu. Click the **Image** button below the preview, then click a highlight area in the preview. Adjust the **Fuzziness** value to limit the selection to only the lightest highlight areas of the photo (**A**, next page), then click OK.

6. On the Masks panel, raise the **Feather** value to between 70 and 90 px to soften the transition between the light and dark areas. Lower the **Density** value slightly to lighten the dark areas in the mask and thereby reveal more of the original color areas of the photo (**B**, next page).

7. To lighten the overall exposure in the photo, duplicate the layer that contains the mask, then lower the Opacity of the new layer until the exposure and highlights look just right (**C**, next page).

A We want to create dramatic lights and darks in this evenly lit portrait.

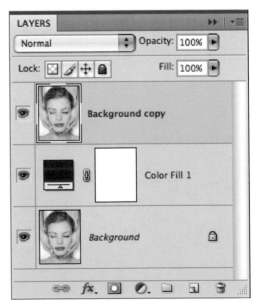

B This is the Layers panel after we created a Solid Color fill layer and restacked the duplicate of the Background.

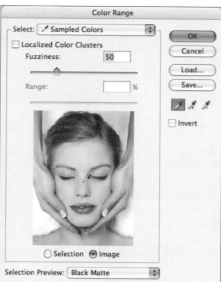

A After opening the Color Range dialog, we clicked the model's forehead in the preview, then chose the settings shown at left to limit the selection to just the lightest highlights.

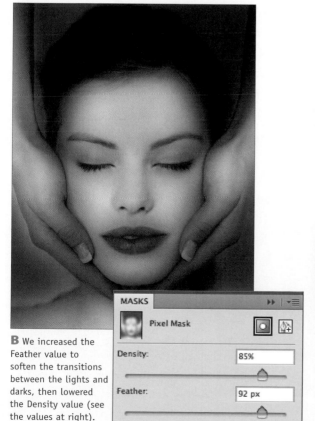

B We increased the Feather value to soften the transitions between the lights and darks, then lowered the Density value (see the values at right).

C Our last edits were to duplicate the mask layer and lower the Opacity of the new layer to 80%. The stronger lights and darks make the shapes look more sculptural and focus attention on the key elements of the portrait.

Creating glowing highlights

Another use we've found for the Masks panel is to create soft and diffused—yet still bright—lighting, with glowing highlights.

To create soft, glowing highlights by using the Masks panel: ★

1. Open an RGB photo that contains good contrast and some bright highlights, such as a product shot.**A**

2. Duplicate the Background (Ctrl-J/Cmd-J). Click the Background, then press Shift-Backspace/ Shift-Delete to open the Fill dialog. Choose Use: White, Normal mode, and 100% Opacity, then click OK.

3. Select the duplicate image layer. On the Masks panel, click the **Add Pixel Mask** button, then click **Color Range**.

4. In the Color Range dialog, click the **Image** button (below the preview) and choose **Black Matte** from the Selection Preview menu.

5. Do either of the following:

   Choose **Highlights** from the Select menu (**A**, next page).

   Uncheck **Localized Color Clusters**, then click a highlight area in the preview. Using the **Fuzziness** slider, expand or contract the selection of highlight areas.

6. Click OK.

7. On the Masks panel, click **Invert** to reverse the black and white areas of the mask (**B**, next page). Raise the **Feather** value to between 70 and 90 px to soften the transitions between light and dark areas. Lower the **Density** value slightly to lighten the dark areas in the mask and thereby reveal more of the original colors in the photo. That's a lot of effect for very little effort! (**C**, next page)

8. *Optional:* To adjust the intensity of the highlights, click Mask Edge on the Masks panel. In the dialog, click Default, raise or lower the Contract/Expand value to lessen or intensify the effect, then click OK.

A Our goal is to bathe this photo in a soft, diffused glow by intensifying the highlights, without losing the beautiful colors in the midtones.

A We added a layer mask, then clicked Color Range on the Masks panel. In the dialog, we chose Highlights from the Select menu. The selection previewed in the document window.

B On the Masks panel, we clicked Invert to reverse the black and white areas in the mask. For the time being, the highlights in the photo are too harsh and transition too abruptly to the midtones.

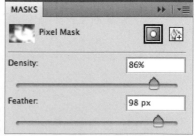

C Finally, we adjusted the Feather value, and then the Density value. As a result, the highlights are softer and transition smoothly to the midtones.

Dodging and burning

For a subtle contrast enhancement, you can lighten or darken areas of an image by drawing strokes with the Brush tool on a removable, editable neutral gray layer. Remember: Dodge to lighten, burn to darken.

To dodge or burn using a neutral color layer:

1. Open an RGB image.**A**

2. Click the Background, then Alt-click/Option-click the **New Layer** button.⬜

3. In the New Layer dialog, choose Mode: **Overlay**, check **Fill with Overlay-Neutral Color (50% gray)** (catchy name, huh?), then click OK.

4. Press Ctrl-J/Cmd-J to duplicate the neutral gray layer.**B**

5. Choose the **Brush** tool 🖌 (B or Shift-B), a large Soft Round tip, Normal mode, a very low tool Opacity of 6–10%, and a Flow setting of 50%. Press D to reset the Foreground and Background colors.

6. Click the lower neutral gray layer, then paint with black to burn (darken) some of the moderately dark shadow areas. The change is subtle.**C–D**

7. Click the upper neutral gray layer. Press X to swap the Foreground and Background colors,

A To create more contrast in this portrait, we'll dodge and burn areas with a brush on two neutral gray layers.

B We created a neutral gray layer, then duplicated it.

C To darken the left side of the face, we clicked the lower of the two neutral gray layers, then painted strokes with black.

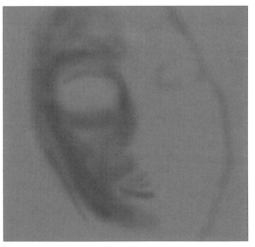

D These are the brush strokes that we applied to the lower neutral gray layer.

then paint with white to subtly dodge (lighten) some of the highlight areas.**A–B**

8. *Optional:* To remove any of your dodge or burn strokes, hide the Background, then Alt-click/ Option-click an unretouched area to sample the neutral gray. Redisplay the Background, choose

an Opacity of 100% for the Brush tool, then paint over any areas to restore them.**C–D**

9. *Optional:* To lessen the overall dodge or burn effect, click one of the neutral gray layers, then either lower the layer Opacity (**A–B**, next page) or choose Soft Light as the layer blending mode.

A To lighten the right side of the face, we clicked the upper neutral gray layer, then painted with white.

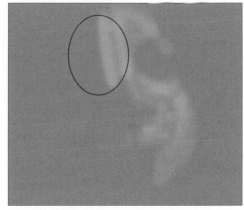

B These are the light paint strokes that we applied to the upper neutral gray layer. Oops! We lightened too much of the forehead. That won't be hard to fix.

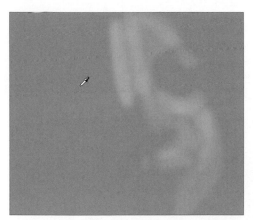

C We hid the Background, then Alt/Option-clicked an area that didn't contain any brush strokes to sample the original neutral gray.

D We redisplayed the Background, chose an Opacity of 100% for the Brush tool, then painted to remove some of the unwanted dodge strokes. Then we pressed D to reset the colors to black and white, lowered the brush Opacity to 8%, and continued to dodge and burn more areas by hand.

See also the figures on the following page

A The original image was a bit humdrum.

B To soften the results of our dodge and burn strokes, we lowered the Opacity of both neutral gray layers to 80%. Overall, our edits enhanced the contrast in the face and added subtle contouring.

Photographers have always found clever ways to enhance their portraits, from the hand tinting of early prints to the digital zapping of blemishes and wrinkles. In this chapter, you'll learn how to correct tonal imbalances, remove imperfections, and improve important facial features, such as the eyes and lips. You'll perform small retouching tasks, such as eliminating under-eye circles and whitening teeth, as well as broader edits, such as correcting a color cast and smoothing out the texture of skin (sometimes the camera is too darn honest!).

To meet these retouching challenges, you'll use a variety of selection and masking methods, and such features as adjustment layers, blending modes, blur filters, healing tools, and the Liquify command. As you work, keep these general guidelines in mind:

➤ Before performing any retouching work, consider cropping the composition to improve it: to create a more intimate close-up, eliminate a distracting background, or trim off superfluous areas.

➤ When determining what kind of corrections to make, keep the "essence" of the subject, your intended audience, and the directives of your client or art director (if any) in mind.

➤ Make broad changes, such as applying color and tonal corrections, before attending to small details, such as the facial features.

➤ Make as few cosmetic corrections as possible. By using the cloning, healing, distortion, and smoothing controls in Photoshop, you can slim a person down, transfer them to a different scene, remove all the nooks, crannies, and pores from their skin (extreme smoothing), perform surreal color shifts (blue hair), or even stick their face on a different body. Take a moment to ask yourself if the alterations you're contemplating are necessary, artistic, appropriate—and legal!

➤ When using a brush, whether on a duplicate image layer or a layer mask, use a delicate touch (e.g., a Soft Round, low-opacity brush). If you have a stylus and graphics tablet, use them.

➤ After performing small touch-ups, evaluate the changes relative to the overall portrait; and conversely, after performing a large-scale correction, such as skin smoothing, make sure the important details are sharp and the eyes, the "window to the soul," look bright and alluring.

Note: For the figures in this chapter, settings were chosen for images that are approximately 3000 x 2000 pixels.

RETOUCHING PORTRAITS

7

IN THIS CHAPTER

Correcting a color cast in a portrait

Sometimes the skin tones in a portrait have a red or yellowish cast. Using the Curves panel to set a neutral gray doesn't usually work as a solution to this problem because finding a neutral gray in a portrait is difficult. To neutralize a color cast in skin tones, we use a Hue/Saturation adjustment layer.

To adjust a color cast in a portrait:

1. Open an RGB image of a face. **A**

2. On the **Adjustments** panel, click the **Hue/Saturation** button, ★ then do the following (drag the slider or use the scrubby slider):

   From the second menu, choose **Reds** (the range that usually needs correcting in a portrait), then lower the **Saturation** to remove red. **B–C**

   To add or remove yellow, choose **Yellows** from the second menu, then adjust the **Lightness** (**A–B**, next page).

3. *Optional:* To make the adjustment more subtle, you can spread it slightly into the adjacent color range (widen the "fall-off" area). With the Reds range chosen on the second menu, drag the rightmost triangle (inside the color bar) into the yellow area; and with the Yellows range chosen (if you adjusted it), drag the leftmost triangle into the red area (**C–D**, next page).

4. *Optional:* Now that the color cast has been corrected, if you want to beef up the skin tones, from the second menu, choose Master, then increase the Saturation slightly.

➤ To correct small areas of sunburned skin, see pages 182–183.

A In this image, the skin has a strong reddish cast.

B For the Hue/Saturation adjustment, we chose Reds from the second menu, then lowered the Saturation to –38.

C The reduction in the saturation of Reds improved the photo considerably.

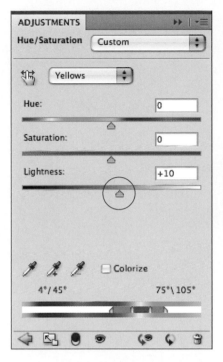

A Next, we chose Yellows from the second menu and increased the Lightness to +10, to restore some warmth to the blonde hair.

B This is the result after we made the edit shown at left.

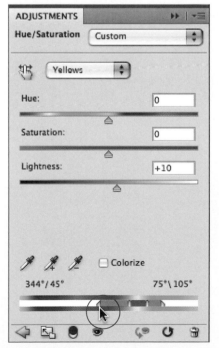

C To smooth the transition of the Yellows range into the Reds range (widen the falloff), we dragged the leftmost triangle on the adjustment slider into the Reds area.

D Our corrections successfully removed the color cast from the woman's skin.

Smoothing skin

If you want to make skin look smoother without using a soft-focus effect on the whole portrait, try the following method. You'll use the Gaussian Blur filter and layer controls, such as Darken and Lighten blending modes, a Black & White adjustment layer, layer masks, and layer opacity.

To smooth skin:

1. Open an RGB image of a face. **A** Press Ctrl-Alt-J/Cmd-Option-J, rename the duplicate layer "blur darken," then click OK.

2. Choose Filter > Blur > **Gaussian Blur**. In the dialog, move the Radius slider until the skin starts to become smooth and blurry (press, then release on the preview to judge the blur effect), then click OK. **B** Don't worry that the face now looks too blurry.

3. Choose **Darken** as the blending mode for the "blur darken" layer, then lower the layer opacity until a hint of the skin texture reappears.

4. Alt-click/Option-click the **Add Layer Mask** button ▣ on the Layers panel to add a black mask, and keep the mask thumbnail selected.

5. Choose the **Brush** tool ✐ (B or Shift-B), a Soft Round tip, Normal mode, and 100% Opacity, and press X to make the Foreground color white.

6. Apply strokes to areas where you want to reveal the smoothing effect, such as on the cheeks and forehead. If you unintentionally paint over any key features, such as the eyes or eyebrows, press X to make the Foreground color black, and paint over your strokes. Press X again to switch to white, and continue revealing skin areas (**A–B**, next page).

   ► Press [to reduce the brush diameter to paint over small areas, such as between the eyes and brows or between the nose and lips, then press] when you need to enlarge it again.

7. Press Ctrl-Alt-J/Cmd-Option-J to duplicate the "blur darken" layer, rename the duplicate layer "blur lighten," then click OK.

8. Change the blending mode of the "blur lighten" layer to **Lighten**. Increase or reduce the layer Opacity until any dark texture marks on the skin look softer (**C-D**, next page).

   The skin should now look smoother. To refine the effect, continue with the steps on page 164.

A We're going to smooth the texture of this woman's skin.

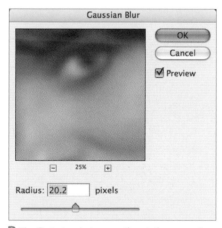

B The first step is to smooth out the pores. In the Gaussian Blur dialog, we chose a Radius of 20.2 pixels.

A To restore details to the shadow areas, we changed the blending mode of the "blur darken" layer to Darken and lowered the layer Opacity to 60%. Then, with the layer mask selected, we applied brush strokes to reveal the smoothing effect on the skin.

B The white areas in the layer mask reveal the smoothing effect (cheeks, chin, and nose); the black areas in the mask protect the rest of the portrait (eyes, lips, and hair) from the smoothing effect.

C We duplicated the "blur darken" layer, changed the blending mode of the new layer to Lighten, and changed the layer Opacity to 52%.

D The two blur layers (one in Lighten mode and the other in Darken mode) made the skin look smoother.

Continued on the following page

9. Click the topmost layer on the Layers panel, then create a **Black & White** adjustment layer. Move the **Reds** slider to between +100 and +120 to eliminate skin imperfections in the midtones, and move the **Yellows** slider to between +80 and +100 to eliminate imperfections in the shadows **A–B** (and **A**, next page).

10. Now the skin looks ghostly. To restore the skin tones, change the blending mode of the Black & White adjustment layer to **Luminosity**, and lower the layer Opacity to around 30%.

11. To group the top three layers, select the adjustment layer, Shift-click the "blur darken" layer, then press Ctrl-G/Cmd-G (**B**, next page). You can control the visibility (or opacity) of the whole layer group via its own control.

   ➤ Click the triangle for the group layer to expand or collapse the group listing.

12. Finally, to make the smoothing effect look more realistic and less "plastic," lower the Opacity for the group layer until you've recovered just the right amount of skin texture (**C–D**, next page). Nice work!

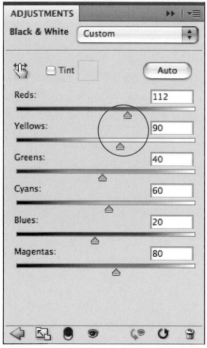

A For the Black & White adjustment, we moved the Reds slider to +112 and the Yellows slider to +90.

B The Reds slider adjustment smoothed the dark skin marks.

SOFTENING OTHER TEXTURES

You can use the same method to soften a texture in a photo of any subject matter: one blur layer in Darken mode to preserve shadow details, and another layer in Lighten mode to preserve highlight details. The Black & White adjustment will help neutralize the colors and refine the texture. And with the layers in a group, it will be easy to hide or show the overall adjustment or to increase or reduce the intensity of the correction.

A The Yellows slider adjustment smoothed the shadow areas.

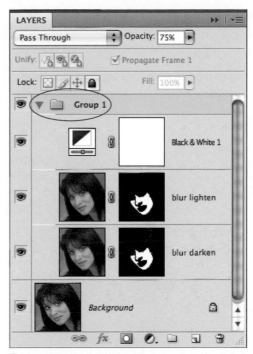

B We put the top three layers in a group (shown expanded) and lowered the Opacity of the group layer to 75% to restore some of the skin texture.

C This is the original image, for comparison.

D And here she is with smoother skin.

Creating a soft-focus portrait

Photographers sometimes use a soft-focus effect to lend an ethereal—and flattering—look to a portrait. In Photoshop, you can achieve a similar dewy glow by using the Diffuse Glow and Gaussian Blur filters to soften the skin texture, choosing Soft Light layer blending mode, and then restoring some sharpness to the facial features by painting on the layer mask.

To create a soft-focus portrait:

1. Open an RGB image of a face.**A** Press Ctrl-Alt-J/ Cmd-Option-J to copy the Background, rename the new layer "diffuse," then click OK.

2. Choose Filter > Distort > **Diffuse Glow**.

3. In the Filter Gallery, choose a zoom level that shows most of the image, then do the following:

   Set the **Graininess** to 1 (you don't want to add more texture).**B**

   Set the **Glow Amount** to around 8, or until the skin tone becomes a soft off-white.

   Set the **Clear Amount** to around 14, or until some skin color begins to reappear.

   Click OK.

4. For the "diffuse" layer, change the blending mode to **Soft Light**.**C**

A We want to soften the facial features and skin texture in this portrait.

B The Diffuse Glow filter (settings shown above) lightened the face and softened her features.

C Changing the blending mode of the Diffuse layer to Soft Light restored some detail and skin tone.

5. Duplicate the Background again. Rename this new layer "blur," then drag the layer listing to the top of the stack.

6. Lower the Opacity of the "blur" layer to 50%.

7. Choose Filter > Blur > **Gaussian Blur**. In the dialog, reduce the zoom level for the preview, drag the Radius slider to blur the edges, then click OK.**A**

8. Click the **Add Layer Mask** button, and keep the mask thumbnail selected.

9. Choose the **Brush** tool (B or Shift-B), a Soft Round tip, Normal mode, and 50% Opacity. Press X to make the Foreground color black. Paint on the image to mask the blur effect from the key features of the portrait, such as the eyes, nose, mouth, jewelry, and possibly a section of hair or a small detail on the clothing.**B–C** (If the results look too harsh, try using a lower-opacity brush.) Dahling, you look faa-bulous!

➤ To restore some color to the skin, lower the Opacity of the "diffuse" layer to around 70%.

A A Gaussian Blur layer further softened the features (we chose a Radius of 15 pixels in the Gaussian Blur dialog).

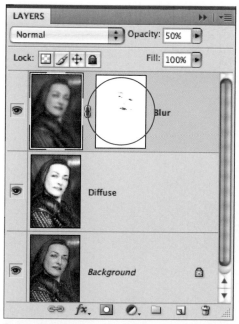

B We used two layers to achieve the final soft-focus effect (shown in **C**): a Blur layer (with brush strokes on the layer mask) and a Diffuse layer.

C The Gaussian Blur filter softened the edges and restored some skin tones. Brush strokes in the layer mask are blocking the blur effect from the pearl earring, nostrils, lips, pupils, and whites of the eyes.

Making eyes look brighter

If the eyes are the focal points of a face, it follows that getting the brightness and tonal contrast right in this area is one of the keys to good portraiture.

To select the eyes:

1. Open an RGB image of a face, then zoom in on the eyes.**A**

2. With the **Quick Selection** tool ![icon] (W or Shift-W)* and a small brush tip, select the whites of one eye (not the tear duct), then drag to select the whites of the other eye. Alt-drag/ Option-drag to subtract from the selection, if needed.**B**

3. On the Options bar, click **Refine Edge**. In the Refine Edge dialog, click Default, then click the Quick Mask preview button. Adjust the Feather value to soften the edge of the selection, and adjust the Contract/Expand value to loosely fit the selection to the eye shapes. This way, the brightening effect will fade softly into the corners of the eyes.**C** Click OK.

4. Press Ctrl-J/Cmd-J to copy the selection to a new layer, and follow the instructions below.

To brighten the eyes:

Method 1

Choose **Screen** as the layer blending mode (temporarily creepy), then lower the Opacity to 30–40% (**A**, next page).

Method 2

1. With the new layer selected, right-click/Control-click and choose **Convert to Smart Object**.

   ► This layer contains only a small area of image pixels, so a Smart Object and Smart Filter won't create a big processing lag.

2. Choose Filter > Distort > **Diffuse Glow**. In the Filter Gallery dialog, choose Graininess 1, Glow Amount 10 (adjust until any redness disappears from the eyes), and Clear Amount 9, then click OK. The eyes should now look softer and whiter. Diffuse Glow will appear as a Smart Filter listing on the Smart Object layer.

3. To soften the brightening effect, choose **Soft Light** as the layer blending mode. You could also lower the layer Opacity to 60–80% (**B–C**, next page).

If you prefer to create the selection by using a Quick Mask, follow steps 2–5 on page 170.

A In the original image, the eyes look a bit dull.

B The first step was to select the eyes with the Quick Selection tool.

C Via the Refine Edge dialog, we applied a Feather value of 5.1 and contracted the selection by –4.

A We copied the selection to a new layer, chose Screen as the blending mode, and reduced the layer Opacity to 30%.

B Here, instead of choosing Screen mode, we applied the Diffuse Glow filter, chose Soft Light as the layer blending mode, and lowered the layer Opacity to 60%.

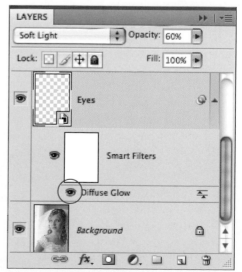

C Because we applied the Diffuse Glow filter to a Smart Object layer, we can double-click the filter listing at any time to edit the settings.

Recoloring eyes

Models can "change" their eye color by wearing colored contact lenses, and you can work similar magic by using the Color Balance dialog in Photoshop. The easiest colors to change are blue eyes to hazel (green), hazel eyes to blue, and blue eyes to brown; brown eyes are more difficult to change.

To recolor eyes:

1. Open an RGB image of a face, **A** and zoom in on the eye area.

2. Click the **Edit in Quick Mask Mode** button 🔘 on the Tools panel (Q).

3. Choose the **Brush** tool 🖌 (B or Shift-B), a small Soft Round brush, Normal mode, and 100% Opacity. Press D, if necessary, to make the Foreground color black.

4. Paint a Quick Mask over the iris of each eye, resizing the brush diameter as needed by pressing [or].**B** You can use multiple strokes. Don't paint over the pupils (you don't want to recolor them). To remove any unwanted Quick Mask strokes, press X and paint with white.

5. Click the **Edit in Standard Mode** button 🔲 (Q) to turn the mask into a selection, then press Ctrl-Shift-I/Cmd-Shift-I to invert it. Now just the irises are selected.**C**

6. On the **Adjustments** panel,⊘ click the **Color Balance** button. 🎚 ★ Click **Tone: Shadows,** and move any of the **Color Levels** sliders. Next, do the same thing for the **Midtones** (**A–C,** next page). We can't recommend a standard formula for choosing the right color.

   ▶ For the most natural appearance, allow flecks of other colors to appear in the irises. To achieve this, fiddle with the sliders in more than one Tone range.

   ▶ You could use a Hue/Saturation adjustment layer for step 6 above instead of Color Balance. For the Hue/Saturation adjustment, choose Master from the second menu, then fiddle with the Hue and Lightness sliders.

A We want to change the eye color of this model from blue to green.

B In Quick Mask mode, we painted a mask over the irises.

C When we clicked the Edit in Standard Mode button, the mask turned into a selection. We then inverted the selection.

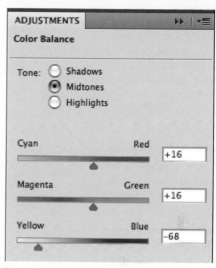

A For the Color Balance adjustment, we chose these settings for the Shadows...

B ...and chose these settings for the Midtones.

DUAL ZOOMS

If you have dual computer displays, you can open another window for the same document in the second display. When performing detail work, choose 100% view for one of the windows and a higher zoom level for the other.

C Now her eyes are soft green.

Removing under-eye circles

Sometimes the area under the eyes needs some touch-up work, such as eliminating bags or dark circles. Although the Clone Stamp or Healing Brush tool might seem like an obvious choice for retouching dark circles, they can leave a visible seam. We think the Patch tool does a better job.

To remove under-eye circles:

1. Open an RGB image of a face.**A** Press Ctrl-J/ Cmd-J to duplicate the Background, then zoom in on the eye area.

2. Choose the **Patch** tool ⌖ (J or Shift-J). On the Options bar, click **Patch: Source.**

3. Drag a marquee around the area to be repaired under one of the eyes.**B** If needed, Shift-drag to add to the selection or Alt-drag/Option-drag to subtract from it.

4. Drag from inside the selection to an area of skin that you want to sample from, preferably an area near the eye that has a similar texture.**C** A second selection marquee will appear temporarily. When you release the mouse (and the correction is done processing), the sampled imagery will appear inside the original selection.

5. Press Ctrl-D/Cmd-D to deselect.

   ➤ If you're not happy with the results, either undo or click the "Patch Tool" state on the History panel, then try again.

A We want to preserve the dramatic contrast in this portrait as we lighten the area under his eyes.

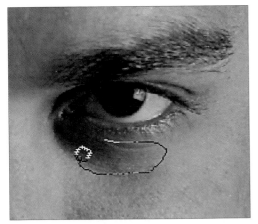

B With the Patch tool, we selected the area below the right eye,...

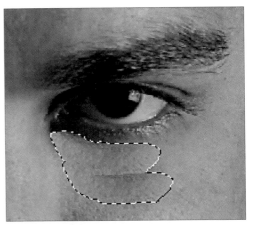

C ...then dragged from the selected area to a nearby area to sample those pixels.

6. Repeat steps 3–5 for the other eye.**A**

7. When your corrections are done, press Ctrl-E/Cmd-E to merge the duplicate layer into the Background.**B**

8. *Optional:* If the Patch tool correction left some dark areas, choose the Lasso tool (L or Shift-L), choose a Feather value of 12 px on the Options bar, then loosely select the area to be corrected. Create a Brightness/Contrast adjustment layer, and increase the Brightness value ever so slightly. Repeat for the other eye.

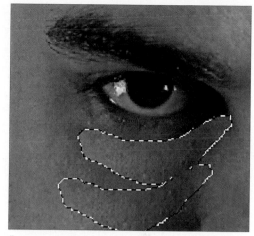

A We repeated the same three steps (3–5) for the left eye.

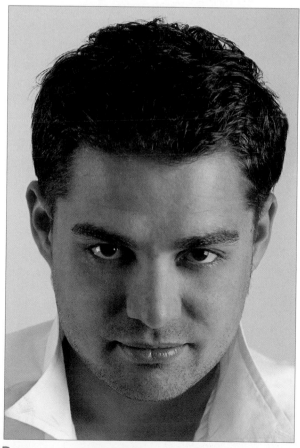

B The under-eye circles are gone.

Changing lipstick color

Digital lipstick!

To apply lipstick:

1. Open an RGB image of a face, then zoom in on the lips.**A**

2. Click the **Edit in Quick Mask Mode** button 🔘 on the Tools panel (Q).

3. Choose the **Brush** tool 🖌 (B or Shift-B), a small Soft Round brush, Normal mode, and 100% Opacity, and press D to make the Foreground color black.

4. Paint a Quick Mask over the lips. Change the brush diameter as needed by pressing [or]. To remove areas of the Quick Mask, press X to paint with white.

5. Click the **Edit in Standard Mode** button 🔲 (Q) to turn the mask into a selection.

6. Press Ctrl-Shift-I/Cmd-Shift-I to invert the selection. Now just the lips are selected.

7. On the **Adjustments** panel,◐ click the **Color Balance** button.⚖ ★ Check **Preserve Luminosity** and move the sliders for each **Tone** range (Shadows, Midtones, and Highlights).**B–C**

8. *Optional:* To darken the lips, Ctrl-click/Cmd-click the layer mask to turn it into a selection, create a Hue/Saturation adjustment layer, and change the Saturation value to between +10 and +20 and the Lightness value to around –5.**D** After performing this step, you may need to tweak the settings for the Color Balance adjustment layer.

A In the original image, the lips look very pale.

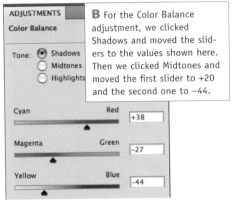

B For the Color Balance adjustment, we clicked Shadows and moved the sliders to the values shown here. Then we clicked Midtones and moved the first slider to +20 and the second one to –44.

C The lips have a new color but still look too pale.

D Via a Hue/Saturation adjustment layer, we changed the Saturation to +19 and the Lightness to –5. Now the lips are a luscious coral.

A VARIATION ON CHANGING THE LIPSTICK COLOR

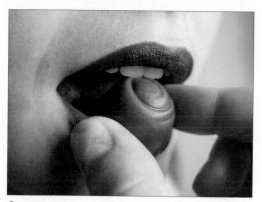

A In the original image, the lip color is too dark and clashes with the color of the chocolate.

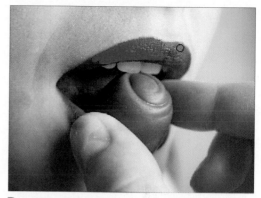

B We followed steps 2–6 on the previous page, including painting a mask over the lips in Quick Mask mode.

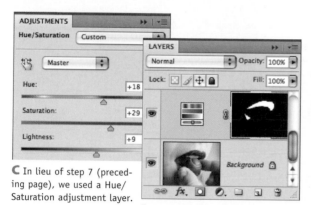

C In lieu of step 7 (preceding page), we used a Hue/Saturation adjustment layer.

D The selection translated into white areas in the layer mask.

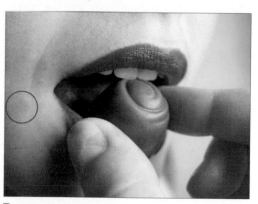

E The new lip color is more in keeping with the rest of the image. We'll make one further correction to remove the small pink spot (a lipstick smudge?) from the cheek.

F We clicked the Background, then with the Spot Healing Brush tool 🖌 (50 px soft brush and Create Texture clicked on the Options bar), clicked once on the smudge. Poof!

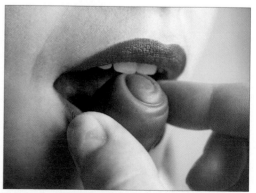

G The corrections are done. Kiss-kiss.

Lightening dark hair roots

In this task, you'll lighten dark roots on blond hair —without using smelly chemicals.

To lighten dark roots in blond hair:

1. Open an RGB portrait of a blonde, **A** and zoom in on the area to be recolored.

2. Create a new blank layer, rename it "recolor," and choose **Soft Light** as its blending mode.

3. Choose the **Brush** tool (B or Shift-B), a small Soft Round tip, Normal mode, Opacity 60%, and Flow 100%. To create strokes that fade gradually, on the Brushes panel, click Other Dynamics; from the Control menu for Opacity Jitter, choose Fade; then enter 60 in the field.

4. To sample the desired color for retouching, Alt-click/Option-click a medium-light area of hair (not a highlight).

5. Draw strokes over the hair in the same direction as the strands. **B** You can build up the color by dragging once or twice more over the same strands (remember, the brush opacity is only 60%). Don't worry that the strokes look too obvious; they'll blend in after the next step.

   ➤ To remove any unwanted brush strokes from the "recolor" layer, use the Eraser tool.

6. Press Ctrl-J/Cmd-J to duplicate the "recolor" layer that you just worked on, then choose Color as the blending mode. Zoom out, then lower the Opacity of the duplicate layer to achieve the desired intensity of coloring. **C–D** (Reset the Opacity Jitter control menu to Off.)

A We want to lighten the dark hair roots.

B Strokes are drawn over the dark strands.

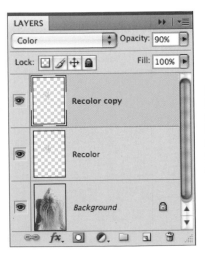

C To blend the brush strokes into the Background image, we lowered the Opacity of the topmost layer to 90%.

D Now the hair color looks more natural.

Using Liquify to trim or tighten

Although Liquify is a very powerful distortion command, it can be used with restraint to gently slim or reshape a waistline, chin, arms, or oddly shaped clothing. With a tool in the Liquify dialog, all you have to do is draw a stroke or two on the area to be reshaped. If only dieting were this easy! A stylus and tablet would come in handy for this task.

To slim a waistline:

1. Open an RGB image of a figure that needs some reshaping.**A** Press Ctrl-J/Cmd-J to duplicate the Background, and keep the duplicate layer selected.

   ➤ The image shown at right (or any silhouette of a figure) will work particularly well for this exercise because we won't have to be concerned about distorting elements in the background.

2. Choose Filter > **Liquify**. The large (resizable) Liquify dialog opens.

3. Zoom in on the waist area (Ctrl-click/Cmd-click).

4. Click the **Push Left** tool ![tool icon] (O).

5. For better control, under **Tool Options** on the right side of the dialog, do the following:

   To increase the amount of feathering and soften the distortion that occurs at the edge of the brush, set the **Brush Density** to between 20 and 40.

   To decrease the speed at which the distortion occurs, set the **Brush Pressure** to between 20 and 40.

   Note: If you're using a stylus, check the Stylus Pressure option and lower the Brush Pressure value.

6. To slim the waistline, position the edge of the brush pointer on the left edge of the figure, choose a brush diameter by pressing] or [, then drag downward.**B–D** Drag in the same direction as many times as necessary to reshape the area.

7. For the right side of the figure, drag upward.

   ➤ To compare the original Background with the liquified layer, check Show Backdrop, choose All Layers from the Use menu, and set the Opacity to 30%. Uncheck and recheck Show Backdrop to toggle between the two views.

Continued on the following page

A The shirt and pants on this fellow are bulging out in an unflattering way.

B With the Push Left tool, we dragged downward along the left side of the shirt a few times (here, the Show Backdrop option is on).

C We used the same tool and a smaller brush to slim down the right side of the shirt...

D ...and to narrow the hip area (here, the Show Backdrop option is off).

8. If the figure has an area that you want to tighten up, such as a belt, blouse, or exposed belly, choose the **Pucker** tool (S). Change the Brush Density to 40 and the Brush Rate to 50. Increase the brush diameter so it covers the area that you want to shrink, then click and hold just once or twice. Instant liposuction! **A**

9. Click OK.**B–C**

➤ To push pixels in the opposite direction from the Push Left tool's normal behavior, hold down Alt/Option while dragging.

HOW TO UNLIQUIFY

To restore pixels to their pre-Liquify state, do any of the following:

➤ In the Reconstruct Options area, choose Revert from the Mode menu, then either choose the Reconstruct tool (R) and drag across the areas to be restored, or click—and keep clicking—Reconstruct to undo your edits in reverse order.

➤ To restore the entire preview image to its undoctored state, click Restore All—and of course you can always Cancel out of the dialog…

A With the Pucker tool, we click and hold on the bulging shirt to contract it inward.

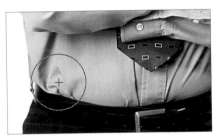

B This is the original image.

C And this is after we used the Liquify filter.

USING LIQUIFY TO TIGHTEN UP A CHIN

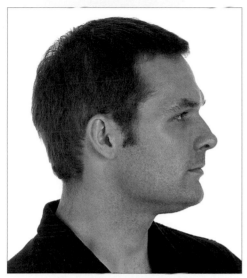

A Another good use for the Liquify filter is to tighten up a chin.

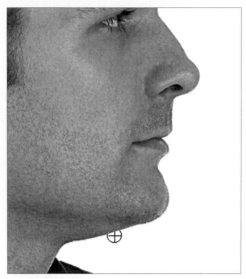

B We dragged the Push Left tool a couple of times from left to right (Brush Size 25, Brush Pressure 50).

C Although Liquify has great distortion power, we use it to make subtle improvements, such as the "chin lift" that we gave this gentleman.

PROTECTING AREAS FROM LIQUIFY

➤ To paint a mask to protect areas of an image from distortion (or to add to an existing mask), choose the Freeze Mask tool ✎ (F), choose Tool Options (including the maximum Brush Pressure), then paint over areas in the preview. Display or hide the mask via the Show Mask check box.

➤ To remove the protection from any frozen areas, choose the Thaw Mask tool ✎ (D), then paint over areas in the preview.

➤ To create a mask based on layer transparency, a layer mask, or an alpha channel in the original image, and thereby prevent those areas from being "liquified," choose that option from the first menu under Mask Options.

➤ To reverse what's masked and what's not, click Invert All; or to unmask the entire image at any time (make all the pixels editable again), click None.

Whitening teeth

In this exercise, you'll whiten teeth by using a Quick Mask and the Hue/Saturation dialog—instant bleaching.

To whiten teeth:

1. Open an RGB image of a smiling figure.**A**

2. Zoom in on the mouth area.

3. Click the **Edit in Quick Mask Mode** button on the Tools panel (Q).

4. Choose the **Brush** tool (B or Shift-B), a small Soft Round brush, Normal mode, and 100% Opacity. Press D to make the Foreground color black.

5. Paint a Quick Mask over the teeth.**B** To remove areas of the Quick Mask, where needed, press X and paint with white.

6. Click the **Edit in Standard Mode** button (Q) to turn the mask into a selection.

7. Press Ctrl-Shift-I/Cmd-Shift-I to invert the selection. Now just the teeth are selected.

8. On the **Adjustments** panel, click the **Hue/Saturation** button. ★ Choose **Yellows** from the second menu, then reduce the **Saturation** and increase the **Lightness.C–D**

➤ In our *Photoshop CS4, volume 1: Visual QuickStart Guide,* we show how to whiten teeth via the Replace Color command; it's an equally good method.

A The teeth in this portrait could use some whitening.

B We painted a mask onto the teeth in Quick Mask mode with the Brush tool (13 px diameter).

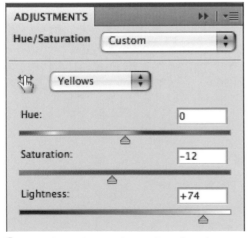

C For Hue/Saturation, we chose Yellows from the menu, then lowered the Saturation and raised the Lightness.

D Whiter, brighter (but still natural-looking) teeth...

Removing blemishes

You can easily zap zits, moles, or crow's-feet with the Spot Healing Brush tool. Using the same photo as in the previous exercise, we'll remove a mole from the man's cheek.

Note: If you're going to continue with the same photo from the previous exercise, you can merge the adjustment layer downward before proceeding with these instructions.

To remove a blemish:

1. Open a portrait in which the figure has a blemish or wrinkle that you want to remove,**A** and press Ctrl-J/Cmd-J to duplicate the Background. Keep the duplicate layer selected.

2. Choose the **Spot Healing Brush** tool 🖌 (J or Shift-J).

3. On the Options bar, choose Mode: Normal and click Type: **Create Texture**. Click the Brush preset picker, and lower the brush Hardness to 0% to create a soft tip.

4. Press [or] to make the brush tip about double the diameter of the blemish.

5. Click on, or drag once across, the blemish.**B** A dark mark will appear, then will disappear when the correction is done processing.**C** How easy was that?

➤ On pages 248–249 you'll find a list of shortcuts for quickly changing brush settings, such as the mode, diameter, and hardness.

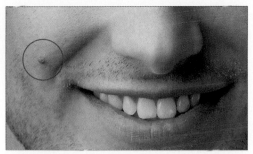

A We want to remove the mole from this man's cheek.

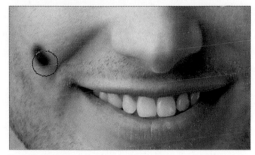

B With the Spot Healing Brush tool (40 px diameter), we drag a short distance — just once.

C The mole is gone. Now, anybody got a razor?!

"Curing" a sunburn

You can use a Hue/Saturation adjustment layer and a layer mask to correct a sunburn, tone down a ruddy complexion, or neutralize the color in any overly red area, such as the cheeks.

To correct sunburned areas:

1. Open an RGB image. **A**

2. On the **Adjustments** panel, ◐ click the **Hue/Saturation** button. ▤ ★ To correct the sunburned areas, choose **Reds** from the second menu, then lower the **Saturation**. You can also increase the **Lightness** slightly or adjust the **Yellows** color range, if needed. **B**

3. Click the adjustment layer mask thumbnail, then press Ctrl-I/Cmd-I to make the mask black.

4. Choose the **Brush** tool ✐ (B or Shift-B), a Soft Round tip, Normal mode, and an Opacity of 50% or less. If necessary, press D to make the Foreground color white.

5. Make sure the adjustment layer mask thumbnail is still selected, adjust the brush diameter by pressing [or], then draw strokes where you want to apply the adjustment, such as the cheeks, forehead, nose, or ears (**A–C**, next page).

6. *Optional:* To reduce the effect of the adjustment layer, lower the layer Opacity.

A We want to tone down the ruddiness of this man's complexion without lightening his rich skin tones.

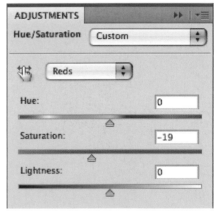

B Via a Hue/Saturation adjustment layer, we lowered the Saturation of the Reds color range.

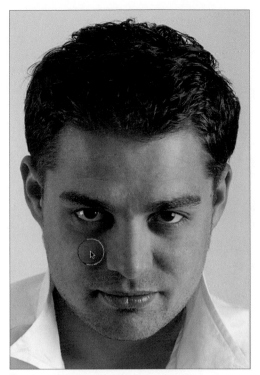

A With the Brush tool and a large Soft Round brush, and with the adjustment layer mask selected, we drew soft, broad strokes on the areas that needed correction.

B The reds are diminished where needed, and the rest of the image is unaltered.

C The adjustment is revealed by the strokes that we applied to the black mask on the Hue/Saturation adjustment layer.

Smoothing out small areas

In this last retouching exercise, we'll show you how to smooth out small areas of a face (or any subject for that matter) by using a feathered selection and the Gaussian Blur filter. Our example will be to smooth out ridges on a woman's eyelids.

To smooth out skin texture:

1. Open a portrait image,**A** and press Ctrl-J/Cmd-J to duplicate the Background.

2. Do either of the following:

   With the **Lasso** tool 𝒫 (L or Shift-L), drag a selection around the area to be corrected, then Shift-drag if you need to select additional areas, such as the second eyelid in a portrait.

   In **Quick Mask** mode, ◻ paint a Quick Mask over the areas to be corrected (as in steps 3–7 on page 180).**B**

3. On the Masks panel, ◻ click the **Add Pixel Mask** button, 🖿 then click **Mask Edge**. In the Refine Mask dialog, click Default, then as you do the following, click between the Quick Mask and On White preview options: Increase the Feather value to 4–9, raise the Contract/Expand value slightly, then click OK. ★

4. *Optional:* To reshape the mask, click the layer mask thumbnail on the Layers panel, then apply strokes with the Brush tool (Soft Round tip).

5. With the layer thumbnail selected, choose Filter > Blur > **Gaussian Blur**. Choose a low Radius value, then click OK. Deselect.**C–D**

6. *Optional:* To lessen the smoothing effect, lower the Opacity of the duplicate layer.

A We want to even out the crepe-like texture of the eyelids without eradicating the iridescent eye shadow.

B We paint over the eyelids in Quick Mask mode.

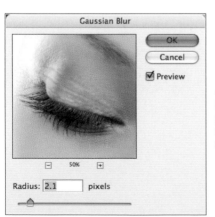

C We chose a Radius of 2.1 pixels in the Gaussian Blur dialog.

D Now the eyelids look slightly smoother.

Images can be combined using various techniques for different goals. In a photo illustration, you can create an illusion by hiding the seams between layers, whereas in an artistic collage, you can leave conspicuous seams "on purpose" to emphasize differences in subject matter, scale, color, and texture. This chapter covers the gamut of compositing tools and techniques, including the Auto-Align Layers command, the Background Eraser tool, drag-and-drop, the Move tool, the Clone Source panel, and the Vanishing Point filter—plus our old standby, layer masks.

Tips for creating montages

➤ Depending on the effect you're after, you can make the edges on an image layer rough or jagged with the Brush tool or filters, or fuse layers together gently via gradients in layer masks.

➤ If you're creating an artistic montage, try venturing out of your comfort zone. For source material, artists have been known to scan everything but the kitchen sink: objects, drawings, paintings, fabric, handmade papers—even their own face or hands. Fiddle with that distortion filter you've always been curious about or apply a surreal color cast via the Color Balance (Color Imbalance!) command. Ultimately, of course, whatever techniques you settle on should serve the greater good of the overall image. We're not advocating a lapse of good taste!

➤ Once all the components are scaled, manipulated, and positioned where you want them, consider using the layer style controls (Blending Options or layer effects), color adjustments, or lighting to create unity and cohesiveness.

➤ To add a handmade touch to your montages, incorporate some of the techniques found in Chapter 11, Fine Art Media.

➤ For inspiration, study the work by montage pros. Look for images labeled "photo illustration" in newsweekly magazines and other media; or browse the websites of our favorite Photoshop "montagists": oldtin.com (Clifford Alejandro), aliciabuelow.com, jeffbrice.com, daltoncowan.com (Stephanie Dalton Cowan), dianefenster.com, naomishea.com, and kerismith.com.

COMBINING IMAGES

8

IN THIS CHAPTER

Aligning and blending shots of the same scene

It can be a challenge to get a whole group of people to smile simultaneously for a portrait (unless there happens to be a comedian in the crowd)—and to keep everyone from blinking when you click the shutter. If you take multiple shots of the same scene, you can blend the choice areas of two of the best photos in Photoshop via the Auto-Align Layers command and a layer mask.

To align and blend two shots of the same scene: ★

1. Open two RGB photos from the same shoot that contain figures or areas that you want to combine the best features of.**A–B** (We'll use a portrait for our illustrations, but other subject matter can be used.)

2. On the **Arrange Documents** menu ▦ on the Application bar, click a 2 Up button. Shift-drag the Background from the Layers panel of one photo onto the document window of the other. Holding down Shift ensures that the copy appears in the correct location.

On the Arrange Documents menu, click the Consolidate All (first) button to restore the single document view.

3. On the Layers panel, Shift-click to select both layers, then choose Edit > **Auto-Align Layers**.

4. In the Auto-Align Layers dialog (**A**, next page), click a **Projection** option: **Reposition** if you used a tripod, or **Auto** for all other shooting situations to let Photoshop choose the best alignment option. Click OK. The Background will be converted to a layer.

A We want to combine the mother and child on the left from this photo...

B ...with the father and child on the right from this photo. The first step is to drag the image layer from one document into the window of the other.

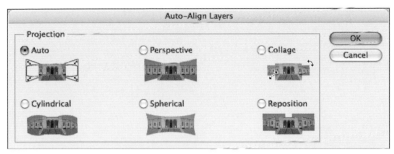

A In the Auto-Align Layers dialog, we clicked Auto as the Projection option.

5. *Optional:* Click the top layer, lower its Opacity (to around 50%) to check the position of the imagery relative to the underlying layer, then restore its Opacity to 100%.

6. Click the top layer, Alt-click/Option-click the **Add Layer Mask** button ⬚ at the bottom of the Layers panel, and keep the mask thumbnail selected. For the moment, the mask is hiding the top layer completely.**B**

7. Choose the **Brush** tool ✎ (B or Shift-B), a Soft Round tip, Normal mode, and 100% Opacity. Zoom in, then paint strokes with white as the Foreground color to reveal the more desirable parts of the top layer.**C–D**

Continued on the following page

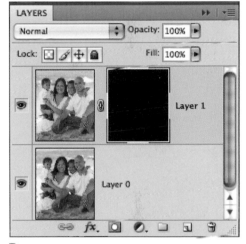

B The Auto-Align Layers command converted the Background to a layer and matched up the two layers. Next, we created a black layer mask, which for the moment is fully blocking the top layer.

C With the Brush tool, we're applying white strokes to the black layer mask to expose just the faces of the father and child from the top layer.

D In the process, we also revealed some of the light background along the edge of the child's face; we'll remedy that next.

8. To touch up the mask, decrease the brush diameter and zoom in further. Paint along the edges of the shapes to reveal more of the top layer, or press X to paint with black to reduce the mask and reveal more areas of the underlying layer.**A–B**

A We zoomed in, reduced the brush diameter, and then, with the layer mask still selected, painted with white (and then black) to correct the masked area between the mother and child.

B The final image is a seamless composite of the two photos, achieved by using the Auto-Align Layers command and brush strokes on a layer mask.

USING AUTO-BLEND LAYERS

You can also use **Auto-Blend Layers** (a cousin of the Auto-Align Layers command) to combine two portraits. Our best results have been with photos in which there's space between the subjects and the background happens to be soft or blurry.

Drag and drop a layer from one document into another. To convert the Background to a layer, double-click it, then click OK in the dialog. With the Rectangular Marquee tool, select and then delete the unwanted portion of each layer (shown as lightened areas here for illustration purposes), making sure to allow the portions that remain to partially overlap.

Deselect. Shift-click the two layers, then choose Edit > Auto-Blend Layers. When the dialog opens, click Panorama and check Seamless Tones and Colors. ★ The command will create a layer mask for each layer to blend the overlapping area between them (it does all the work for you!).

Using the Background Eraser tool

When you click or drag with the Background Eraser tool, colored pixels are replaced with transparent ones. This tool gives you greater control than the plain old Eraser tool, because it lets you sample the color to be erased and also lets you choose whether adjacent colors will be erased, within a specific range of the sampled color.

To use the Background Eraser tool:

1. Open an RGB image.**A** Press Ctrl-J/Cmd-J to duplicate the Background, then hide the Background.

2. Choose the **Background Eraser** tool (E or Shift-E) and a brush tip. If you have a pressure-sensitive tablet, via the Brush preset picker, set the brush Size and Tolerance to Pen Pressure.

3. On the Options bar, click a **Sampling** button to control the tool behavior:

   Continuous to replace all the colored pixels directly under the pointer with transparent ones, as well as adjacent colors that are within the current Tolerance range.

   Once to replace only pixels that closely match the first color you click with transparent pixels.

   Background Swatch to erase only pixels that match the current Background color. For this option, pick a Background color now.

4. To control which pixels can be erased, choose from the **Limits** menu:

   Discontiguous to erase all pixels within the current Tolerance range that the tool passes over; pixels don't have to be adjacent to one another.

   Contiguous to erase only pixels adjacent to the one you click, within the Tolerance range.

   Find Edges to erase pixels contiguous to the one you click, while preserving shape edges.

5. Choose a **Tolerance** percentage to control how widely the colors to be erased can differ from the first color you click. For the Continuous sampling option, use a low Tolerance (less than 8%); for the Once option, use a moderate Tolerance of around 20–30%.

6. Click or drag in the document window **B** (also **A–E**, next page, and **A–D**, page 191). You can change the Sampling option, Tolerance, brush diameter, or brush hardness between strokes.

A We are going to erase the sky in this photo (a stock photo taken in Angkor, Cambodia, in case you're wondering).

B With the Background Eraser tool, we dragged horizontally from the sky into the trees. Because the tool setting was Sampling: Once, it sampled the sky color only from the point where we started dragging and erased only colors that were close in value to the sampled color, within our chosen Tolerance range of 30%.

ERASING SKY BEHIND FOLIAGE

A The Background Eraser tool is successfully removing the sky colors while preserving the leaves. Since the sky contains multiple colors, we will need to click and drag multiple times to sample and erase.

B Next, we clicked the left side of the image with the Background Eraser tool to sample that part of the sky.

C Dragging across the tree removed sky colors within the chosen Tolerance range, while preserving the leaves.

D Using a smaller brush (and a lower Tolerance range, to avoid erasing the highlight colors on the buildings), we erased the sky near the buildings, then dragged from the sky toward the buildings to sample and erase only the sky color.

E Next, we dragged a layer of sky imagery from another document into this one, then restacked it below the layer that we erased pixels from. The new sky looks too bright and saturated, though, so we'll fix that problem next.

A We created a Hue/Saturation adjustment layer above the sky layer, and with Master chosen on the second menu, lowered the Saturation.

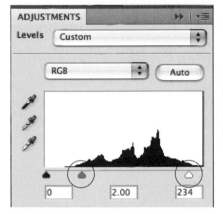

B To lighten the sky, we created a Levels adjustment layer and moved the gray and white Input Levels sliders.

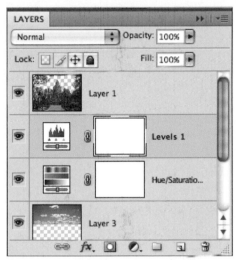

C This is the Layers panel for the final image, which is shown below.

D In the final montage, the two image layers meld successfully: the trees and temple from the original image together with the new sky layer.

Enlarging the canvas area

Before creating a montage, you may need to enlarge the canvas area—that is, add a blank area to one or more sides of the image—to accommodate more imagery. When you draw a marquee with the Crop tool that's larger than the image, you effectively increase the canvas size. Unlike the Canvas Size command, this technique gives you manual control over the size and location of the added canvas area. Another use for this technique is to reveal imagery that extends beyond the live canvas, which may result when you drag and drop or paste in a layer from a larger document.

To enlarge the canvas area using the Crop tool:

1. Open an image, then choose a Background color.**A**

2. Change the zoom level, if necessary, to show some gray area around the image.

3. Choose the **Crop** tool (C or Shift-C).

4. Drag a crop marquee within the image.

5. Drag any of the handles of the marquee beyond the live canvas area (**A–B**, next page).

6. To accept the edit, do one of the following (**C**, next page):

   Double-click inside the marquee.

   Press Enter/Return.

   Right-click/Control-click the image and choose Crop.

   If the image has a Background (Layers panel), the added canvas area will fill with the current Background color; if not, it will fill with transparent pixels. Pixels that were previously located outside the edge of the canvas area may now display within it.

➤ To cancel the crop marquee before accepting it, press Esc.

A We want to add blank space around this image to accommodate other image layers that we're going to add to it.

OVERRIDING THE SNAP

Normally, if you resize a crop marquee near the edge of the canvas area and the View > Snap To > Document Bounds feature is on, the marquee will snap to the edge of the canvas area. To override this snap function (say you want to crop ever so slightly inside or outside the edge of the image), either turn Snap To > Document Bounds off, or start dragging a handle on the marquee, then hold down Ctrl/Control as you continue to drag.

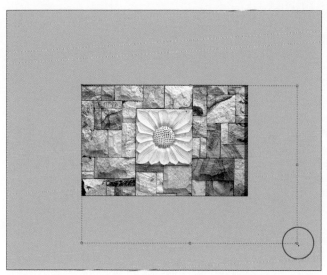

A We lowered the zoom level and chose white as the Background color. With the Crop tool, we drew a marquee within the image, then dragged the lower right handle of the marquee to enlarge it.

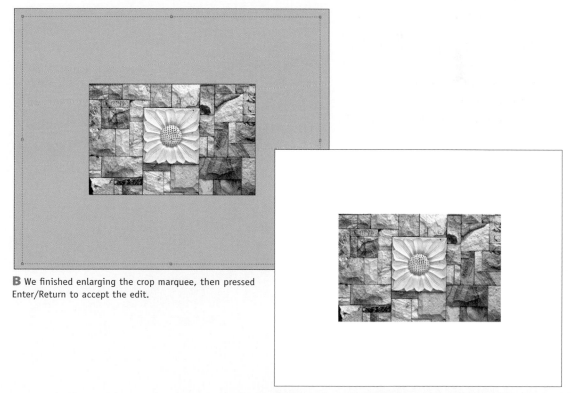

B We finished enlarging the crop marquee, then pressed Enter/Return to accept the edit.

C The canvas area now includes a white area around the original imagery.

Blending imagery via layer masks

When you create a montage from multiple image layers, you can let the seams stay visible or you can apply a gradient to each layer mask to meld the imagery together, as we show you how to do here.

To combine images into a composite:

1. Open an RGB image to be used as a background for a composite image (e.g., a soft-focus image or a photo of a texture), and make sure it's large enough to contain the other images that you're going to add. If you need to enlarge the canvas area, see the preceding two pages. Alternatively, you can create a blank document and fill it with a solid color or a gradient.

2. Open two or more smaller RGB images to be placed on top of the master background image. To make your job easier, make sure all the files have the same resolution (Image > Image Size).

   On the **Arrange Documents** menu 🔲 on the Application bar, click an available "Up" button. ★

3. Click in one of the smaller images, then drag the Background or a layer from the Layers panel into the document window of the master image. If desired, use the Move tool (V) to scale any of the imported layers.* Repeat to add imagery from the other files, then close all but the master file. **A–B**

4. Save the master file, then hide all but one of the new layers.

5. Choose the **Move** tool ⊹ (V). Click the visible image layer, then drag it to one side of the document. Click the **Add Layer Mask** button 🔘 on the Layers panel.

A Into a horizontal document that contains a background texture, we dragged a portrait layer and a watches layer.

B The two layers that we imported appear on the Layers panel.

If you find that you need to enlarge any layer by a substantial amount, do so in the original file via Image > Image Size, and then reimport it.

6. Choose the **Gradient** tool ▢ (G or Shift-G). On the Options bar, click the Black, White preset in the Gradient preset picker, click the Linear Gradient button, ▢ set the Mode to Normal, set the Opacity to 100%, and uncheck Reverse.**A**

7. In the document window, start dragging horizontally from where you want the imagery to be transparent (the black area of the mask), and stop dragging where you want the image to remain fully opaque (the white area of the mask).**B** A representation of the gradient will appear in the layer mask thumbnail.**C**

8. To transform the mask to control where the fadeout occurs on any layer, do the following:

   Click the **Link** button ▨ between the layer and layer mask thumbnails to unlink them, then click the layer mask thumbnail.

Continued on the following page

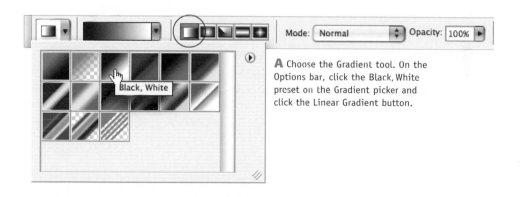

A Choose the Gradient tool. On the Options bar, click the Black, White preset on the Gradient picker and click the Linear Gradient button.

B We scaled and repositioned the face, then hid the watches layer. Next, we added a layer mask to the face layer, then dragged with the Gradient tool to fade the right side of the man's face.

C The linear gradient appears in the layer mask thumbnail for the face layer.

Choose the **Move** tool ⊹ (V). On the Options bar, check **Show Transform Controls**. Drag the middle handle on the transform box (to control where the fadeout is),**A** then double-click inside the transform box to accept the edit. Click between the image and mask thumbnails to relink them.

9. To fade a corner of the same image layer, do the following:

   Click the layer mask thumbnail. Choose the **Gradient** tool and the same settings as in step

6, except this time choose **Multiply** as the tool Mode (Normal mode would replace the existing gradient, whereas Multiply mode will combine the new and existing ones).

Drag from the edge of the imagery toward the middle.**B–C**

10. Redisplay the hidden image layer(s), and repeat steps 5–9 to add a layer mask and gradients to those layers.

➤ If you need to redo a gradient, press Ctrl-Z/Cmd-Z to remove the current one, then reapply it.

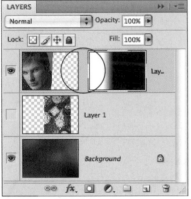

A We unlinked the layer mask from the layer and then, with the Move tool, adjusted the position of the fadeout by dragging a handle on the transform box (as shown by the white arrow).

C The diagonal gradient appears in the layer mask for the portrait layer.

B With the Gradient tool Mode set to Multiply, we added another gradient to the layer mask to fade the bottom left corner.

To fade a layer from its center:

1. Click an image layer on the Layers panel (a different layer, if you're continuing with the preceding task), then click the **Add Layer Mask** button.

2. Choose the **Gradient** tool. On the Options bar, click the **Black**, **White** preset on the Gradient preset picker, click the **Reflected Gradient** button, set the Mode to Normal and the Opacity to 100%, and check **Reverse**.

3. In the document window, drag horizontally from the center of the imagery to the edge.**A** Note how the gradient looks in the layer mask thumbnail.**B**

4. To blend the imagery, on the Masks panel, ★ increase the **Feather** value to soften the edge of the mask. Also lower the layer Opacity.**C**

To refine the lighting, follow the steps on the next page.

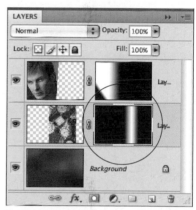

B The reflected gradient is fading to black on both sides of the layer mask.

A We made the watches layer visible and repositioned and scaled it. Next, we added a layer mask, then dragged the Gradient tool (with the Reflected Gradient style chosen) to fade both sides of the watches layer.

C On the Masks panel, we increased the Feather value to 130 px and reduced the layer Opacity to 80%. The layer could use some lighting refinements (see the following page).

For a finishing touch, add some subtle lighting tweaks to the composite image.

To refine the lighting on an image layer:

1. Click the layer that contains the reflected gradient in its mask, then press Ctrl-J/Cmd-J to copy it.**A**

2. Click the layer mask thumbnail for the duplicate layer. To make the layer look brighter, on the Masks panel, reduce the Feather value. Whitening the center of the mask reveals more of the image.**B**

3. *Optional:* To intensify the light, choose a different blending mode for the duplicate layer, such as Hard Light or Luminosity, and adjust the layer Opacity.**C**

4. *Optional:* To narrow the lighting effect on the duplicate layer, make the white area in the mask narrower. Click the mask thumbnail, then click Mask Edge on the Masks panel. In the dialog, click Default, lower the Contrast/Expand value (try a value between –25 and –40), then click OK.

A We duplicated the watches layer.

B We clicked the mask on the duplicate watches layer, then reduced the Feather value to 65 px (Masks panel) to lighten the middle of that layer.

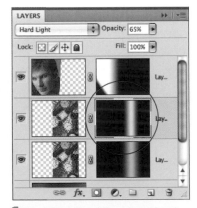

C The sharper transitions are evident in the layer mask. Finally, we chose the Hard Light blending mode for the duplicate layer and reduced the layer Opacity to 65%.

QUICK SUMMARY: USING THE MOVE TOOL

Once your imagery has been collected into one document — whether via the Clone Stamp tool, drag-and-drop, or copy-and-paste — you can use the Move tool ⊕ to reposition or transform each layer individually. For the following tasks (except the first one), choose the Move tool.

TASK	METHOD
Temporary Move tool	Ctrl/Cmd (this works with most tools); or hold down V to spring-load the tool. ★
Drag-copy a selection with a temporary Move tool	Ctrl-Alt-drag/Cmd-Option-drag the selection.
Move imagery or a layer mask separately	Unlink the two thumbnails by clicking the link icon between them, click a thumbnail, then drag.
Copy a layer or a selection	Alt-drag/Option-drag in the document window.
Nudge a layer or a selection	Press (or Shift-press) an arrow key.
Align or distribute multiple layers	Ctrl-click/Cmd-click multiple layers, then click one or more align or distribute buttons on the Options bar.
Select (and move) the uppermost layer or layer group that contains the most opaque pixels below the pointer	Check Auto-Select on the Options bar, choose Layer or Group from the menu, then click or drag.
Turn on the Auto Select Layer option for the Move tool temporarily when that option is unchecked	Ctrl/Cmd click or drag.
Select a layer via a menu	Right-click/Control-click in the document window where the layer imagery is located and choose a layer from the context menu.
Transform a layer or selection	Check Show Transform Controls on the Options bar, click a layer, then do any of the following: to scale proportionally, Shift-drag a corner handle; to skew, Ctrl/Cmd drag a side handle; to distort, Ctrl/Cmd drag a corner handle; to apply perspective, Ctrl-Alt-Shift/Cmd-Option-Shift drag a corner handle; or to rotate, position the pointer just outside the transform box, then drag. To accept the transformation, press Enter/Return.

Using the Clone Source panel

To gather fragments from multiple images, you can copy and paste or drag and drop selections or layers from other documents, or use the Clone Stamp tool, which we feature here. With this tool, you can clone imagery from one layer to another within the same file or between files. The Clone Source panel lets you keep track of up to five different clone sources (represented by a row of buttons at the top of the panel); assign different sources; clone repeatedly from the same source; and best of all, scale, rotate, or reposition the source pixels before or as you're cloning them.

To use the Clone Stamp tool and the Clone Source panel:

1. Open one or more RGB documents to use as source imagery, and create or open the document that you want to clone imagery to. **A**

2. Choose the **Clone Stamp** tool ![clone stamp icon] (S or Shift-S) and then, on the Options bar, choose a large Soft Round brush tip; choose a Mode; choose Opacity and Flow values; and check Aligned.

3. Display the **Clone Source** panel. ![icon] By default, the first clone source button is selected.

4. Check **Show Overlay** and **Auto Hide**, then set the **Opacity** to 35–40% so you'll be able to preview the source as an overlay (a faint version of the source layer below the pointer) while you clone.

5. In the document you're going to clone to, create a new blank layer, and keep it selected.

   ▶ For the next two steps, you can either display all the open documents simultaneously by clicking an "Up" icon on the Arrange Documents menu ![icon] on the Application bar ★ or click back and forth between the documents by clicking their tabs.

6. Click in the document that you want to clone from and then, from the **Sample** menu on the Options bar, choose **Current Layer, Current & Below,** or **All Layers,** depending on what you want to clone, and if necessary click the desired layer.

   Alt-click/Option-click an area to establish it as a source point for cloning. The document (and layer name, if you didn't click the Background) will be assigned to, and listed below, the first clone source button on the panel. **B**

A Our first step was to open some files to be used as source material for a piece on green energy (we clicked a 3 Up icon on the Arrange Documents menu).

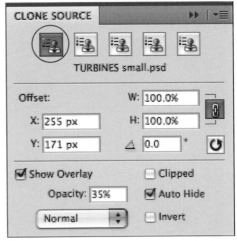

B We chose the Clone Stamp tool, clicked the first clone source button on the Clone Source panel, then Alt/Option clicked to set a source point in another document. The name of the source document appeared below the buttons.

7. Click in the document the imagery is going to be cloned to.

8. Move the pointer over the image without clicking to position the clone overlay, then drag to start cloning.**A–B** The overlay will disappear temporarily (because you checked Auto Hide), and then will reappear when you release the mouse. Note: When you start dragging, the position of the source overlay will become fixed. To reposition it, see the instructions on the next page.

➤ Check Clipped on the Clone Source panel if you prefer to display the overlay only within the brush tip. ★

9. Before or while cloning, you can do any of the following:

Change the **Rotate** value △ on the Clone Source panel, or hold down Alt-Shift/Option-Shift and press < or >.

To **scale** the clone source, change the W or H value on the Clone Source panel, or hold down Alt-Shift/Option-Shift and press [or]. Activate the Maintain Aspect Ratio button ▨ to preserve the current aspect ratio as you change the W or H value. Avoid scaling beyond 150 or –150%.

To **flip** the clone source, choose negative W and/or H values on the panel.

➤ To restore the default rotation and scale settings at any time, click the Reset Transform button on the panel.↻

➤ To change values quickly on the Clone Source panel, use the scrubby sliders.

Continued on the following page

A After we Alt/Option clicked in a source image with the Clone Stamp tool, we positioned the overlay in our destination file...

B ...then dragged with the tool to make a portion of the source image appear.

10. To clone from more sources, click the second source button,**A** create a new layer in the target document, and repeat steps 6–9.**B–C**

Note! The Clone Source panel keeps the links active only while the source document is open.

➤ To switch between source files while cloning, click a different source button. The new source will display within the overlay.

➤ When using the Clone Stamp tool, check the Ignore Adjustment Layers When Cloning button ![icon] on the Options bar if you want to exclude adjustment layer data from the source file.

As soon as you begin cloning, the position of the source overlay becomes fixed. However, you can clone the source imagery in a new location by repositioning the source overlay.

To reposition the source overlay after you've begun cloning:

1. With the overlay visible in the document you're cloning to, do either of the following:

Change the **Offset:** X and/or Y value on the Clone Source panel.

Alt-Shift-drag/Option-Shift-drag the overlay.

2. Click, then drag to clone in the new location.

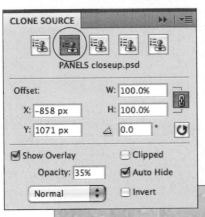

A We clicked the second clone source button to clone an image of solar panels, positioned the overlay...

B ...then dragged long strokes to make part of the second clone source imagery appear.

C We also added editable type, drag-and-dropped silhouetted image layers from three other files (the recycle symbol, wind turbine, and bamboo), and used a Hue/Saturation adjustment layer to make the Background (the large leaf) lighter and less saturated.

ADDING FINISHING TOUCHES TO A MONTAGE

A With a few alterations, the image is now complete.

To create depth, we applied the Drop Shadow layer effect to the recycle symbol layer and then, to create unity in the image, we Alt/Option dragged the effect to copy it to the type layer.

To hide the center of the solar panels layer, we added a layer mask and then, with the Gradient tool, applied a radial gradient to the mask.

For an interesting color shift, we chose Luminosity blending mode for the bamboo layer.

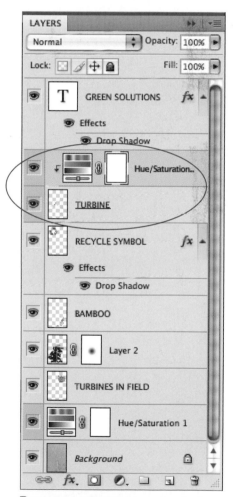

B We used an adjustment layer to make the turbine layer whiter. To limit the effect of the adjustment layer to just the layer below it, we clicked the Clip to Layer button ⬛ ★ on the Adjustments panel (to create a clipping group).

Using the Vanishing Point filter

The Vanishing Point filter lets you paste imagery or a pattern into a perspective plane, such as a building facade, wall, floor, or object. It can't compare to a dedicated drafting or 3D modeling program that an interior designer, architect, or package designer might use—and it doesn't always work perfectly—but you might find a use for it. You can work with multiple source and destination surfaces.

To place imagery into perspective:

1. Open the file that contains the imagery to be pasted, and make sure its resolution is similar to that of the destination document. With a selection tool, select the area to be pasted, then copy it (Ctrl-C/Cmd-C).**A** Or to select text instead, Ctrl-click/Cmd-click the T icon on the Layers panel before using the Copy command.

2. Open a document that you want to paste imagery into. Create a new, blank layer, and keep it selected. *Optional:* Select an area of the layer that you want the copied imagery to fit into.**B**

3. Choose Filter > **Vanishing Point**. The Vanishing Point dialog opens. Press Ctrl- –/ Cmd- – (hyphen) once to reduce the preview size.**C**

A We are planning to paste the striped "wallpaper" onto the side and back walls of the kitchen image. We created the stripes in Adobe Illustrator, placed the file into a blank Photoshop document, then selected and copied it.

B With the Polygonal Lasso tool, we selected the areas that we're going to apply the wallpaper to.

C The image displays in the preview in the Vanishing Point dialog.

4. To define the perspective grid for the imagery to be pasted onto, choose the **Create Plane** tool ⊞ (C), click in the preview to place the first corner node for the perspective grid, then click to place three more nodes to complete the four-sided blue grid.**A** The Edit Plane tool ↖ becomes selected automatically.

➤ Press and hold down X to zoom in temporarily, click to place a node, then release X. (To delete the last node, press Backspace/Delete, then click to place new nodes.)

5. With the **Edit Plane** tool, ↖ do any of the following (Note: To undo any of these edits, press Ctrl-Z/Cmd-Z):

To **reshape** the grid, drag a corner point.

To **reposition** the whole grid, drag it.

The grid should still be **blue** (signifying that it's a valid plane). If it's yellow or red, drag a corner handle until the grid becomes blue.**B–C**

Continued on the following page

A With the Create Plane tool, we placed four corner points to create a grid.

B With the Edit Plane tool, we dragged a corner of the yellow grid...

C ...until it turned blue.

To connect a **second plane** to the existing one, Ctrl-drag/Cmd-drag a midpoint handle away from the edge of the grid.

To change the **angle** of the new plane relative to the first one, Alt-drag/Option-drag a midpoint handle.**A–B**

6. Press Ctrl-V/Cmd-V to **paste** the imagery from the Clipboard. Don't deselect the new floating selection! The **Marquee** tool [⬚] becomes selected automatically. Drag the pasted imagery onto the first grid you defined (**A**, next page).

7. Choose the **Transform** tool [⊹] (T), then do either or both of the following:

   Reposition the pasted imagery within the planes by dragging it.

   Scale the pasted imagery by dragging any of the small white handles on its edge (**B**, next page). (If you don't see any of those handles,

drag the imagery to bring one or more into view.)

➤ To blend the pasted imagery into the background, choose the Marquee tool (M), then choose Luminance from the Heal menu to blend lights and darks, or choose On to blend lights, darks, and colors. These options take time to process.

8. Click OK (**C**, next page). For a way to enhance the Vanishing Point results, see page 208.

➤ To hide and show the grid and any selection while in the Vanishing Point dialog, press Ctrl-H/Cmd-H.

➤ At the top of the Vanishing Point dialog, read a hint for the currently selected tool.

➤ To learn more about the Vanishing Point filter, see Adobe Photoshop CS4 Help > Retouching & Transforming.

A We Ctrl/Cmd dragged the left midpoint on the grid to add a second (connected) plane to define the left wall. Then we fine-tuned the angle of the new plane by Alt/Option dragging a midpoint (the plane swung like a door).

B Now the grid is ready for us to paste in the imagery.

A We pressed Ctrl-V/Cmd-V to paste the imagery we copied into the grid and then, with the Marquee tool, dragged the selection into the first plane that we defined.

B With the Transform tool, we dragged the midpoint handle to the left to fill the grid.

C Our use of the Vanishing Point filter produced this result. We think it could use a lighting enhancement, though, to make the wallpaper look more realistic (see the next page).

ADDING REALISM TO VANISHING POINT RESULTS WITH LIGHTING

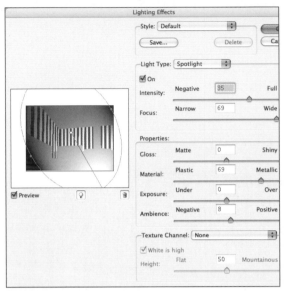

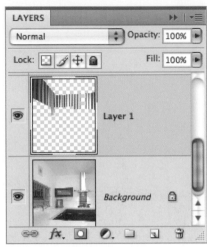

A To add realism to the scene, we applied Filter > Render > Lighting Effects, using the default Spotlight type (we widened the lighting ellipse slightly).

B This is the Layers panel for the final image, which is shown below.

C That's better!

► As an alternative to using the Lighting Effects filter, change the mode of the layer you applied the Vanishing Point filter to (try Multiply), and see if that does the trick.

REVEALING UNDERLYING IMAGERY

If you want to reveal more of the underlying layer (such as an object on a wall or floor that protrudes into the vanishing point imagery), after exiting the Vanishing Point dialog, add a layer mask to the vanishing point layer. Lower the layer opacity temporarily so you can see part of the underlying layer and then, with the mask selected, paint with black.

The difference between an unsharpened photo and a sharpened one may be subtle, but the former will look blah and undefined and the latter will have that extra, well, edge. In this chapter, you'll learn how to use three sharpening filters in Photoshop: Unsharp Mask, High Pass, and Smart Sharpen.

If you're wondering whether to use the sharpening controls in Camera Raw or in Photoshop, the answer is "both." Use Camera Raw to apply a moderate amount of "capture" sharpening to your image, as described in Chapter 3; then, after completing all your tonal and color correction, image edits, and noise reduction work and any scaling or transformations that cause resampling, sharpen the image again in Photoshop. For the latter, follow the instructions in this chapter.

Before exporting your file, you should apply a last round of sharpening to a copy of it (see page 325). For Web output, do this after downsizing the image to 72 ppi. For print output, the extra sharpening will help compensate for the fact that when digital images are converted to dots of ink on paper, the details are softened slightly.

The two powerhouse sharpening filters that we use most often are Unsharp Mask and Smart Sharpen. We'll show you how to use Unsharp Mask once for overall sharpening and then a second time to sharpen a specific tonal range further, and how to use the Smart Sharpen filter to target the sharpening effect to specific tonal ranges. We've also included instructions for applying the High Pass filter and Unsharp Mask to sharpen edges.

In Photoshop, you can apply sharpening to the entire image or, as we'll show you in this chapter, to targeted areas or tonal ranges. You'll learn how to control where the sharpening is applied as well as how to regulate the intensity of the effect.

SHARPENING

9

IN THIS CHAPTER

Note: Settings listed in the captions in this chapter were chosen for photos that are approximately 3000 x 2000 pixels.

Sharpening a whole image with the Unsharp Mask filter

The best time to sharpen an overall image with the Unsharp Mask filter is after applying capture sharpening in Camera Raw, reducing noise, and performing color corrections and other image edits, and before outputting or exporting your file. To achieve a sharpening effect, Unsharp Mask increases the contrast between adjacent pixels. Dialog options let you control the increase in contrast (the Amount), the width of the area of surrounding pixels the filter affects (the Radius), and the level of contrast needed between adjacent pixels for an area to be sharpened (the Threshold).

To apply the Unsharp Mask filter:

1. Open an RGB image, and flatten it if it contains layers. Choose a zoom level of 50% (**A**, next page).

2. Press Ctrl-J/Cmd-J to duplicate the Background. Change the blending mode of the duplicate layer to **Luminosity** to allow the sharpening to affect only its tonal values. Keep the duplicate layer selected.

3. Choose Filter > Sharpen > **Unsharp Mask**.

4. In the Unsharp Mask dialog, choose an **Amount** value to control the intensity of the sharpening (**B**, next page). For a high-resolution portrait or landscape (2000 x 3000 pixels or higher), use a low setting of around 80–120; for an image containing hard-edged objects, use a higher setting of 150–170.

5. The **Radius** setting controls how wide an area of pixels surrounding high-contrast edges will be sharpened (**C**, next page). Two variables to consider are the pixel count of the file (the higher the pixel count, the higher the Radius value needed) and its subject matter. For a low-contrast image that contains large, simple objects and smooth color transitions, a high Radius of 1.5–2 is usually effective; for an intricate, high-contrast image with sharp transitions, a lower Radius of around 1 would probably work better. You may need to experiment.

CHOOSING A ZOOM LEVEL FOR SHARPENING
When judging a sharpening effect on images that are 3000 x 2000 pixels or larger, choose a zoom level of 50%. At this level, you'll see just the right amount of detail, whereas at a zoom level of 100%, you would see too much detail (you would be viewing the image at a much closer range than you'd normally view a printout). Zoom to 100% only in the event that you need to judge whether sharpening has added noise to the midtones and shadows.

▶ Think of the Amount and Radius settings as interdependent. If you adjust one value, you should also readjust the other (**A**, page 212).

6. Choose a **Threshold** value for the degree of contrast an area must contain in order to be sharpened. Start with a Threshold of 0 (which would sharpen the entire image), then raise the value slowly. At a Threshold between 5 and 10, high-contrast areas will be sharpened and areas of lesser contrast will receive very little sharpening. At higher Threshold values, only high-contrast edges will be sharpened, in which case you can also increase the Amount and Radius to apply more sharpening to just those areas without oversharpening the lower-contrast areas (**B**, page 212).

7. Uncheck, then recheck Preview to compare the original and sharpened versions of the image.

   ▶ To inspect a different part of the image, click in the document window; that area will display in the preview window in the dialog. To compare the unsharpened and sharpened images, click and hold on the dialog preview, then release.

8. Click OK, then flatten the document (choose Flatten Image from the Layers panel menu).

A The details in this original image look too soft.

B We chose a high Amount value of 200 in the Unsharp Mask dialog temporarily to better judge the Radius and Threshold values that we'll set next.

C We can see that a Radius value of 2.5 is too high, because it produced halos along the edges of some of the shapes.

See also the figures on the following page

A We lowered the Amount value to 160 to lessen the overall sharpening and lowered the Radius value to 1.3 to remove the halos.

B Our final Unsharp Mask filter edits were to raise the Threshold value to 3 to restrict the sharpening to just high-contrast edges and to raise the Amount value to 170 to slightly increase the sharpening of those edges. Now you can practically smell the chile powder.

SUGGESTED UNSHARP MASK FILTER SETTINGS FOR DIFFERENT TYPES OF IMAGES*

Landscapes containing sharp details

A For "high-frequency" images that contain numerous fine details, try an Amount of 120–170, a Radius just below 1.0, and a Threshold of 3 or 4.

Subjects containing soft edges

B For images that contain mostly soft textures with a few distinct edges here or there, try a high Threshold of 6–8 to preserve the softness, an Amount of 100–150, and a Radius of 1.

Buildings and other high-contrast subjects

C To preserve the contrast, surface detail, and well-defined edges in a subject like this one, try a high Amount of 170, a high Radius of 2–3, and a low Threshold of 0–3.

Portraits

D To control the softness or sharpness of a portrait, try an Amount of 90–120. Set the Radius to 1–2 to make the hair and facial details crisp, and set the Threshold to 3–6 (to the point where the skin begins to look smoother).

These settings apply to high-resolution images.

SHARPENING MIDTONES WITH THE UNSHARP MASK FILTER

After using the Unsharp Mask filter once, you can refine the results by further sharpening just the midtone areas (not the highlights and shadows). In the second round, apply the filter to a duplicate layer, **A–D** then use the Blend If sliders in the Layer Style dialog to control which more-sharpened pixels in the duplicate layer stay visible and which less-sharpened pixels from the Background show through (**A–C**, next page).

A This image is sharpened adequately, but we want to further enhance the surface detail in the midtones.

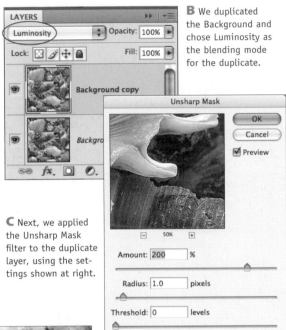

B We duplicated the Background and chose Luminosity as the blending mode for the duplicate.

C Next, we applied the Unsharp Mask filter to the duplicate layer, using the settings shown at right.

D In this close-up of the image after the Unsharp Mask filter was applied, you can see that the highlight and shadow areas look oversharpened (it's especially noticeable on the two shells in the center).

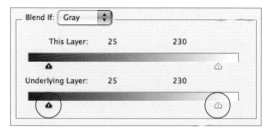

A We double-clicked the duplicate layer to open the Layer Style dialog, and clicked Blending Options on the left side. In the Blend If area, we set both black sliders to 25 and both white sliders to 230, to enable the less-sharp shadow and highlight pixels from the Background to show through the duplicate layer.

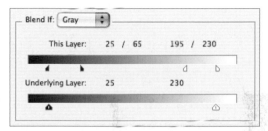

B Finally, we held down Alt/Option and dragged the right part of the black This Layer slider to 65 and the left part of the white This Layer slider to 195. These changes allowed the extra-sharp midtone areas on the duplicate layer to stay visible but also fade into the less-sharpened areas.

C After the Blend If adjustments, in this closeup you can see that the midtones are still very sharp and the highlights and shadows display neither oversharpening nor unwanted noise. Compare the red shell on the left side and the interior of the striped shell with the same areas in figure **D** on the preceding page.

Enhancing details with the High Pass filter

The High Pass filter is a simple but effective tool for increasing the edge contrast and enhancing details in an image. If you apply the filter to a duplicate layer, you'll be able to control not only the intensity of the sharpening, but also which areas become sharpened.

To apply sharpening using the High Pass filter:

1. In an RGB image that needs sharpening,**A** press Ctrl-J/Cmd-J to duplicate the Background, and keep the duplicate layer selected.

2. Choose Filter > Other > **High Pass**. The High Pass dialog opens.**B**

3. For a high-resolution image (300 ppi, or 2000 x 3000 pixels or larger), choose a **Radius** value of 4; for a low-resolution image (150 ppi or lower), set the Radius to 2. Click OK.

4. To restore color to the image and control the effect of the High Pass filter, choose one of the following blending modes for the duplicate layer:

   To display the sharpening effect, choose **Overlay** (**A**, next page).

   To intensify the sharpening effect, choose **Hard Light** or **Vivid Light** (**B**, next page).

   To soften the sharpening effect, choose **Soft Light**.

A This image could use some extra sharpening.

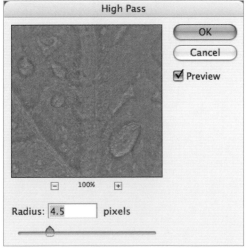

B We duplicated the Background, then applied the High Pass filter at a Radius of 4.5 pixels.

5. Set the zoom level to 50% or 100% to judge the amount of sharpening, and then, if needed, lower the **Opacity** of the layer to compensate for any oversharpening. **C**

6. *Optional:* To restrict the sharpening effect to specific areas of the image, click the duplicate layer, then Alt-click/Option-click the Add Layer Mask button 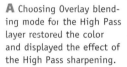 at the bottom of the Layers panel to add a black mask. Choose the Brush tool 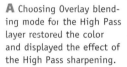 (B or Shift-B), a Soft Round tip, Normal mode, and a brush Opacity of 80%, and press D, if necessary, to make the Foreground color white. Draw strokes where you want to reveal the sharpening effect. If you need to remask any of the sharpened areas, press X to paint with black.

A Choosing Overlay blending mode for the High Pass layer restored the color and displayed the effect of the High Pass sharpening.

B We settled on Vivid Light blending mode for the High Pass layer to increase the sharpening effect...

C ...but lowered the High Pass layer Opacity to 50% to soften the sharpening by half.

Sharpening areas selectively

One way to give an image more punch is by applying extra sharpening to select areas. To control which areas receive the extra sharpening, you'll use a layer mask (of course!). You can exercise some creative license with this approach, depending on the image content—or in a commercial setting, how much latitude you're allowed.

To sharpen areas selectively:

1. Open an RGB image that has areas that could benefit from an extra sharpening boost.

2. If you already applied some capture sharpening via Camera Raw, skip this step. If not, choose Filter > **Unsharp Mask** and apply a moderate amount of sharpening.**A**

3. Press Ctrl-J/Cmd-J to duplicate the Background. Keep the the duplicate layer selected, and change its blending mode to **Luminosity**.

4. Choose Filter > Sharpen > **Unsharp Mask**. In the dialog, set the **Amount** to 200%, the **Radius** to 1–1.5, and the **Threshold** to 3, then click OK.**B** Don't worry if the image now looks too sharp.

5. Alt-click/Option-click the **Add Layer Mask** button ◻ on the Layers panel to add a black mask, which will hide the extra sharpening that you just applied.

A Some capture sharpening was applied to this photo in Camera Raw. To emphasize the food details in the center, we'll apply some extra sharpening to just those areas.

B We duplicated the Background, chose Luminosity as the blending mode for the duplicate layer, and applied the Unsharp Mask filter using the settings shown at right.

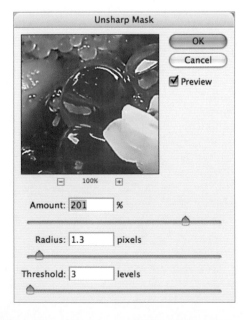

6. Choose the **Brush** tool 🖌 (B or Shift-B), a Soft Round tip, Normal mode, and 80% Opacity. Press D to make the Foreground color white. Draw strokes in areas where you want to reveal the extra sharpening.**A–B** Reapply your brush strokes to any areas that need an extra boost. If you need to remask any sharpened areas, press X to paint with black.

7. *Optional:* To soften the transition between the masked and unmasked areas, display the Masks panel,⬛ then increase the Feather value.★

A We added a layer mask, then painted with a soft-edged brush (Foreground color white) to reveal the heightened sharpening along the edges of the flowers, roe, cucumber, and pieces of sushi.

B The extra sharpening heightened the edge details and textures in the center of this image. (Question: Are the flowers edible?)

Using the Smart Sharpen filter

Although the Unsharp Mask filter is fast, powerful, and a good tool for sharpening an overall image, when you want to apply selective sharpening without having to use a selection or mask, we recommend using the Smart Sharpen filter instead. Via the Smart Sharpen controls, you can target more sharpening to a particular tonal range, such as the midtones, and less sharpening to the highlights and shadows. It's particularly useful when you need to sharpen some areas in an image more than others, such as key features in a portrait.

Smart Sharpen offers several advantages:

➤ **More control**: Via the Tonal Width control in the Smart Sharpen dialog, you can widen or narrow the range of tonal values that receive sharpening. Also, Smart Sharpen lets you fade the sharpening in the shadow and highlight areas separately, whereas Unsharp Mask does not.

➤ **More muscle**: The More Accurate option in the Smart Sharpen dialog applies sharpening in multiple passes.

➤ **Fewer halos**: Because it has the ability to detect edges, Smart Sharpen produces fewer color halos than Unsharp Mask.

➤ **Flexibility**: Smart Sharpen corrects Gaussian blur, lens blur, or motion blur, depending on your choice of three algorithms, whereas Unsharp Mask corrects only Gaussian blur.

➤ **Improved workflow**: Smart Sharpen lets you save your settings, so you can apply them to other images.

Continued on the following page

To sharpen areas selectively with the Smart Sharpen filter:

1. Open an RGB image that needs sharpening.**A** On the Layers panel, click an image layer or the Background, then press Ctrl-J/Cmd-J to duplicate it. Right-click/Control-click the duplicate layer and choose **Convert to Smart Object**, then click OK if an alert dialog appears.

2. Choose Filter > Sharpen > **Smart Sharpen**. In the Smart Sharpen dialog,**B** keep the zoom level for the preview at 100%.

3. Check **More Accurate** to allow multiple passes of the filter, for higher-quality sharpening (it's worth the extra processing time).

4. From the **Remove** menu, choose an algorithm for the correction:

   Gaussian Blur uses a sharpening method similar to that of the Unsharp Mask filter.

   Lens Blur (our favorite) does a superior job of detecting edges and produces fewer color halos.

   Motion Blur is useful if the blurring was caused by a slight movement of the camera or subject and you know the angle at which that movement occurred.

A This image looks too soft.

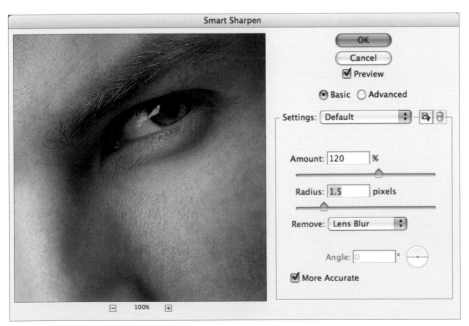

B The settings shown in the Basic pane of the Smart Sharpen dialog properly sharpened the facial details (eyes, teeth, and lips) but also oversharpened the skin.

5. Try an **Amount** of 100–140% and a **Radius** of 1–2 pixels (you can use the scrubby slider to set values in this dialog). The image should now look slightly oversharpened. **A**

6. Next, you'll fade the effect. To control the amount of sharpening in the shadow and highlight areas, click **Advanced**, then click the **Shadow** tab. Drag in the preview to display an area of the image that contains both shadows and midtones, then do the following:

Raise the **Fade Amount** to reduce any over-sharpening in the shadows.

Choose a **Tonal Width** to control the range of midtones that are affected by the Fade Amount. The higher the Tonal Width, the wider the range of midtones in which the sharpening will be reduced, and the more smoothly the reduction will fade to no sharpening in the shadows.

Choose a **Radius** between 5 and 15 to control how many neighboring pixels will be compared to a sharpened pixel. The higher the Radius, the larger the area that will be compared.

7. Click the **Highlight** tab. Drag the image in the preview to display an area that contains both highlights and midtones. Adjust the Fade Amount, Tonal Width, and Radius settings, as in the preceding step.

8. Hopefully, the key details (e.g., the eyes and mouth, in a portrait) are now sharpened properly, and the larger expanses (e.g., cheeks and forehead) are smooth. If the overall image looks too sharp, click the **Sharpen** tab and lower the **Amount** value slightly. After making adjustments in one tab, you may need to readjust the settings in the other two.

➤ To save your Smart Sharpen settings for future use, click the Save a Copy of the Current Settings button, ➡ type a name in the New Filter Settings dialog, then click OK. Saved settings can be chosen from the Settings menu for any image.

9. To compare the unsharpened and sharpened images, click and hold on the dialog preview, then release. Click OK (**A–C**, next page).

➤ To restore all the options in the dialog box to the default settings, hold down Alt/Option and click Reset; or if a preset is chosen on the Settings menu, choose Default from that menu.

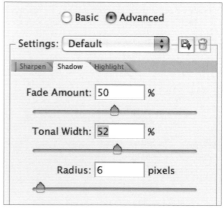

A To apply the Smart Sharpen filter selectively and fade the sharpening, we clicked the Shadow tab and chose the settings shown above. A Tonal Width of 52% reduced the sharpening completely in the shadow areas (the side of the face and around the eyes) but preserved it in the midtones.

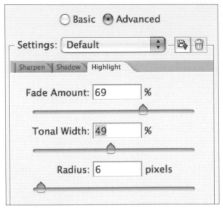

A In the Highlight tab of the Smart Sharpen dialog, we chose a high Fade Amount to reduce the sharpening and a medium Tonal Width value to fade the sharpening partially in the lighter midtones and completely in the highlights. At these settings, less sharpening is being applied to the cheeks and lower eyelids. The final image is shown at right and in figure **C**.

B This is the original image before the Smart Sharpen filter was applied.

C Using Smart Sharpen, we were able to successfully sharpen the eyes, eyebrows, nose, lips, and hair without oversharpening the skin.

Selecting edges for sharpening

Sometimes you can achieve better sharpening results by limiting the correction to just the edges of shapes (the areas of highest contrast) and leaving the lower-contrast areas unsharpened. The method given here for selecting only high-contrast edges works best on images that have large swaths of low-contrast color, such as a hazy sky or a portrait with soft skin tones, and a small proportion of contrasty edges. If used on an image that contains many intricate details, too many edges will become selected.

To select the edges of shapes: ★

1. Open an RGB image that needs sharpening. **A** Click the Background layer, then press Ctrl-J/ Cmd-J twice. Rename the topmost duplicate "find edges," and keep it selected.

2. Choose Filter > Stylize > **Find Edges** to reduce the layer to line work. **B**

3. To increase the contrast and discard the thinnest edges, choose Image > Adjustments > **Levels** (don't create an adjustment layer), then do the following: **C**

   Move the **white Input Levels** slider to the left to remove the thinnest lines in areas of low contrast (e.g., the cheeks and forehead, or details in the foreground). The three Input Levels sliders should now be closer together.

   Move the **black Input Levels** slider to the right to darken the line work.

   Move the **gray Input Levels** slider slightly to the right to further darken the line work.

   Click OK.

Continued on the following page

A We will select just the high-contrast edges in this image, for targeted sharpening.

B We applied the Find Edges filter to a duplicate layer.

Input Levels:

172   0.83   206

C We used these Levels dialog settings to boost the contrast in our "find edges" layer and to reduce it to just high-contrast line work.

4. On the Adjustments panel, ◪ click the **Black & White** button, ◣ then do the following:

   For a portrait, move just the **Yellows** slider to the right (to around 130) to remove the thinnest lines.

   For a landscape, move the **Yellows** slider to the right to remove the finest lines and the **Blues** slider to the left to darken the line work.

5. Choose the **Magic Wand** tool ✦ (W or Shift-W). On the Options bar, set the Tolerance to around 60 and uncheck Contiguous.

6. Click one of the thick black lines in the image, then choose Select > **Similar** to select all the other medium to heavyweight lines.

7. Hide both the adjustment layer and the "find edges" layer. Click the Background copy layer.

8. On the Masks panel, ◪ click the **Add Pixel Mask** button. ◪ **A**

9. Click **Mask Edge**. In the Refine Mask dialog, click **Default**, then do the following:

   Click the **Mask** preview button (the last button in the row) to see how your mask edges will be modified.

   To preserve fine details, such as strands of hair, choose a **Radius** value of around 2 px.

   Keep the **Contrast** value at 0%.

   To eliminate thin edges in areas of low contrast, choose a **Smooth** value between 5 and 10. **B**

   To soften the transition between the selected and unselected areas, choose a **Feather** value between 1 and 1.6 px (**A–B**, next page).

   To widen the selection lines, choose a **Contract/Expand** value between +5 and +12%.

   By feathering and expanding the edges of the mask, you enlarged the editable area slightly. The result will be a smoother transition between the edited and unedited areas.

   Click OK.

To sharpen the image using the new layer mask, follow the instructions on the next two pages.

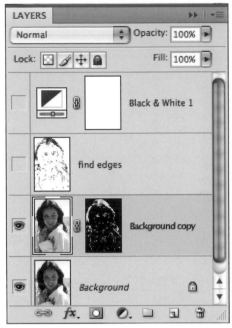

A We duplicated the Background and added a mask to the duplicate layer.

B In the Refine Mask dialog, we clicked the Mask preview button (to view the edges of the mask more clearly). Setting the Radius value to 2.1 px and the Contrast value to 0% preserved the fine details, such as the hair, and setting the Smooth value to 7 eliminated edges from low-contrast areas.

A For our final Refine Mask adjustments, we set the Feather value to 1.6 px to soften the transition between the selected and unselected areas, and set the Contract/Expand value to +11% to expand the layer mask. Now there are fewer lines in the broad area of the mask and the remaining line work is softer.

B For comparison, the mask is shown here without any Refine Mask adjustments. The mask contains both moderate and high-contrast edges, and the edge transitions are abrupt.

Sharpening edges

In the preceding instructions, we showed you how to select only the high-contrast edges in an image and then convert your selection to a layer mask. Here we'll show you how to use that mask to limit sharpening to the edges of shapes when applying the Unsharp Mask filter. Sharpening that is applied subsequently will affect only the sharp details and will blend smoothly into the low-contrast areas. This method works well for sharpening a portrait, in which you typically want to emphasize facial features (edges) and de-emphasize the skin texture (pores and blemishes).

To sharpen edges:

1. Open an RGB image,**C** and follow the steps on the preceding two pages to create a selection of edges and a layer mask.
2. Click the layer thumbnail for the Background copy (**A**, next page) and zoom to 50%.
3. Choose Filter > Sharpen > **Unsharp Mask**.

Continued on the following page

C We'll apply some targeted sharpening to this image using our saved selection (shown as a close-up).

4. You can use higher Amount and Radius values in the Unsharp Mask dialog than usual because the filter will affect only the selection of edges:

Set the **Amount** to 150–180%.

Set the **Radius** to 1.3 pixels.

Set the **Threshold** value to between 1 and 4. Judge the Threshold effect in the document window, not in the dialog; the preview won't show the effect of the layer mask.**B** (Don't use a Threshold value of 0, which would apply full sharpening to all the edges.)

Optional: Increase the Amount value if you want to increase the edge sharpening. Click OK.

5. *Optional:* To soften the overall sharpening effect, lower the Opacity of the duplicate layer.**C**

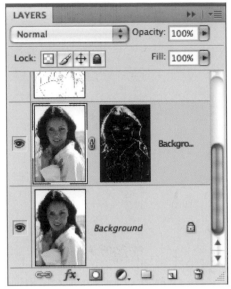

A We clicked the layer thumbnail for the Background copy.

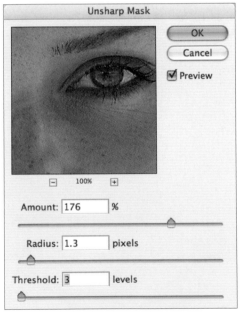

B We chose these Amount and Radius values in the Unsharp Mask dialog. Note: Although the dialog preview displays sharpening in the whole image, in actuality, the layer mask is limiting the effect.

C A Threshold value of 3 sharpened the soft, low-contrast edges. We also lowered the layer Opacity to 80% to soften the overall sharpening effect.

Sometimes a photo speaks for itself and is best left as is, and sometimes a little extra processing, such as applying a tint or a photo filter, can elevate an ordinary photo into an extraordinary one or help your viewers see a subject from a new perspective.

A few of the tasks in this chapter, such as layering gradients in the background with the Gradient tool, involve adding colors to an image to round out the scene. Most of the tasks, however, involve paring colors down to grayscale in one way or another, and then judiciously reintroducing color by using adjustment layers, such as Hue/Saturation, Black & White, or Photo Filter, or filters, such as Lighting Effects. The final task involves choosing settings for commercial duotone printing, a technique in which a subtle color tint is added to a grayscale print by using an extra plate and ink color.

What formerly took many hours of experimentation in the darkroom can now be accomplished with a few clicks of the mouse in Photoshop. To get good results with the techniques you'll learn in this chapter, try to choose a method that suits the subject matter of the image. For example, it would be overkill to apply a gradient to a photo of a brightly colored or complex object, but it might add just the right kick to a simple or ordinary one. If you want to showcase a particular area in a landscape or product shot, try the "Restoring color selectively" method on page 238.

Although the technical aspects of photography, such as lighting, exposure, focus, depth of field, and timing—and equipment—do affect the outcome dramatically, no amount of postcapture processing and image editing can compensate for a poorly framed shot. A photo that has "good bones"—meaning a good composition and strong linear elements—will be a great candidate for the color reduction methods covered in this chapter, such as the faux infrared effect, whereas the same technique might just accentuate and magnify the flaws in a weaker photo. When browsing through prospective photos for tinting or color reduction, try to imagine what they would look like in grayscale (see them as a cat would!).

Note: Settings listed in the captions in this chapter were chosen for photos that are approximately 3000 x 2000 pixels.

TINTING & BLENDING

10

IN THIS CHAPTER

Layering gradients

In this task, you'll learn how to create a complex, blended background using multiple Gradient Fill layers. A subject that is silhouetted on a white background, such as a high-tech product or fashion shot, would be an excellent candidate for this treatment. The advantage of using Gradient Fill layers is that you can reopen the Gradient Fill dialog at any time to edit the gradients.

To layer multiple gradients:

1. Create an RGB document that has a white Background and a silhouetted object on a layer. On the Layers panel, click the Background.**A**

2. If it's not already active, click the Foreground color square on the **Color** panel. Click a color on the Swatches panel; or create a color via the Color panel, then save it to the **Swatches** panel by clicking the **New Swatch of Foreground Color** button.

3. From the **New Fill/Adjustment Layer** menu on the Layers panel, choose **Gradient.** The Gradient Fill dialog opens.

4. Click the arrowhead to the right of the gradient thumbnail to open the Gradient preset picker, click the **Foreground to Transparent** preset,**B** then click again in the dialog.

   Choose **Linear** from the Style menu, rotate the **Angle** dial to set the angle of the gradient, adjust the **Scale** value via the slider to control where the color transitions to transparency on the image,**C** keep **Dither** checked for better print results, and click OK.**D**

A This photo of a compact fluorescent bulb consists of a silhouetted object on a layer and a white Background below it.

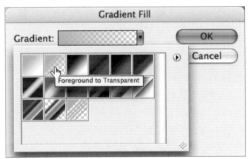

B After choosing a Foreground color, we created a Gradient Fill layer, then chose the Foreground to Transparent preset from the Gradient preset picker.

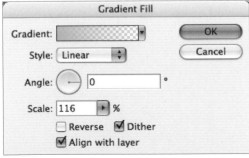

C We also chose these Style, Angle, and Scale settings for the first Gradient Fill layer.

D The first Gradient Fill layer (Style: Linear) is visible behind the bulb.

5. To create another fill layer, repeat steps 2–4 on the preceding page. Experiment with different Style, Angle, and Scale settings.**A–B**

➤ For added depth or contrast, apply layer effects to the silhouetted object.**C–D**

➤ To change the Foreground color in the Gradient Fill layer, double-click the layer thumbnail, click the gradient thumbnail in the Gradient Fill dialog, click the left color stop below the gradient bar in the Gradient Editor dialog, then click the Color swatch at the bottom of the dialog to open the Color Picker. After choosing a color, click OK twice.

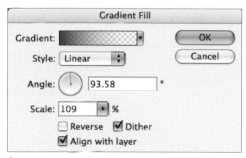

A For our second Gradient Fill layer, we chose these dialog settings and a new Foreground color.

B The two gradient fill layers create a beautiful glow in the background.

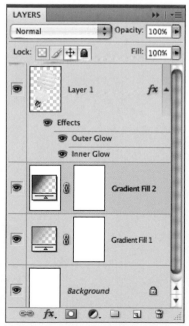

C This is the Layers panel for the final image, which is shown at right.

D To add depth and contrast to produce this final image, we added two layer effects — Inner Glow and Outer Glow.

Lighting a background

Another way to enhance a silhouetted object is by adding dramatic background lighting. This is easy to achieve with the Lighting Effects filter.

To apply lighting and create a reflection:

1. Create an RGB document that consists of a Background plus a silhouetted object positioned on a layer approximately two-thirds of the way down from the top.

2. On the **Color** panel, 🎨 click the Foreground color square to open the Color Picker. Click to sample a medium-light color in the image, then click OK.

3. On the **Layers** panel, click the Background.

4. Press Shift-Backspace/Shift-Delete to open the **Fill** dialog. Choose Use: Foreground Color, Mode: Normal, and Opacity: 100%. Click OK.**A**

5. To apply lighting, choose Filter > Render > **Lighting Effects**. The Lighting Effects dialog opens.**B**

6. From the **Style** menu, choose **Soft Omni**. In the lighting preview, drag the bottom handle on the circle downward or upward until the side handles touch the edges of the dark area, then drag the white center point to just above the center of the dark area. Click OK.**C**

A Via the Fill dialog, we filled the Background with a Foreground color that we sampled from the image layer.

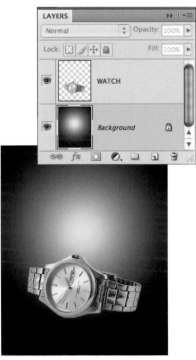

C The results of the Lighting Effects filter appeared in the Background.

B In the Lighting Effects dialog, we chose Style: Soft Omni. We dragged the bottom handle of the circle until the side handles touched the edges of the preview and repositioned the center of the circle slightly above the middle of the preview.

7. Press Ctrl-J/Cmd-J to duplicate the Background.

8. For the duplicate layer, change the blending mode to **Lighten**. Choose the **Move** tool (V) and uncheck Show Transform Controls on the Options bar. Start dragging in the document window, then hold down Shift and continue to drag to move the duplicate lighting layer downward until you see a subtle dark seam.**A** Lower the layer Opacity to a value that looks good.

9. Finally, you'll create a reflection of the object to create the appearance of a shiny surface:

Click the object silhouette layer, press Ctrl-J/Cmd-J to duplicate it, then choose Edit > Transform > **Flip Vertical**.

With the **Move** tool, Shift-drag the reflection downward until the bottom lines up with the bottom of the duplicate object.

Choose **Overlay** as the layer blending mode, and lower the layer **Opacity** to 20–40%. Voilà!**B**

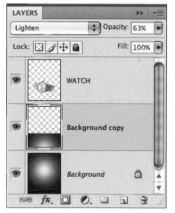

A We changed the blending mode of the duplicate lighting layer to Lighten, then moved the layer downward until a subtle seam appeared between the two lighting layers (see the arrow at left). We also lowered the layer Opacity.

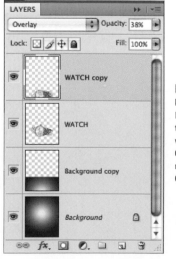

B We duplicated the object layer, applied Transform > Flip Vertical, and dragged the duplicate layer downward. Finally, we chose Overlay as the blending mode and lowered the layer Opacity to 38%.

Desaturating colors selectively

One way to emphasize part of an image is by desaturating most of the colors while preserving, or even heightening, the saturation in a specific color range. In this task, you'll use a Hue/Saturation adjustment layer to subdue the less important colors and intensify the more important ones.

To desaturate colors selectively: ★

1. Open an RGB image that has strong coloration.**A**

2. On the Adjustments panel,⬤ click the **Hue/Saturation** button.▦ Just to demonstrate a point, with **Master** chosen on the second menu, move the **Saturation** slider to the left.

As you can see, this generalized approach to desaturation won't allow you to de-emphasize some colors while selectively preserving others.**B** Click the **Reset to Adjustment Defaults** button ↺ to reset the Saturation to 0.

A Because this whole image is highly saturated, no single area is taking center stage. Our goal is to tone down the greens and yellows while preserving some of the reds in the most important part of the image: the flower petals.

B Via a Hue/Saturation adjustment layer, we tried reducing the Saturation for the Master color range (all the colors). Now the whole image looks dull, including the rose petals, so we'll reset the Saturation for the Master range to 0 and try a more selective approach instead.

A To subdue the colors of the leaves, we reduced the Saturation for the Greens color range to –80 and reduced the Saturation for the Yellows color range to –60.

3. From the second menu, choose a color range to be desaturated, then reduce the **Saturation.A** Repeat for any other ranges.

4. *Optional:* Try increasing the Lightness value slightly for any range you desaturated.**B**

5. *Optional:* To enhance the results, for the Hue/Saturation adjustment layer, choose Saturation as the blending mode.**C**

B Next, we reduced the Saturation and increased the Lightness for the Reds color range, using the settings shown above. This improved the coloration in the rose petals.

C Finally, we chose Saturation as the blending mode for the Hue/Saturation adjustment layer, which muted the greens even more and softened the transition between the strong reds and desaturated yellows in the rose petals.

Tinting an image

When you replace all the color in an image with a color tint, instead of the color drawing the eye through the composition, the pattern of lights and darks orchestrates the scene. Here, you'll use a Black & White adjustment layer to convert an image to grayscale and intensify the contrast, and apply a tint and a Photo Filter to neutralize the highlights.

To apply a tint to an image: ★

1. Open an RGB image. **A**

2. On the Adjustments panel,⬤ click the **Black & White** button.◣

3. The image is converted to grayscale. Do either or both of the following:

   Heighten the contrast by moving the sliders. **B–C**

A This image is a good candidate for tinting because it contains strong sculptural forms and has good tonal contrast in the two main color areas (the stone pillars and sky).

B The Black & White adjustment converted the photo to grayscale. We reduced the Cyans and Blues values to intensify the contrast in the sky.

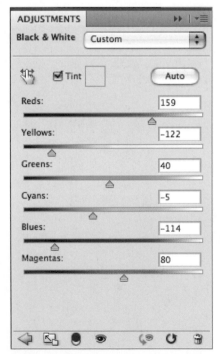

C Next, we moved the Reds and Yellows sliders in opposite directions to create subtle contrast and to enhance the detail in the columns.

Click the **On-Image Adjustment** tool on the panel, then in the document window, drag to the right or left over a grayscale shade that you want to lighten or darken; this will move the corresponding color slider in the dialog.

4. Check **Tint.A** Click the color swatch to open the Color Picker, choose a color, then click OK.

   ➤ For a sepia or earth-toned hue, try values of H: 38, S: 20, and B: 78.

5. *Optional:* On the Layers panel, click the Black & White layer, and lower its Opacity slightly.**B**

6. On the Adjustments panel, click the **Return to Adjustment List** button, then click the **Photo Filter** button.

7. From the **Filter** menu, choose a filter that has an opposite color temperature (warm or cool) from the tint color that you applied. Set the **Density** slider to 20–30% and check **Preserve Luminosity**.

8. Lower the **Opacity** of the Photo Filter layer to around 50–60%.**C**

   See also the optional step and illustrations on the following page, and see also page 237.

A With the Black & White dialog still open, we applied a Tint (as shown in **C** on the preceding page).

B We lowered the Opacity of the adjustment layer to 82% to reveal a bit of color from the original photo.

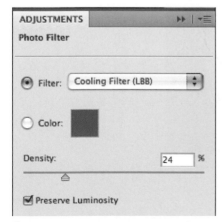

C Finally, to neutralize the colors and counterbalance the warm Tint, we applied a cooling filter via a Photo Filter adjustment layer, then lowered the adjustment layer Opacity to 50%. The tints enhance the stunning architecture.

9. *Optional:* Restack the Photo Filter adjustment layer below the Black & White adjustment layer, and see if you like how it alters the colors.**A**

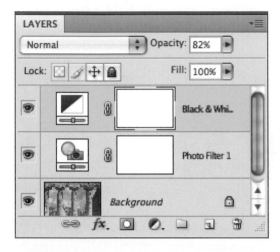

A We discovered that the simple step of restacking the Photo Filter layer below the Black & White layer produced better contrast and added a silvery quality to the highlights.

ANOTHER IMAGE TINTED THE SAME WAY

A We'll apply the same "silver" tinting method to this photo, which has two dominant color ranges (oranges and blues) plus white, and strong lighting contrasts.

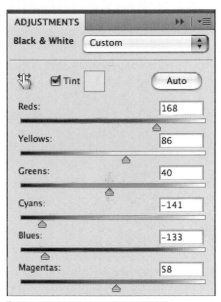

B Via a Black & White adjustment layer, we lowered the Cyans and Blues to intensify the contrast in the sky (as in **B** on page 234), and increased the Reds and Yellows to lighten the midtones and highlights. We applied a pale yellowish tint, and left the layer Opacity at 100%.

C Just as in **C** on page 235, we applied a cooling filter via a Photo Filter adjustment layer, then lowered the adjustment layer Opacity to 50%. This time, however, we kept the Photo Filter layer stacked above the Black & White layer.

Restoring color selectively

In the photo shown at right, A the path is a strong geometric element that anchors the whole image, but it's overpowered by all the greenery. We'll enhance it by applying a sympathetic color tint while desaturating the rest of the photo.

To restore a color to a desaturated image: ★

1. Open an RGB photo that contains a distinct color area that you want to emphasize.

2. To make it easier to select the area to be tinted, on the Adjustments panel, ○ click the **Black & White** button. ◤ Use the sliders to intensify the contrast between the area to be tinted and the surrounding areas.

3. With the **Quick Selection** tool ◣ or **Magic Wand** tool, ◥ click or drag to select the area to be tinted. B

4. On the Adjustments panel, click the **Return to Adjustment List** button, ◤ then click the **Black & White** button ◤ to create a second adjustment layer.

5. Display the Masks panel, ◻ click **Invert**, then redisplay the Adjustments panel.

6. Delete the original (lower) Black & White adjustment layer. C For the remaining Black

A The path in this photo is a strong compositional element. To emphasize it, we'll heighten its color while converting the rest of the photo to grayscale.

B We used a Black & White adjustment layer to increase the contrast, to make it easier to select the path via the Quick Selection tool.

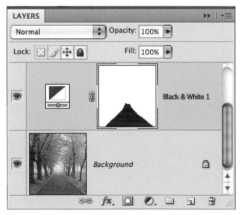

C With the selection active, we created a new adjustment layer and inverted its mask. The selected area (grass and trees) corresponds to the white area in the mask, whereas the black area is masking the path. Next, we deleted the original Black & White layer.

& White layer, use the sliders to create a well-balanced black and white conversion.**A**

Check **Tint**. Click the color swatch to open the Color Picker, choose a low saturation color that won't compete with the color being preserved by the mask, then click OK.**B**

7. *Optional:* To boost the contrast and intensity, click the Return to Adjustment List button ◁ on the Adjustments panel, create a Brightness/Contrast adjustment layer,▦ and increase the Brightness value. On the Layers panel, change the blending mode for this adjustment layer to Soft Light and change the layer Opacity to 70–80%.**C**

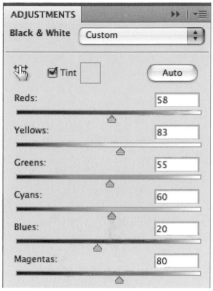

A For the second Black & White adjustment, we used the sliders to lighten the grays in the leaves and grass and also applied a Tint similar to the original path color to unify the image.

B This is the image after we applied the second Black & White adjustment, which includes a subtle tint.

C Finally, we used a Brightness/Contrast adjustment layer (Brightness +100) to lighten the entire photo and chose Soft Light mode for the layer (80% Opacity) to enrich the color and tint. Now the delicate, intricate trees are balanced by the solid geometric path.

Creating an infrared effect

Normally, infrared light waves aren't visible to the human eye, but photographers can capture images in this wavelength by using special infrared filters. In Photoshop, you can simulate the surreal effect of infrared photography by using the Monochrome option in the Channel Mixer, followed by the Diffuse Glow filter.

To create an infrared effect: ★

1. Open an RGB landscape photo that has some green areas and good contrast, and is sharp.**A** Press Ctrl-J/Cmd-J to duplicate the Background, and keep the duplicate layer selected.

2. On the Adjustments panel,⬤ click the **Channel Mixer** button.🔲

3. Check **Monochrome** to convert the photo to grayscale. Move the **Green** slider almost all the way to the right to lighten the greens, move the **Red** slider slightly to the left or right, and move the **Blue** slider to the left. The aim is to create contrast between the light greens and the other colors. We've gotten good results by keeping the Total of the three sliders (listed below the sliders) at or below 100% **B** (and **A**, next page).

> **INFRARED IN A LITTLE NUTSHELL**
> The specialized filters used in infrared photography block blue wavelengths while allowing near infrared (IR) light to pass through. Factoid: With thermal imaging equipment, scientists also can capture far infrared wavelengths.

If you also want to darken the entire photo, drag the **Constant** slider to between –1 and –5.

4. *Optional:* You're going to merge the adjustment layer downward in the next step, but before doing so, you may want to duplicate it and then hide the duplicate, to preserve the option to edit it later.

5. Select the visible adjustment layer, then press Ctrl-E/Cmd-E to **merge** it with the duplicate of the Background.

6. Right-click/Control-click the duplicate layer and choose **Convert to Smart Object**. This conversion will enable the filter that you're going to apply next to remain editable.

A An infrared treatment is going to transform this ordinary image.

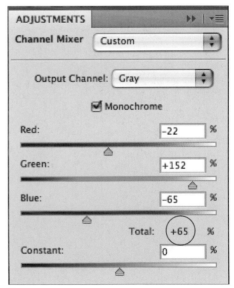

B For the Channel Mixer adjustment, we checked Monochrome. To increase the contrast, we moved the Green slider to the far right, and moved the Red and Blue sliders to the left by differing amounts.

7. To simulate the glow that infrared photos develop (due to the requisite long exposure times), choose Filter > Distort > **Diffuse Glow**.

8. In the **Filter Gallery**, do the following: **B**

Click the **Hide Thumbnails** ▲ button to hide the pane of thumbnails, and lower the zoom level for the preview.

Adjust the three sliders to achieve the desired amount of graininess and glow. As you raise the Glow Amount, you'll also need to raise the Clear Amount. Click OK. Don't worry if the highlights now lack detail; you can correct that somewhat in the next step.

Continued on the following page

A Our Channel Mixer adjustment produced this grayscale image and a simplified composition. Now the strong highlights (former green areas) are taking center stage.

B In the Filter Gallery, we chose these settings for the Diffuse Glow filter: Graininess 2; Glow Amount 5 (to create a glow without clipping too many highlights); and Clear Amount 8 (to lighten the entire photo).

9. If the Diffuse Glow filter clipped the highlights, double-click the **Edit Blending Options** button 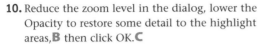 (to the right of the filter name listing on the Layers panel) **A** to open the Blending Options [filter name] dialog.

10. Reduce the zoom level in the dialog, lower the Opacity to restore some detail to the highlight areas,**B** then click OK.**C**

➤ Each Smart Filter can be edited individually: Double-click the filter name to edit the filter settings; or choose a different blending mode or Opacity via the Blending Options dialog; or hide the filter effect by clicking its visibility icon.

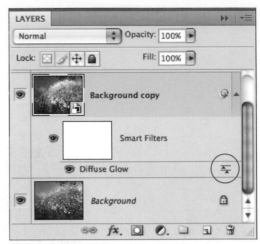

A On the Layers panel, we'll double-click the Edit Blending Options button to open the Blending Options dialog.

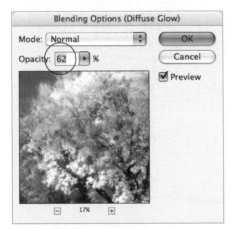

B In the Blending Options dialog, we lowered the Opacity for the Diffuse Glow filter to restore some detail to the highlights.

C By simplifying and intensifying the lights and darks, the infrared effect produced this luminous, surreal image.

A VARIATION ON THE INFRARED EFFECT

ADJUSTMENTS

Channel Mixer   Custom

Output Channel: Gray

☑ Monochrome

Red: +6   %

Green: +200 %

Blue: -127 %

Total: +79 %

Constant: -4   %

A We followed the steps on pages 240–242 to create this infrared effect. We chose the settings shown at left for the Channel Mixer, then merged it into a copy of the Background.

B To restore some color to the distant mountains and sky (the nongreen areas in the original photo), we chose Lighter Color as the blending mode for the Smart Object layer.

Creating a duotone

To create a duotone, commercial printers use one or more additional plates and ink colors for a grayscale image to lend it added depth and richness and to extend its tonal range (especially in the midtones). Via the Duotone Options dialog, you can specify settings for printing a duotone (two plates), tritone (three plates), or quadtone (four plates). Although you could choose custom colors and control how they're distributed across the tonal range, it will be easier—and, more important, will help prevent printing problems—if you use a preset.

Note: The only way to proof a duotone is via a press proof (it can't be done via a PostScript color printer).

To create a duotone by using a preset:

1. Open an RGB image, and make sure it has good contrast, so it will look good after the grayscale conversion in the next step. If you need to adjust (e.g., increase) the contrast, use a Black & White adjustment layer, then merge it downward.**A**

2. Choose Image > Mode > **Grayscale** to convert the image to grayscale.**B** Click Discard in the alert dialog.

3. Choose Image > Mode > **Duotone**. The Duotone Options dialog opens.

4. Choose **Duotone** from the **Type** menu to create a duotone that uses Black and one color.

5. From the **Preset** menu, ★ choose one of the presets that ends in 1. A tint will be applied to the image (**A**, next page), and swatches will display for the Ink 1 and Ink 2 colors (**B**, next page).

6. To view a preset that has a more muted color scheme for comparison, from the Preset menu, choose a preset that ends in 2.

7. Sample other duotone presets, if desired. When you settle on one that you like, click OK to close the Duotone Options dialog (**C–D**, next page).

➤ The duotone presets that end with a 1 apply the most color, whereas the presets ending in 2, 3, and 4 apply progressively less color to a smaller range of midtones.

➤ To edit the existing duotone settings for an image, reopen the Duotone Options dialog by choosing Image > Mode > Duotone.

A This is the original image.

B We used a Black & White adjustment layer to correct the contrast before converting the image mode to Grayscale.

➤ The presets differ not only in the color that they apply, but also in the shape of the curves, which display in the Ink 1 and Ink 2 thumbnails.

Continued on the following page

A We converted the image to Duotone mode, and applied the 478 brown (100%) bl 1 duotone preset.

C For comparison, this is the 478 brown (100%) bl 2 duotone preset (well...actually, these are simulated duotones).

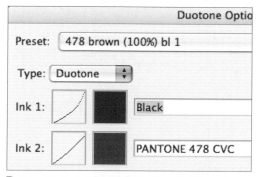

Duotone Optio

Preset: 478 brown (100%) bl 1

Type: Duotone

Ink 1: Black

Ink 2: PANTONE 478 CVC

B The settings for the 478 brown (100%) bl 1 preset display in the Duotone Options dialog.

Duotone Optio

Preset: 478 brown (100%) bl 2

Type: Duotone

Ink 1: Black

Ink 2: PANTONE 478 CVC

D Note that although the same PANTONE color is being used for this 478 brown (100%) bl 2 preset as the one shown at left, the Ink 1 and Ink 2 curves have a different shape. This preset applies less color to the midtones (the Ink 2 curve is lower).

To choose a file format for a duotone:

If you're going to print your duotone file directly from Photoshop, save it in the PSD format.

If you're going to import the duotone file into a page layout program, do either of the following:

To import the file into an InDesign CS3 or CS4 layout for two-color printing (black plus one color), save it in either the Photoshop (PSD) or Photoshop PDF format. For other layout programs, use the Photoshop EPS format (see step 6 in the instructions below).

To import the file into a page layout program for printing with four-color process inks, first convert it to CMYK mode (Image > Mode > CMYK Color), then save it in the PSD, PDF, or TIFF format, depending on which format the layout program supports.

To ensure that your commercial printer outputs your duotone using two plates, tell them the duotone is set up with black as Ink 1, and ask which format you should save the file in. The order of inks and the screen angles will affect the outcome, so also ask if they'll take care of choosing screen angles for the colored ink, or if they would rather provide you with the necessary information so you can do it. In the latter case, follow the instructions below.

To choose options for duotone printing:

1. With the duotone file open, choose File > **Print**.

2. In the Print dialog, choose **Output** from the menu in the upper right, then click **Screen.A**

3. The Halftone Screen dialog opens.**B** Uncheck **Use Printer's Default Screen**, then click **Auto**.

4. In the Auto Screens dialog,**C** enter the **Printer** resolution and lines/inch **Screen** setting as specified by your print shop, check **Use Accurate Screens**, then click OK.

5. Click OK to close the Halftone Screen dialog, then click Done to close the Print dialog.

6. Save the file in the format your print shop has specified, which will be either Photoshop PSD (so the print shop can make screen adjustments) or Photoshop EPS. For the latter, when you choose Photoshop EPS as the Format in the Save As dialog, the EPS Options dialog opens;**D** check Include Halftone Screen to embed the screen settings into the file, then click OK.

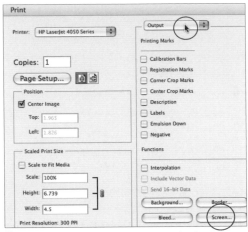

A To establish the necessary screen angles for duotone printing, open the Print dialog, choose Output from the menu in the upper right, then click Screen.

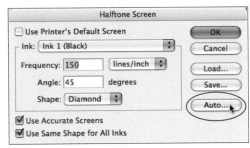

B In the Halftone Screen dialog, uncheck Use Printer's Default Screen, then click Auto.

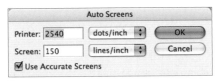

C In the Auto Screens dialog, enter the Printer resolution and Screen frequency and check Use Accurate Screens.

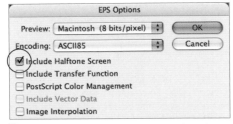

D If you're told to save the file in the Photoshop EPS format, check Include Halftone Screen in the EPS Options dialog.

This chapter covers painting techniques that are the antithesis of high tech—well, except that they're all done in Photoshop. One advantage to working electronically is that you can create images that have a handmade look without slavishly trying to mimic a specific medium.

This chapter begins with an introduction (or rehash, if you're already experienced with brushes in Photoshop) to brushes and painting techniques, which you can use as a reference guide. The first exercise is to create a brush from imagery and use it in a composition. This is a great way to apply a single shape repetitively or to apply a texture.

If you're not confident about your artistic skills or your ability to handle a brush, don't worry: You can easily simulate a fine art look by using filters. For example, we'll show you how to create a sketch by using the Gaussian Blur and Glowing Edges filters, then polish it off with a few brush strokes on a layer mask. To simulate pastels, you'll apply the Rough Pastels filter. For a more painterly look (similar to gouache or crayon), you'll use a combination of the Colored Pencil, Paint Daubs, and Smudge Stick filters. And finally, to create the look of a watercolor, you'll use the Noise Median, Poster Edges, and Glowing Edges filters. In most of the exercises, you'll apply multiple filters to a single image. Our experience has been that applying filters in twos, threes, or more often yields the best results.

We like the effects that can be achieved with brushes and filters in Photoshop, but tend to shy away from simulating thick surfaces, such as oil paint or impasto, because the faux versions lack three-dimensionality. Working on the flat plane of a computer screen, we gravitate to media that are traditionally applied to paper, such as pencil, charcoal, watercolor, and gouache (but hey, that's just our bias).

There are no hard and fast rules in the world of electronic or traditional art-making. You can develop your own electronic art media in any way that appeals to you. And remember that in addition to giving whole images a more handmade look, you can apply the techniques that you learn in this chapter (or your own variations thereof) to sections of an image, such as to individual layers in a collage.

Note: Settings listed in the captions in this chapter were chosen for photos that are approximately 3000 x 2000 pixels.

FINE ART MEDIA

11

IN THIS CHAPTER

QUICK SUMMARY: USING BRUSHES

TASK	METHOD
Using and choosing brushes	
Display the Brushes panel	Choose Window > Brushes (F5) or click the Brushes panel icon, 🖌 if it's docked
Open a temporary Brush preset picker	Choose a tool that uses brushes, then click the Brush preset picker 🔳 on the Options bar or right-click/Control-click in the document window
Load brush tips	Choose from the bottom of the Brush preset picker menu
Select the next brush tip on the Brushes panel	. (period)
Select the previous brush tip on the Brushes panel	, (comma)
Select the first tip on the Brushes panel	Shift-, (comma)
Select the last tip on the Brushes panel	Shift-. (period)
Save all the tips on the Brushes panel	Choose Save Brushes from the Brushes panel menu
Save select brush tips on the Brushes panel	Use Edit > Preset Manager (see pages 112–113)
Save the current brush settings, including the tip, mode, opacity, flow, etc., as a preset to the Tool preset picker	Open a temporary Tool preset picker from the left side of the Options bar or display the Tool Presets panel, 🖌 then click the New Tool Preset button 🔳
Create a brush tip from an image	Select an area of an image, then choose Edit > Define Brush Preset
Delete a brush tip from the Brushes panel	Alt-click/Option-click the tip
Changing brush variables	
Control the rate of buildup	Change the Flow and Airbrush settings on the Options bar (use a higher Flow for quick strokes)
Control the softness of the edge of the brush stroke	Change the Hardness setting on the Brush preset picker; or check or uncheck Noise, Wet Edges, or Smoothing on the Brushes panel; or try using Dissolve mode (Options bar)
Control the color variation	Change the Jitter values in the Color Dynamics panel of the Brushes panel
Choose a color from the image with a temporary Eyedropper tool	Alt-click/Option-click a color in the document window
Choose settings for a stylus	Use the Control menus on individual panels of the Brushes panel

QUICK SUMMARY: SHORTCUTS FOR CHANGING TOOL SETTINGS

You can use shortcuts to change settings for many tools, such as the Brush, Pencil, Color Replacement, Clone Stamp, Pattern Stamp, Smudge, Dodge, Burn, History Brush, Art History Brush, Spot Healing Brush, Healing Brush, Eraser, Magic Eraser, or Background Eraser, if the tool has that feature:

TASK	METHOD
Cycle through the blending modes for the tool	Shift-+ (plus) or Shift - – (minus)
Decrease or increase the Master Diameter	[or]
Resize a brush interactively (check OpenGL drawing in Preferences > Performance) ★	Right-click-Alt/Control-Option drag to the left or right in the image
Decrease or increase the Hardness	Shift-[or Shift-]
Change the Opacity, Exposure, or Strength percentage (Shift-press a number to change the Flow level)*	0–9 (e.g., 2 = 20%), or quickly type a percentage (e.g., "38")

If the Airbrush option is on, press a number to change the Flow percentage or Shift-press a number to change the Opacity percentage. Note: When Shift-pressing in Windows, use the numbers on the main keyboard, not on the keypad.

QUICK SUMMARY: PAINTING TECHNIQUES

TASK	METHOD
Restore areas	Set the History Source icon to a snapshot or state on the History panel, then draw strokes with the History Brush tool (Y) (create snapshots periodically as you work)
Erase areas to transparency	Use the Eraser (drag), Background Eraser (click), or Magic Eraser (click) tool
Repaint an image in stylized strokes	Add a new blank layer above an image layer, then draw strokes with the Art History Brush tool; or use the Pattern Stamp tool with the Impressionist option on
Smudge colors	Use the Smudge tool on a new layer with the Finger Painting option on
Add an overall paper color or texture	Apply a Solid Color or Pattern Fill layer via the New Fill/Adjustment Layer menu on the Layers panel, and change the layer blending mode and/or lower the layer Opacity

Creating brush tips from imagery

After creating a brush tip from a selected area of an image, you can click or drag with the Brush tool to quickly create multiple monochromatic repeats of that tip in the current Foreground color.

To create a brush tip from an image:

1. With the **Quick Selection** ✎ or **Magic Wand** tool ✎, select a small area of a picture.**A**

2. Choose Edit > **Define Brush Preset**. The Brush Name dialog opens.**B** Enter a Name, then click OK.

3. To practice using the tip, choose the **Brush** tool ✎ and a Foreground color, click the tip on the Brush preset picker (the last preset on the picker),**C** turn on the Airbrush option, ✎ if desired, then click or drag in another image (see the illustrations on the next two pages).

➤ When you use a brush tip that you've created from an image, you can reset the brush diameter to the original sample size by clicking Use Sample Size on the Brush preset picker.

A We selected some leaf shapes, which will be made into a brush tip.

B We chose Edit > Define Brush Preset and then, in the Brush Name dialog, entered a name for our custom brush.

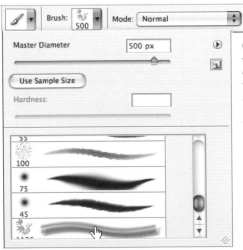

C After choosing the Brush tool, we clicked our new brush tip on the Brush preset picker, set the Opacity and Flow to 100%, and clicked the Airbrush option. (Stroke Thumbnail view is chosen for this picker.)

PAINTING WITH A BRUSH MADE FROM AN IMAGE

A To create the semitransparent brush mark (leaf shapes) in the center of this image, we created a new, blank layer, chose a Foreground color, then clicked with the Brush tool. To create the more opaque marks in the lower right, we held the mouse down (the marks gradually became darker, due to the Airbrush function).

CREATING VARIETY WITH BRUSHES

➤ Change the Foreground color between clicks or strokes.

➤ Use the mouse in different ways: Click; click and hold for a long or short interval with the Airbrush option on; or drag.

➤ Via the Brushes panel, choose settings to increase the randomness of various properties. Increase the Spacing value in the Brush Tip Shape panel, or the Opacity Jitter or Flow Jitter value in the Other Dynamics panel. Or for more variably sized strokes, increase the Size Jitter in the Shape Dynamics panel.

➤ Place your brush marks on separate layers, then transform, restack, or adjust the Opacity or blending mode for, or apply layer effects to, any of those layers.

B We changed the Foreground color to gold, then clicked again to create another brush mark. To rotate all the marks on that layer, we chose the Move tool, then dragged a corner handle on the transform box.

See also the figures on the following page

A Next, we created a second new layer and stacked it below the first one. We pressed [to reduce the brush diameter, changed the Foreground color to tan and then, to create a trail of leaves and a feeling of movement, dragged horizontally across the bottom of the image.

B We created one more layer, pressed] to increase the brush diameter, then added green, orange, and red brush marks. Finally, to change the orientation of that layer and make the leaves look as though they're swirling in an autumn breeze, we chose Edit > Transform > Flip Horizontal and Flip Vertical.

Creating a sketch by using filters

In the remaining exercises in this chapter, you'll reinterpret a photo as a sketch, painting, or watercolor. In this exercise and the next, you'll reduce an image to a line art sketch by using filters and by drawing a few strokes on a layer mask.

To create a line art sketch:

1. Open an RGB image.**A** Press Ctrl-Alt-J/Cmd-Option-J to duplicate the Background. In the dialog, name the layer "blur," then click OK. Keep the layer selected.

2. Lower the Opacity of the blurred layer to 50%.

3. Choose Filter > Blur > **Gaussian Blur**. Set the Radius value to around 20 pixels, then click OK.**B**

4. The blur layer will supply the color, whereas a line art layer will supply the necessary details. Duplicate the Background again, then drag the second duplicate layer to the top of the stack.

Continued on the following page

A This image will convert well to a sketch because it has strong contrast and broad color areas.

B To create a layer of soft color, we duplicated the Background, lowered the layer opacity to 50%, then applied the Gaussian Blur filter at a Radius of 20 px.

5. Choose Filter > Stylize > **Glowing Edges**. In the Filter Gallery dialog, click the Hide Thumbnails button to expand the preview panel, and lower the zoom level for the preview. Increase the **Edge Brightness** and **Smoothness** values to create bright, crisp lines without too many tiny details. Click OK.**A**

6. Press Ctrl-I/Cmd-I to **invert** the layer (the background switches to white).**B** And to allow some color from the blurred layer to show through, choose **Overlay** as the layer blending mode.**C**

7. To restore some underlying color by hand, with the topmost layer still selected, click the **Add Layer Mask** button.🔲 With the **Brush** tool,🖌 a large, Soft Round, low-opacity tip, and Black as the Foreground color, drag across areas that you want to restore color to (**A–B**, next page). To remove any of your strokes, paint with white.

➤ If you need to brighten the sketch, see **C** on the next page.

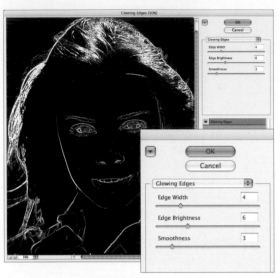

A In the Filter > Stylize > Glowing Edges dialog, we increased the Edge Brightness to make the line work brighter and set the Smoothness to eliminate superfluous lines from low-contrast areas.

B Next, we pressed Ctrl-I/Cmd-I to invert the colors.

C Overlay, the blending mode of the line art layer, allows color from the blurred layer to show through.

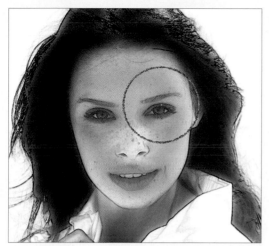

A To restore more color and detail from the underlying layers, we added a layer mask and then, with the Brush tool (Soft Round 200 Pixels tip, Opacity 65%, Flow 50%), drew horizontal strokes across the face. Next, we lowered the brush Opacity to 30% and painted a stroke across the eyes and the mouth (see the layer mask insert at right).

B The partial mask is allowing some color and some details from the lower layers to show through.

C To brighten the final sketch, we created a Levels adjustment layer, and set the white Input Levels slider to 222. We also chose Soft Light as the blending mode for the adjustment layer.

CREATING A LINE ART SKETCH: A VARIATION ON THE PRIOR EXERCISE

The main difference between this method for converting a photo to a line art sketch and the previous one is that here you'll restore colors from the original Background image, whereas in the previous exercise colors were restored from a blurred layer **A–B** (and **A–C**, next page).

A With its strong geometry, color, and linear details, this photo of Nyhavn harbor in Copenhagen, Denmark, will translate beautifully into a sketch.

WHICH FILTER HAS THE EDGE?

When converting a photo to a sketch, we use the Glowing Edges filter instead of Find Edges because the former lets us eliminate extraneous fine lines and control the line thickness, whereas the latter has no dialog or controls.

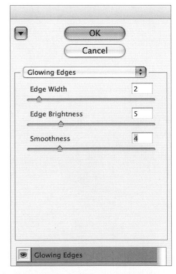

B We duplicated the Background, then used the Glowing Edges filter to convert the duplicate layer to line art. In this image (unlike the portrait on the preceding page), we wanted to preserve most of the delicate lines, so we chose low settings for all three options.

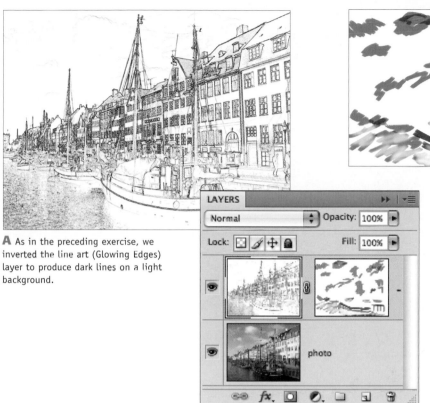

A As in the preceding exercise, we inverted the line art (Glowing Edges) layer to produce dark lines on a light background.

B We added a layer mask to the line art layer and kept the mask thumbnail selected. We chose the Brush tool, the brush tip called "Chalk 60 Pixels," and a Flow value of 50%. Using different brush Opacities between 25% and 50%, we added strokes to remove areas of the mask.

C The strokes that we applied to the layer mask restored color from the Background, which added a watercolor-like effect to the line art.

Simulating pastels

Another fine art medium that can be simulated in Photoshop is pastels. The way we suggest doing so is to apply the Rough Pastels filter to a desaturated copy of the Background. You can leave the desaturated effect as is or change the layer mode to allow colors from the Background to peek through.

To create a pastel sketch:

1. Open an RGB image. **A** Press Ctrl-J/Cmd-J to duplicate the Background, and keep the copy selected.

2. On the Adjustments panel, ⬚ click the **Black & White** button. ◣ ★ Use the sliders to create adequate contrast in the grayscale layer. **B**

3. Press Ctrl-E/Cmd-E to merge the adjustment layer into the duplicate layer.

A With its clearly defined color areas and good contrast, this photo will convert well to a pastel.

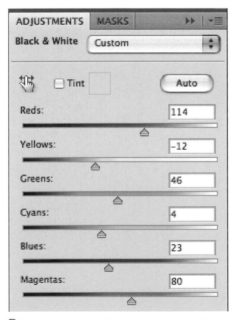

B To produce the results at right, we chose the settings shown above for our Black & White adjustment layer: To darken the midtones, we moved a few sliders slightly to the left; to lighten the face, we moved the Reds slider to the right.

4. To enable editing of the filter you're going to apply, choose Filter > **Convert for Smart Filters** to create a Smart Object layer (click OK in any alerts).

5. Choose Filter > Artistic > **Rough Pastels**. In the dialog, drag a key area of the image into view.**A** Adjust the Stroke Length and Stroke Detail values, and use the Texture sliders to control the graininess and roughness of the strokes. Click OK (**A–B**, next page).

A We converted the duplicate layer to a Smart Object. Via the Filter Gallery, we applied the Rough Pastels filter, increasing these values: Stroke Length and Stroke Detail to make the strokes more clearly defined; Scaling to make the Canvas texture more prominent; and Relief to accentuate the strokes.

A The final pastels image is shown above.

B As a variation, to allow traces of color from the Background to show through, we changed the blending mode for the Smart Object layer to Luminosity and changed the layer Opacity to 80%.

SMART FILTERS: SOLO OR ON ONE LAYER

In the next task, as you apply multiple filters using the Filter Gallery, consider these points:

➤ One advantage of applying multiple filters to a single Smart Object layer via the Filter Gallery is that you need to open the gallery only once to edit the filter visibility, stacking order, and settings. This is faster than opening the gallery separately for each individual Smart Filter listing. Another advantage is that the preview in the gallery will show the combined effect of all the filters.

➤ A disadvantage of applying multiple filters to a single layer is that you can't change the blending mode or opacity for individual Smart Filters. You can't have everything!

Turning a photo into a painting

To create a painting, you'll start with a grayscale layer, as in the previous exercise, but apply a different series of filters and then add a texture. You won't have to use the Brush tool!

To turn a photo into a painting:

1. Open an RGB photo that has bright, clearly defined color areas.**A** Duplicate the Background (Ctrl-J/Cmd-J).

2. Follow steps 2–4 on pages 258–259 to create a grayscale **Smart Object** layer, and to reveal some color from the Background, choose Luminosity as the layer blending mode.

3. Choose Filter > **Filter Gallery**. In the dialog, click the Hide Thumbnails button ▾ to expand the preview panel and choose **Paint Daubs** from the menu. Set the sliders to convert the shapes into smooth, blocky areas.**B** Keep the dialog open!

Continued on the following page

A We'll use this photo again because its vivid colors and geometric shapes will also translate well into a painting.

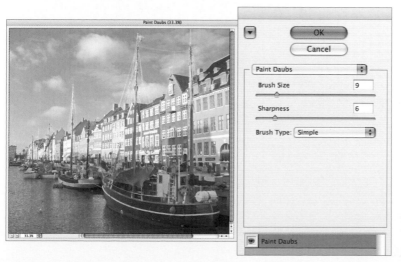

B We converted a duplicate image layer to grayscale and then to a Smart Object, and chose Luminosity as the layer blending mode. Next, we chose Filter > Filter Gallery and applied the Paint Daubs filter. To soften the details while preserving shapes, we chose low Brush Size and Sharpness settings.

4. Click the **New Effect** button 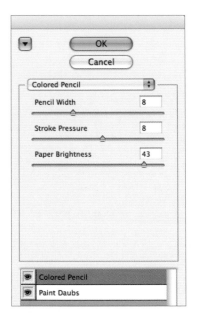 at the bottom of the dialog, then choose **Colored Pencil** from the menu. Choose settings to turn the paint daubs into a collection of strokes.**A**

5. Click the **New Effect** button once more, and choose **Smudge Stick** from the menu. Choose settings to increase the contrast and make the strokes look more expressive.**B** Click OK (**A**, next page).

A Next, we applied the Colored Pencil filter to break up the paint daubs into strokes: a Pencil Width value of 8 for moderately thick strokes, a Stroke Pressure value of 8 for good contrast, and a very high Paper Brightness value of 43 to lighten the image.

B The last filter effect we applied was Smudge Stick, to boost the contrast and make the strokes look more expressive. We chose a low Stroke Length because the line work was already present, a low Highlight Area value to produce fewer highlights, and a high Intensity value to preserve the contrast.

6. *Optional:* To add texture to the image, click the filter effects mask thumbnail on the Layers panel. Choose Filter > Sketch > Conté Crayon. Set the Foreground Level slider to around 8 and the Background Level slider to a low value of 2 or 3. Choose a Texture option and a Light direction option **B** (we like Bottom Left). Click OK.**C**

7. *Optional:* To restore more color from the Background image, lower the opacity of the Smart Object layer to around 70%.

A This is the result after we applied the three filters via the Filter Gallery and lowered the Opacity of the Smart Object layer to 70%. The image has an Impressionist feel but still plenty of detail.

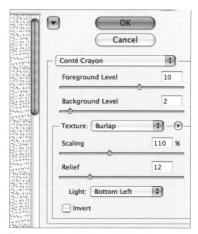

B To add a texture to the image, we clicked the filter effects mask thumbnail on the Layers panel, then applied the Conté Crayon filter.

C In this closeup view of the image, you can see that the Conté Crayon filter (burlap texture) added a "tactile" quality to the painting.

Creating a watercolor

If you don't have the time, patience, or skill to paint a watercolor with a brush, you can simulate a watercolor effect by using just filters.

To create a watercolor by using filters:

1. Open an RGB image, preferably one that has clearly defined color areas.**A** Press Ctrl-J/Cmd-J to duplicate the Background, and keep the duplicate layer selected.

2. To keep the filters you're going to apply editable, Ctrl-click/Cmd-click the layer and choose **Convert to Smart Object.**

3. To convert the colors into blocky shapes, choose Filter > Noise > **Median**. In the dialog, choose a Radius of 10–12 pixels, then click OK.

4. To posterize the colors, choose Filter > Artistic > **Poster Edges**. In the Filter Gallery dialog, set the Edge Thickness and Edge Intensity to 0 and the Posterization to 2, then click OK.**B**

A Our watercolor effect will work well on this image because it has clearly defined colors.

B After creating a Smart Object layer, we applied the Median and Poster Edges filters. The color transitions are no longer smooth or continuous, and color areas are now separate, distinct shapes.

5. *Optional:* To lighten areas and restore some of the white of the "paper" background, choose Filter > Sharpen > Unsharp Mask. In the dialog, set the Amount to 125, the Radius to 20, and the Threshold to 3–4, then click OK. To soften the sharpening effect, on the Layers panel, drag Unsharp Mask to the bottom of the list of Smart Filters.**A** Note: If the Unsharp Mask filter made the highlights too bright, double-click the Edit Blend Options icon ≆ for that filter on the Layers panel, lower the Opacity to 60–70%, then click OK.

6. To add lines along the edges of the shapes, click the Background, press Ctrl-J/Cmd-J to duplicate it once more, then choose Filter > Stylize > **Glowing Edges**. Set the Edge Width to around 3, the Edge Brightness to around 5, and the Smoothness to around 7–9, then click OK.

7. Press Ctrl-I/Cmd-I to **invert** the Glowing Edges layer, then drag it to the top of the layer stack. Change the layer blending mode to **Multiply**, and adjust the layer Opacity as needed.**B** Done!

A We applied the Unsharp Mask filter to intensify the brightness and contrast, but restacked it to the bottom of the list of Smart Filters to lessen its effect.

B Finally, we applied the Glowing Edges filter to a duplicate of the Background, inverted the duplicate layer, dragged it to the top of the layer stack, changed its mode to Multiply, and lowered its Opacity to 60%. Now the line work blends beautifully with the colors on the Smart Object layer.

In traditional watercoloring, pigment has a tendency to pool, or collect, at the edges of the brush strokes. In Photoshop, you can mimic this effect in a unique way: Create a pattern preset from an entire photo, then with the Pattern Stamp tool and an assortment of brushes, paint (stamp, actually) the image onto a new layer.

To create a watercolor with the Pattern Stamp tool:

1. Open an RGB photo that contains broad color areas.**A**

2. Without selecting anything first, choose Edit > **Define Pattern**. In the Pattern Name dialog, enter a name or keep the default name, then click OK.

3. Choose the **Pattern Stamp** tool 🖌 (S or Shift-S).

4. On the Options bar,**B** do all of the following:

   Click the brush thumbnail to open the Brush preset picker. From the picker menu,⊙ choose **Wet Media Brushes**. In the alert, click Append to add the brush library to the existing presets.

   Scroll to the bottom of the picker, then click the last brush tip, which is **Watercolor Light Opacity**. (You'll be using the last five "Watercolor" brushes in this exercise.)

   Choose Mode: Normal, Opacity 60%, and Flow 50%, and check **Aligned** and **Impressionist**.

   Click the Pattern thumbnail to open the **Pattern preset** picker. Click the pattern you defined (the last preset on the picker).

A To reinterpret this still life as a watercolor, the first step will be to create a pattern preset from the whole image.

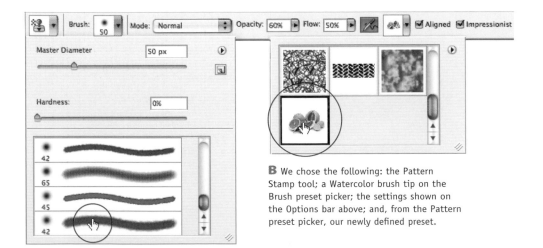

B We chose the following: the Pattern Stamp tool; a Watercolor brush tip on the Brush preset picker; the settings shown on the Options bar above; and, from the Pattern preset picker, our newly defined preset.

5. Create a new, blank layer. Press Shift-Backspace/Shift-Delete to open the **Fill** dialog. Choose these settings: Use: White, Mode: Normal, and Opacity: 100%, then click OK.

6. Lower the layer Opacity to 85%. You'll use this faint version of the image as a guide as you apply strokes.

7. Press] to enlarge the brush tip, then fill in the main shapes in the image.**A** For an authentic watercolor look, leave some of the white (paper) showing and use distinct, separate strokes.**B**

8. Once the main areas have been blocked in, right-click/Control-click on the image to open the Brush preset picker, then click the **Watercolor Textured Surface** brush tip.

9. Increase the brush Opacity via the Options bar, then paint in details on the edges or interiors of the shapes. You can switch to other Watercolor brushes and brush settings between strokes (**A–B**, next page) and periodically raise, (then lower) the layer opacity to check your progress.

Instructions continue on page 269

A To use a faint version of the image as a guide for painting, we created a new layer, filled it with white, and lowered its Opacity to 85%. We chose the Watercolor Light Opacity brush tip, increased the brush size, and then "painted in" the grapefruit. The color derived from the pattern preset automatically.

B We continued to paint in the other large fruit shapes, pressing [or] as needed to resize the brush tip in order to fit the sizes of the different shapes.

SEEING DOUBLE

If your computer display is large enough or you have dual displays, open a copy of the original image and keep it onscreen, to refer to as you stamp in the details. Don't be a slave to the original image, though; you can be selective about which details you decide to omit or restore.

A We switched to the Watercolor Textured Surface brush tip to add details along the edges and surfaces of the fruit.

B To concentrate more on the watercolor that was starting to take form, we reset the layer Opacity to 100% to hide the Background. We chose the Watercolor Heavy Pigments brush tip, lowered the brush Opacity, and increased the brush size, then added a light color wash along each fruit shape. To add final details, we used the Watercolor Textured Surface brush tip again.

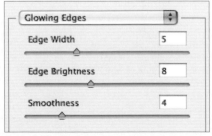

C We duplicated the paint layer, applied the Stylize > Glowing Edges filter to the duplicate (settings shown above), then inverted the layer to restore the white background.

10. When you're done painting in the image, press Ctrl-J/Cmd-J to duplicate the paint layer, and keep the duplicate selected.

11. To enhance the watercolor look, choose Filter > Stylize > **Glowing Edges**, choose settings, then click OK. Press Ctrl-I/Cmd-I to **invert** the layer colors (**C**, previous page), change the layer blending mode to **Multiply** to blend the lines with the paint layer, **A** then press Ctrl-E/Cmd-E to merge the line art layer into the paint layer.

12. To heighten the color contrast and saturation, use the Adjustments panel to create a **Levels** adjustment layer, ★ and move the black and gray Input Levels sliders to the right. To lessen the impact of the adjustment layer, lower its Opacity slightly. **B**

13. Your watercolor is almost done. To add a texture to the white "paper" background, double-click the paint layer to open the Layer Style dialog, then click **Pattern Overlay**.

14. In the Pattern Overlay panel, click the pattern thumbnail to open the Pattern preset picker. From the picker menu, choose **Artist Surfaces**, then click Append to add the pattern library to the existing presets. Click the **Watercolor** pattern thumbnail. Set the Scale to around 132, the blending mode to Multiply (to blend the pattern with the paint layer), and the Opacity to 100%, then click OK.

Your watercolor is finished (**A**, next page).

A We chose Multiply mode for the line art layer to blend the line work with the underlying paint layer. Now the edges and details look more crisp and provide a needed counterpoint to the broad shapes.

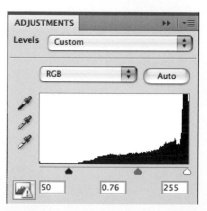

B We used a Levels adjustment layer to heighten the color contrast and saturation, then lowered the Opacity of the adjustment layer to 90%.

A This is our final watercolor, complete with a subtle Pattern Overlay paper texture.

In this chapter, you will learn how to make type characters look as if they're carved into granite, embossed into leather, stamped onto a cracker, illuminated, spray painted, scratched off a surface, cut out of paper, printed on porcelain, screened back, and written in the sky. To accomplish these feats, you'll use a variety of Photoshop features, such as layer styles, filters, masks, and gradients. You can use these methods as a springboard for developing a personal repertoire of type treatments.

Note: This chapter requires familiarity with the basic typesetting features of Photoshop, which we cover thoroughly in our *Photoshop CS4, volume 1: Visual QuickStart Guide*.

Tips for designing with type

➤ Think thematically. Choose a font—be it formal, casual, high-tech, calligraphic, historical, simple, or ornate—that relates to the background image.

➤ Chubby is good. Chunky letters will give you more surface area to alter or apply effects to.

➤ Make sure the type is legible, and not a struggle to decipher.

➤ For a sophisticated, cohesive look, take your color cues from the background image. You can sample a type color from the image with the Eyedropper tool.

➤ Improvise with Photoshop features in unconventional ways. For example, to create informal "hand" lettering, such as spray paint or chalk, instead of using the Type tool, you could draw the letters by hand with the Pencil or Brush tool (preferably with a graphics tablet and stylus).

➤ Be concise. To create more than a few words or a short phrase for print output, export your Photoshop image to a page layout program and typeset the text there instead.

➤ Keep your type treatments editable, if possible, by using flexible features, such as layer effects.

➤ Keep records. Take notes of your editing sequences and settings, for future reference. Save your favorite layer style settings to the Styles panel, for future use. Or record your successful editing steps in an action (see Chapter 14).

CREATIVE TYPE

12

IN THIS CHAPTER

Using layer effects

A layer style encompasses all the settings that you can apply via the Layer Style dialog (**A–B**, next page), including Blending Options, such as layer opacity and fill opacity, and layer effects, such as a Drop Shadow or Inner Glow. Although layer effects can be applied to any kind of layer (image layer, shape layer, Smart Object, etc.), we feature them in this chapter because they work magic on type. They're easy to apply and edit, singly or in combination, and will transform automatically if you transform the layer they're applied to.

➤ As you'll see from many of the exercises in this chapter, our experience has been that applying layer effects in twos, threes, or more produces the best results. And don't be afraid to use non-default settings. For example, you can lighten the shadow for a bevel by changing the mode.

LAYER TYPES FOR LAYER EFFECTS

➤ Apply the layer effects that work inward or outward from edges — Drop Shadow, Inner Shadow, Outer Glow, Inner Glow, Bevel and Emboss, and Stroke — to a type layer, shape layer, or any layer imagery that's surrounded by transparent pixels. You can select an area of a layer, then use Layer via Copy (Ctrl-J/Cmd-J) to isolate a subject from its background first.

➤ You can apply the Satin, Color Overlay, Gradient Overlay, and Pattern Overlay effects either to fully opaque layers or to layers that contain transparency.

QUICK SUMMARY: LAYER EFFECTS

TASK	METHOD
Apply a layer effect (you don't need to create a selection first; selections will be ignored)	Double-click next to any layer name (not a locked layer or the Background); or double-click the thumbnail for an image layer; or click a layer, then choose from the Add Layer Style menu *fx* on the Layers panel. Click an effect name and choose settings.
Change the layer effect settings or add more effects	Double-click next to or below the layer name; or double-click the Effects bar or an effect name that's nested below the layer name.
Restore settings that were in place (in all the panels) when you opened the Layer Style dialog	Alt-click/Option-click Reset.
Copy an individual effect from one layer to another	Alt-drag/Option-drag an effect name (to move an effect without copying it, don't hold down Alt/Option).
Move all the effects from one layer to another (replacing the existing effects)	Drag the Effects bar.
Change the opacity of a layer and its effects	Adjust the Opacity slider on the Layers panel (the Fill slider controls the opacity only of layer imagery, not of layer effects).
Adjust the lighting	Use the Angle to control the direction, and the Altitude (if available) to control the height of the light source, to create highlights and shading. To unify the lighting for all effects, adjust the Angle for an individual effect, then check Use Global Light; other effects for which Use Global Light is enabled will update accordingly.
Scale a layer effect (except those defined by a percentage)	Right-click/Control-click the *fx* icon on the layer and choose Scale Effects (a dialog opens).
Remove a layer effect or effects	Drag the effect name or Effects bar to the Delete Layer button.

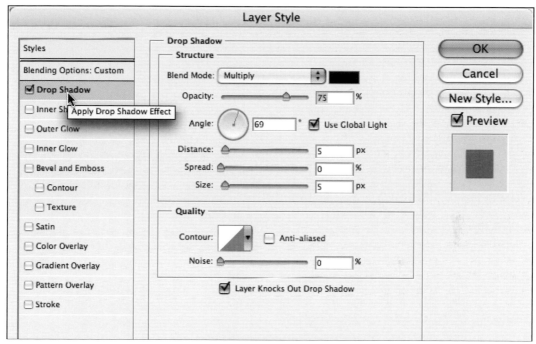

A In the Layer Style dialog, click an effect name (the box checks automatically) to view and edit the settings.

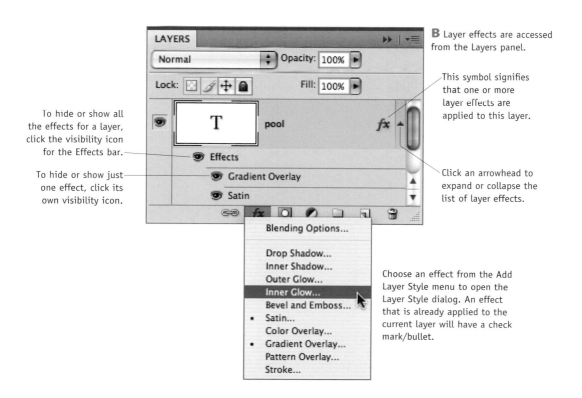

To hide or show all the effects for a layer, click the visibility icon for the Effects bar.

To hide or show just one effect, click its own visibility icon.

B Layer effects are accessed from the Layers panel.

This symbol signifies that one or more layer effects are applied to this layer.

Click an arrowhead to expand or collapse the list of layer effects.

Choose an effect from the Add Layer Style menu to open the Layer Style dialog. An effect that is already applied to the current layer will have a check mark/bullet.

One way to modify the edges of a layer effect (except for Overlay or Stroke) is by choosing a different contour in the Contour preset picker.

To choose a contour for a layer effect:

1. On the Layers panel, double-click a layer or an effect name to open the Layer Style dialog.

2. Apply one of the first six effects, and click the arrowhead next to the **Contour** thumbnail  (or for the Bevel and Emboss effect, click the **Gloss Contour** arrowhead) to open the Contour preset picker.

   ➤ For the Bevel and Emboss effect, you can also click the nested Contour option on the left side of the Layer Style dialog to add an extra contour.**A–D**

3. Click a contour thumbnail.

4. Click away from the picker to close the menu.

➤ When applying multiple layer effects, we recommend using the following strategy. Change the contour in just one or two of the effects. If Bevel and Emboss is applied, change its contour first; if Inner Glow is applied, change its contour next; if neither of those effects are applied, change the contour in one of the other "Inner" effects. The contours for Drop Shadow and Outer Glow control how the "Outer" effects follow the edge of an object; change the contour for only one of the two effects.

USING THE CONTOUR OPTION THAT'S NESTED UNDER THE BEVEL AND EMBOSS EFFECT

—Opaque pixels

A This is the default Linear contour for the Bevel and Emboss layer effect (Inner Bevel style).

B The Cone contour reversed the highlights and shadows in the bevel and moved the bevel inward.

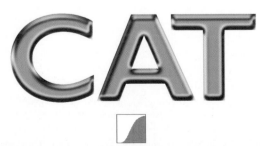

C The Gaussian contour rounded and softened the bevel.

D The Ring contour sharpened the edge of the bevel and moved it inward.

Using layer styles

You can conveniently store any collection of Blending Options and layer effects (Layer Style dialog settings) for future use as a layer style on the Styles panel. A saved style can be applied quickly to any layer in any document. To acquaint yourself with this panel, apply a preset style first.

To apply a style to a layer:

1. Show the **Styles** panel. *fx*
   ► From the panel menu, choose a thumbnail size or a list display mode for the panel.

2. Do either of the following:

   Click a layer (not the Background) on the **Layers** panel, then click a style on the **Styles** panel. **A–C**

   Drag a style name or thumbnail from the **Styles** panel over any selected or unselected layer on the **Layers** panel.

   ► Styles can also be applied via the Layer Styles dialog (click Styles at the top of the dialog).

   ► Normally, when you apply a style, it replaces any existing effects on the current layer. To add a style without replacing existing effects, Shift-click or Shift-drag the style. Whether you hold down Shift or not, if the new and existing effects have the same name, the new effects will replace the old.

As you save a layer style to the Styles panel, you have the option to include the layer effects and/ or Blending Options settings (such as layer opacity, blending mode, and fill opacity) that are currently applied to the selected layer.

To save a style to the Styles panel:

1. *Optional:* To give yourself a head start, apply an existing style to type, then modify the settings or apply additional effects.

2. Do either of the following:

   On the **Layers** panel, click a layer that contains the desired layer style settings (layer effects, layer opacity, blending mode, fill opacity, etc.), then click a blank area on the **Styles** panel or click the **New Style** button. 🔳

   On the **Layers** panel, double-click a layer that contains the desired layer style settings. In the Layer Style dialog, click **New Style**.

3. In the New Style dialog, type a **Name** for the new style, check whether you want to **Include Layer Effects** and/or **Include Layer Blending Options** in the style, then click OK. If the Layer Style dialog is open, click OK to exit that dialog. Your new style will appear as the last listing or thumbnail on the Styles panel.

   ► You can load other style libraries from the bottom of the Styles panel menu or from the Styles menu in the Layer Style dialog. To create a library of style presets, see page 112. The preset styles that are supplied with Photoshop are stored in Adobe Photoshop CS4/Presets/Styles.

   ► To remove a style from a layer (including reverting the layer blending mode to None and the layer Opacity to 100%), right-click/Control-click the layer and choose Clear Layer Style.

A This is the original, plain editable type.

B With the type layer selected, we clicked a style thumbnail on the Styles panel.

C The Swimming Pool layer style in the Text Effects library is applied.

Applying layer effects to type

Next, we'll show you ways to use layer effects to add depth and volume to type, to make it look three-dimensional. For good-quality print results, choose a resolution for your file of 250–300 ppi.

To create beveled type:

1. Create editable type.

2. From the **Add Layer Style** menu *fx* on the Layers panel, choose **Drop Shadow**.

3. In the Layer Style dialog, Drop Shadow is selected; choose **Drop Shadow** settings.**A** Keep the dialog open.

4. Click **Bevel and Emboss**. Choose Style: Inner Bevel and Technique: Chisel Hard, and choose Depth, Size, and Soften settings.**B**

5. Click **Inner Glow** and choose settings (**A**, next page).

6. Click OK. If desired, you can also apply a gradient to the Background, as we did (**B–D**, next page).

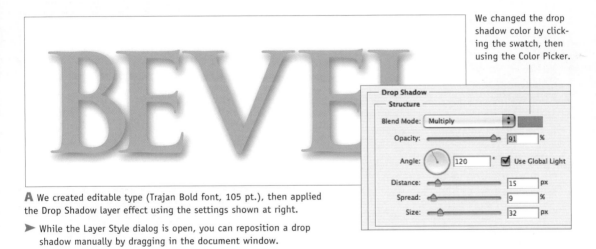

We changed the drop shadow color by clicking the swatch, then using the Color Picker.

A We created editable type (Trajan Bold font, 105 pt.), then applied the Drop Shadow layer effect using the settings shown at right.

▶ While the Layer Style dialog is open, you can reposition a drop shadow manually by dragging in the document window.

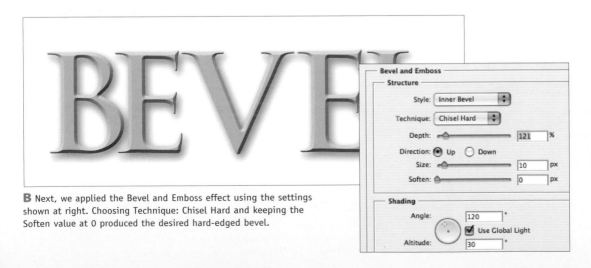

B Next, we applied the Bevel and Emboss effect using the settings shown at right. Choosing Technique: Chisel Hard and keeping the Soften value at 0 produced the desired hard-edged bevel.

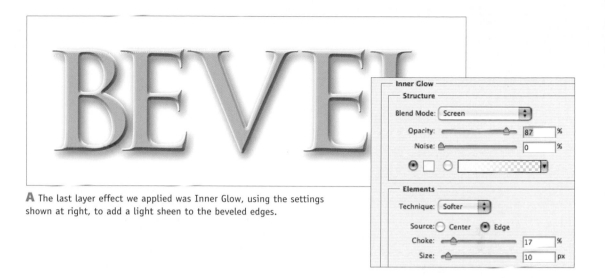

A The last layer effect we applied was Inner Glow, using the settings shown at right, to add a light sheen to the beveled edges.

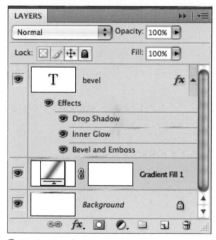

B Finally, we added a gradient above the background in coordinating colors via a Gradient Fill layer (see page 228).

C This is the Layers panel for the final image, which is shown below.

D The final image contains three layer effects, plus a Gradient Fill layer above the Background.

Now that you know how to apply layer effects, you can explore some variations. You'll need to adjust the settings for your document dimensions and resolution, the colors on the Background, and the font, font size, and type color. The type images in this chapter have a file resolution of 300 ppi.

Carving letters in stone

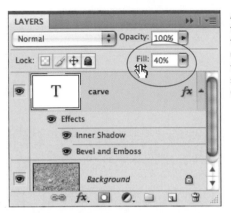

A We created editable type (Trajan Bold font, 93 pt.) above a photo of granite on the Background. To reveal some of the underlying layer inside the type, we lowered its Fill percentage on the Layers panel (this setting can also be accessed in the Blending Options area of the Layer Style dialog).

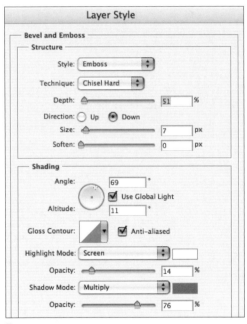

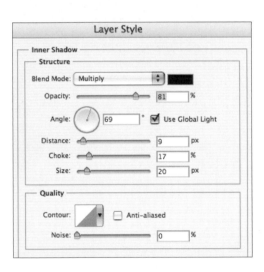

B We applied the Inner Shadow and Emboss effects. For Emboss, note the Opacity setting for Highlight Mode and the Color we chose for Shadow Mode.

C The type looks as though it's carved into the stone.

WARPING THE CARVED LETTERS

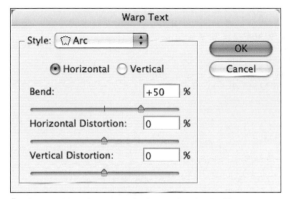

A After applying the Inner Shadow and Emboss effects, we chose Layer > Type > Warp Text and the settings shown above.

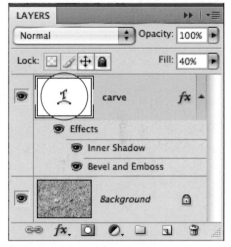

B The warp text icon appeared in the layer thumbnail.

C To reopen the Warp Text dialog at any time to edit the settings, double-click the type layer thumbnail, then click this button on the Options bar.

D This is the same image as shown on the previous page, except with the Warp Text command applied (Arc style).

Making type look like rusted metal

CREATING TYPE WITH A RUSTED METAL EDGE

A We created editable type (Bauhaus 93 Regular font, 223 pt.) above a photo of rusted metal.

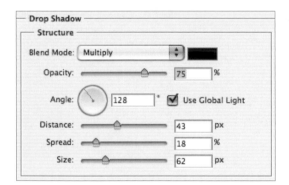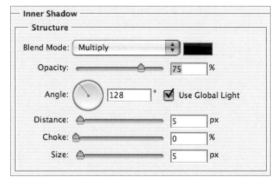

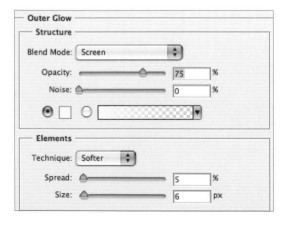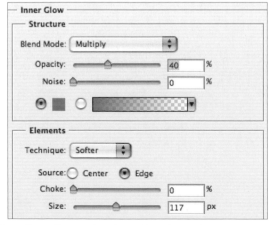

B We applied the Drop Shadow, Inner Shadow, Outer Glow, and Inner Glow effects, using the settings shown above.

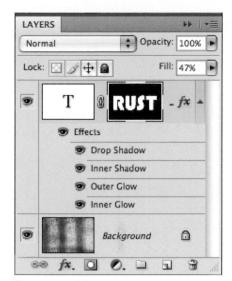

A To reveal some of the underlying layer, we lowered the Fill percentage of the type layer. The results are acceptable, but we want to make the letters look more corroded.

B To "corrode" the edges of the type, we Ctrl/ Cmd clicked the type layer thumbnail, clicked the Add Layer Mask button, then applied Filter > Brush Strokes > Spatter. This is the Layers panel for the final image, which is shown below.

C The Spatter filter added just the finishing touch we were after. (The Distort > Glass filter would also work well.)

Note: If you followed along with these steps, save your file and keep it open for the instructions on the following page.

FILLING TYPE WITH A RUSTED METAL TEXTURE

As a variation on the previous task, we'll show you how to fill the type characters with a texture by using a clipping mask, and intensify the texture by applying the Lighting Effects filter in a texture channel.

1. Save a copy of the file from the exercise on the preceding two pages, and make sure RGB Color is chosen on the Image > Mode submenu. Under the Effects bar, drag the Inner Glow listing to the Delete Layer button. 🗑

2. On the Layers panel, reset the **Fill** value to 100%.

3. Duplicate the Background (Ctrl-J/Cmd-J), then restack the duplicate layer above the type layer.

4. Click the Background. Choose a new Foreground color, then press Alt-Backspace/Option-Delete to fill the Background with the current Foreground color.

5. Alt-click/Option-click the line between the top two layers to create a clipping mask. **A**

6. Click the Background copy (topmost) layer, then choose Filter > Render > **Lighting Effects**.

7. In the Lighting Effects dialog, choose **Style: 2 O'clock Spotlight** and **Texture Channel: Blue**, then click OK.

8. To roughen the edges of the type, click the mask thumbnail on the type layer, then choose Filter > Distort > **Glass**. Adjust the sliders, set the Texture option to Frosted, then click OK.

9. Double-click the **Effects** bar for the type layer. For Drop Shadow, lower the Opacity to around 55% and increase the Size to 85 px. For Inner Shadow, set the Distance to 7 px and the Size to 16 px. For Outer Glow, set both the Spread and Size to 7. Also apply the Bevel and Emboss effect (**A–C**, next page). Click OK.

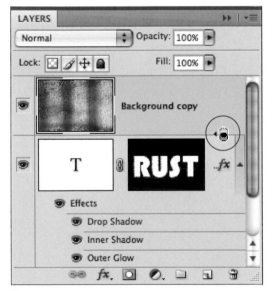

A To create a clipping mask, Alt/Option click the line between two layers.

MOVING IMAGERY WITHIN A CLIPPING MASK

Click the Background copy and then, with the Move tool, ▶⊕ drag in the document window to reposition the imagery within the type shapes.

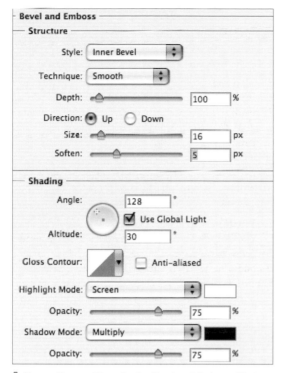

Bevel and Emboss

Structure

Style: Inner Bevel

Technique: Smooth

Depth: 100 %

Direction: ● Up ○ Down

Size: 16 px

Soften: 5 px

Shading

Angle: 128 °

☑ Use Global Light

Altitude: 30 °

Gloss Contour: ☐ Anti-aliased

Highlight Mode: Screen

Opacity: 75 %

Shadow Mode: Multiply

Opacity: 75 %

A Choose these settings for the Bevel and Emboss effect.

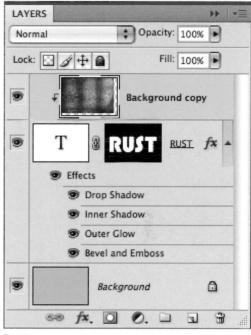

LAYERS

Normal | Opacity: 100%

Lock: ☐ ☐ ☐ ☐ | Fill: 100%

👁 Background copy

👁 T 🔗 **RUST** RUST fx ▲

👁 Effects

👁 Drop Shadow

👁 Inner Shadow

👁 Outer Glow

👁 Bevel and Emboss

👁 Background 🔒

B This is the Layers panel for the final image, which is shown below.

C In this final image, the type is filled with the rusted metal texture, and it looks more corroded than in **C** on page 281.

Embossing leather

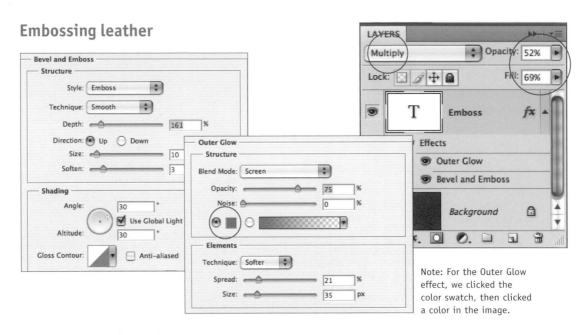

Note: For the Outer Glow effect, we clicked the color swatch, then clicked a color in the image.

A To create these embossed letters, we opened a photo of leather, and created type (Trajan Bold font, 112 pt.). We chose the Move tool, clicked the Color swatch on the Character panel, then chose a color for the type by clicking in the image (eyedropper pointer). We chose the Bevel and Emboss and Outer Glow settings shown above, chose Multiply mode for the type layer, and lowered the layer Opacity and Fill settings.

B We saved the settings shown above as a layer style (see page 275), then applied it to a type layer above a Background photo of a leather-covered book.

▶ We added the fleur-de-lis at the top of this image by using the Custom Shape tool and the Fleur-De-Lis shape preset (see pages 307–308). We copied the layer effects from the type layer to the shape layer by Alt/Option dragging the Effects bar, and then we lowered the layer Opacity to 67%. Finally, for the Outer Glow effect for the shape and type layers, we changed the color to an orangey brown.

Creating metallic type

ADDING A METALLIC SHEEN TO TYPE

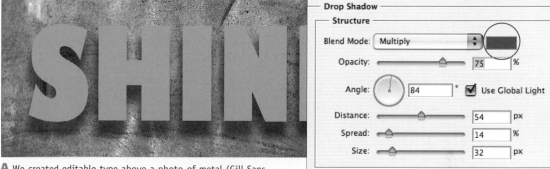

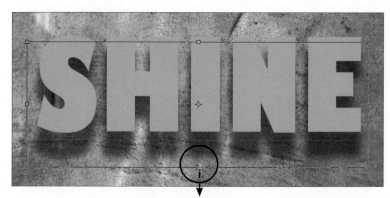

A We created editable type above a photo of metal (Gill Sans Ultra Bold Condensed font, 109 pt.), then applied the Drop Shadow effect to the type.

B For the Drop Shadow, we clicked the color swatch, then clicked a dark color in the document window.

C We transferred the shadow effect to its own layer via Layer > Layer Style > Create Layer. Next, we clicked the drop shadow layer, chose Edit > Free Transform (Ctrl-T/Cmd-T), dragged the midpoint handle downward, then pressed Enter/Return (the fully transformed shadow is shown in **C** on the next page).

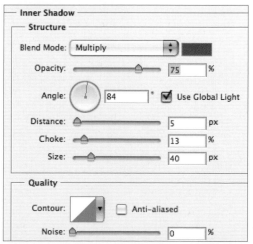

D The drop shadow appeared as a new rasterized layer above the image layer. We chose a Fill value for the shadow layer of 53%.

E Next, we clicked the type layer, then applied the Inner Shadow effect.

See also the figures on the following two pages

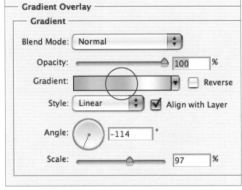

A Next, we applied the Bevel and Emboss effect (Inner Bevel style).

Note the Opacity setting we chose for Shadow Mode.

B We also applied the Gradient Overlay style (note the Angle setting). We clicked the Gradient bar to open the Gradient Editor dialog.

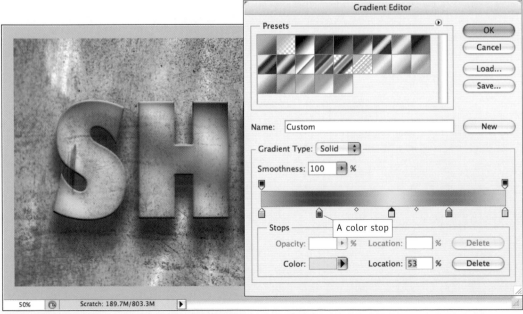

C In the Gradient Editor dialog for the Gradient Overlay style, we clicked below the gradient bar to add color stops and, for each stop, clicked a color in the document window.

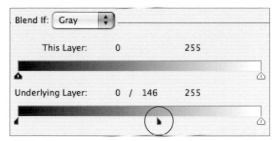

Blend If: Gray

This Layer: 0   255

Underlying Layer: 0 / 146   255

A Finally, in Blending Options, we held down Alt/Option and dragged the right part of the black Underlying Layer slider to reveal some of the image layer within the type (depending on the type color, you may not need to drag your slider as far as ours).

B The shiny metallic type is completed.

CREATING METALLIC TYPE WITH GROMMETS

1. Open an image to serve as a background, then create editable type.**A**

2. To create the metal texture, open a photograph of metal and then, with the **Rectangular Marquee** tool, select all or most of the image.

3. Choose Edit > **Define Pattern**.

4. In the **Pattern Name** dialog, enter a descriptive name, then click OK.**B**

5. Click in the image that contains the type, and click the type layer. Apply the **Drop Shadow**, **Emboss**, and **Pattern Overlay** layer effects (settings shown below).**C** For the Pattern Overlay

A Create editable type (this is the Helvetica Bold Condensed font, 196 pt.).

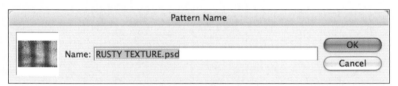

B Define an area of a background image as a pattern preset.

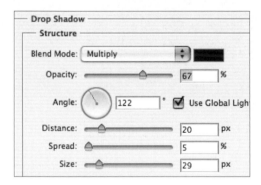

C Apply the Drop Shadow, Emboss, and Pattern Overlay effects.

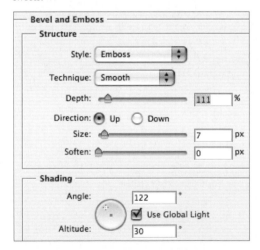

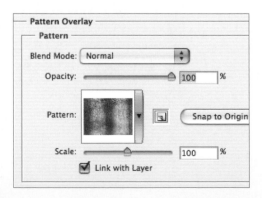

USING PATTERN OVERLAY

When you apply a pattern via the Pattern Overlay effect, you can adjust the Blend Mode, Opacity, and Scale settings for it. You can also drag the pattern in the document window while the Layer Style dialog is open.

effect, choose your custom pattern from the Pattern preset picker. Click OK.

6. To create one of the grommets, click the type layer, then create a new blank layer. With the **Elliptical Marquee** tool,◯ Shift-drag to create a small circle. Choose a Foreground color (we chose a deep russet), then press Alt-Backspace/Option-Delete to fill the selection with the current Foreground color. Keep the circle selected!

7. With the **Move** tool ⊹ (V), Alt-drag/Option-drag as many copies of the selection as you need. To copy it on the same axis, also hold down Shift. Now you can deselect.

8. Alt-drag/Option-drag the **Effects** bar from the type layer to the "Grommets" layer.

9. For the "Grommets" layer, hide the Pattern Overlay effect by clicking its visibility icon. Double-click the **Bevel and Emboss** effect, change the Style to Pillow Emboss, click the Down button, then click OK.

10. Apply the **Outer Glow** effect to the "Grommets" layer (settings shown below).**A–C**

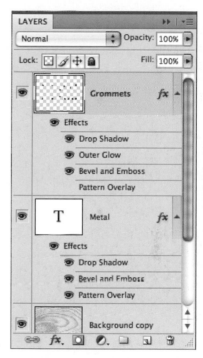

B This is the Layers panel for the final image, which is shown below.

A In addition to the effects that you copy from the type layer to the "Grommets" layer, also apply the Outer Glow effect.

C This is the final image. We happen to like the contrast that the photo of wood provides as a background, but other texture imagery would also be suitable.

Stamping a product name

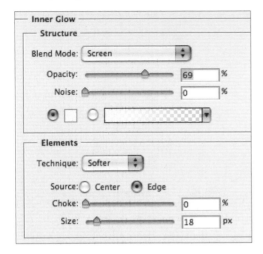

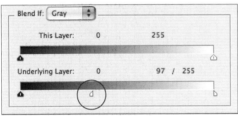

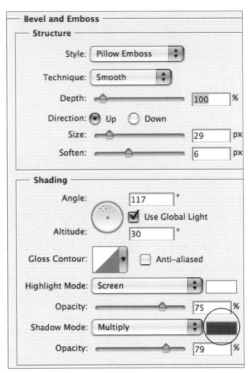

A We created editable type above an image layer (a photo of a cracker) in the Helvetica Extra Compressed font, 165 pt. To choose a color for the selected type layer, we clicked the Color swatch on the Character panel, then clicked a medium tan color in the image. Next, we applied the Inner Glow and Bevel and Emboss effects. For the Bevel and Emboss effect, we chose the Pillow Emboss style, clicked the Shadow Mode color swatch, then clicked a dark color in the image. Finally, in Blending Options, we Alt/Option dragged the left part of the white Underlying Layer slider about halfway to the left.

B The type looks as though it's been stamped into the cracker.

Making type glow

Another way to manipulate type in Photoshop is by applying filters and/or gradients. The possible variations are virtually unlimited. On this page and the next two pages are a few ideas, for inspiration.

To illuminate type with gradients and a filter:

1. Create editable type for the top word in an orange color. Copy the type layer, then hide the original (keep it for potential future edits).

2. Right-click/Control-click the layer copy and choose **Convert to Smart Object**, then choose Filter > Blur > **Gaussian Blur**. Adjust the Radius slider to blur the type,**A** then click OK.

3. With the **Horizontal Type** tool, **T** type the bottom word, then press Ctrl-Enter/Cmd-Return. Right-click/Control-click this new type layer and choose **Rasterize Type** from the context menu.

4. Choose the **Gradient** tool ▦ (G or Shift-G) and click the Linear Gradient button on the Options bar. From the Gradient preset picker menu, choose **Color Harmonies 1**, then click Append. Click the **Orange, Blue** gradient on the picker.**B**

5. Click the **Lock Transparent Pixels** button on the Layers panel, then Shift-drag a short distance from the top of the new word downward.

6. *Optional:* Click the Background, then via a Gradient Fill layer, apply a light-toned gradient.**C–D**

➤ To customize a gradient, double-click the Gradient preset picker thumbnail on the Options bar, click any gradient stop below the bar in the Gradient Editor, click the Color swatch, then click a color in the Color Picker or in the document window.

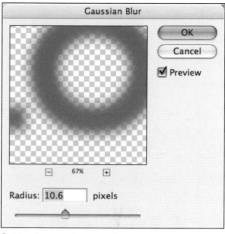

A Blur the type layer via the Gaussian Blur dialog.

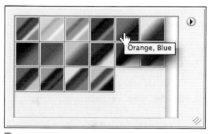

B We applied the Orange, Blue gradient preset to the type...

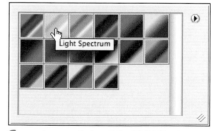

C ...and we applied and the Light Spectrum gradient to the Background.

D You can easily create variations on this idea by changing the colors in the gradients (we used the Futura Extra Bold font, 86 pt.).

Creating graffiti

To create graffiti:

1. Open a background image that contains some texture, and create a new, blank layer.

2. Choose the **Brush** tool ✒ (B or Shift-B), choose a rough-edged brush tip,**A** click the Airbrush option on the Options bar (so the letters will look spray painted), and choose a Foreground color. Scribble some letters on the new layer.

3. To create another layer of graffiti, create a new, blank layer, choose a new Foreground color, then scribble more letters.

4. To "corrode" the letters, double-click a graffiti layer and then, in the **Blend If** area of the Layer Style dialog, Alt-drag/Option-drag the black or white **Underlying Layer** slider a long or short distance, depending on which works best for the type color and background colors.**B–D** Repeat for the other graffiti layer.

5. *Optional:* To make the paint "drip," choose Filter > Liquify. In the dialog, choose the Forward Warp Tool 🖉 (W) and choose Brush Size, Density, and Pressure settings. Drag from the end of a few characters downward—multiple times if necessary—to mimic the pull of gravity (**A–B**, next page).

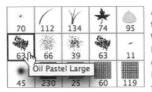

A Click a brush preset on the Brush preset picker. We chose the Oil Pastel Large preset for the white graffiti and the Watercolor Loaded Wet Flat Tip for the red graffiti.

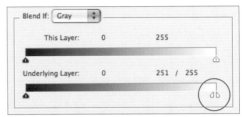

B We moved the left part of the white Underlying Layer slider slightly to the left for the red letters...

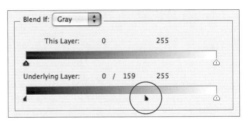

C ...and moved the right part of the black Underlying Layer slider to the right for the white letters.

D To create the graffiti in this image, we drew letters with the Brush tool, then used the Blend If sliders in the Layer Style dialog for each graffiti layer to partially reveal the underlying image layer.

MAKING DRIP MARKS

A To make the paint drips, we opened the Liquify dialog and dragged downward several times with the Forward Warp tool in a few areas.

B The final graffiti image has paint drips, and the letters look as if they've been slightly weathered by the elements.

Making type look corroded

By hiding pixels from a type layer, you can make the type look as if it's been worn away or eroded. We'll show you two different ways to do this: by using a layer mask and by using the Blend If sliders in the Layer Style dialog. Shop and compare.

To create corroded type:

Method 1

1. Open a photo of a surface texture, and create editable type in a contrasting color.**A**

2. Do either of the following:

   Choose the **Pencil** tool and a very small brush tip.

   Choose the **Brush** tool and a small rough-edged brush tip, such as one of the Spatter tips.

3. With the type layer selected, click the **Add Layer Mask** button on the Layers panel.

4. Choose an Opacity of 40–50% on the Options bar, click the layer mask thumbnail, make the Foreground color black, then draw quick scratches or scribbles in the document window.**B** To add variety, switch the tool and/or brush tip and apply more strokes.

   ➤ To undo the last stroke, either click an earlier state on the History panel or press X and paint over any unwanted strokes with white (brush Opacity of 100%).

A We created an editable type layer (Brush Script font, 109 pt.) on top of a photo of a textured wall on the Background.

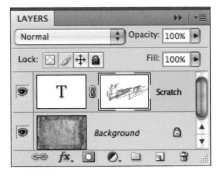

B Pencil and Brush tool strokes that we applied to the mask on the type layer are partially hiding the type and partially revealing the Background.

Method 2

1. Open a photo of a surface texture, then create editable type in a contrasting color.

2. To distress the type, you'll force dark or light colors from the image to show through the type. Double-click the type layer to open the Layer Style dialog.

3. If the type is darker than the background, in the **Blend If** area, drag the **black Underlying Layer** slider to the right until some dark (underlying) colors start to show through the type layer, **A** then Alt-drag/Option-drag the right half of the black slider farther to the right. **B** If the type is lighter than the background, do the same thing with the **white Underlying Layer** slider instead.

4. Click OK.

A In the Blend If area of the Layer Style dialog, we dragged the black Underlying Layer slider to the right. Dark colors from the texture layer now show through the type layer.

B Next, we Alt/Option dragged the Underlying Layer sliders to enable midtone colors from the underlying texture layer to show through the type layer. (If you want to let highlight areas show through, drag the white Underlying Layer slider.)

Cutting up a rasterized type layer

If you can't achieve the desired type treatment by using layer effects, filters, or masks, another option is to rasterize the type layer, then "attack" the type characters with knives (well, actually, a lasso tool)!

To create a cut paper effect:

1. Create an editable type layer, duplicate it, and right-click/Control-click the layer and choose **Rasterize Type**. Hide the editable type layer.

2. To select a portion of a type character, drag with the **Lasso** tool ρ (L or Shift-L) or click with the **Polygonal Lasso** tool. ✄ **A**

3. Choose the **Move** tool ⊹ (V), then drag the selection in the document window or press any arrow key. **B–D**

4. Repeat steps 2–3 for other characters to create a pleasing arrangement (**A**, next page).

A We created editable type (Futura Extra Bold font, 102 pt.), duplicated and hid the type layer, and rasterized the duplicate. With the Polygonal Lasso tool, we created a straight-edged selection of the stem on the letter P.

B We repositioned the selection with the Move tool.

C We used the Lasso tool to create an irregular selection of the top of the letter A...

D ...then repositioned the selection by pressing the up and right arrow keys.

A This is the final "cut paper" image after we moved more straight-edged and irregularly shaped selections of the rasterized type layer.

PUTTING SECTIONS OF RASTERIZED TYPE ON SEPARATE LAYERS

B With the Magic Wand tool (Tolerance 0, Contiguous checked), we clicked each piece of "paper" separately, then pressed Ctrl-J/Cmd-J to put it on a separate layer.

C With the sections on different layers, we were able to apply a different Color Overlay and the Drop Shadow layer effect to each one, and move each layer individually. Fun!

Transforming type to fit onto a perspective plane

In this example, we'll "adhere" type to a photo of a porcelain bowl. These steps would also work with a photo of a vehicle, package, billboard, interior wall—you get the idea.

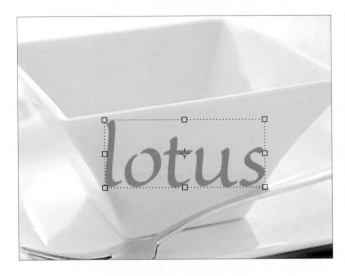

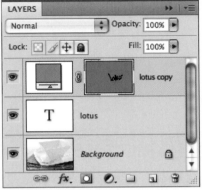

A We entered type (Sanvito Roman font, 81 pt.) above an image layer, then chose the Move tool. To apply a color to the selected type layer, we clicked the Color swatch on the Character panel, clicked a green area of the napkin in the image (not shown), then clicked OK to exit the Color Picker. Next, we duplicated the type layer, kept the duplicate layer selected, right/Control clicked the layer and chose Convert to Shape, then hid the original type layer.

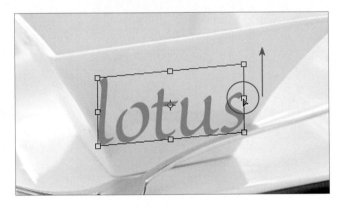

B We clicked the vector mask thumbnail, then pressed Ctrl-T/Cmd-T to display the transform box for the Free Transform command. To make the type conform to the angle of the top of the bowl, we Ctrl/Cmd dragged the middle handle on the right side upward (a skew transformation).

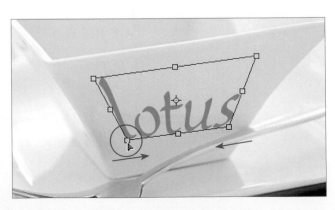

C To make the type conform even more closely to the bowl shape, we Ctrl-Alt-Shift/Cmd-Option-Shift dragged a bottom corner handle of the transform box inward (to apply perspective).

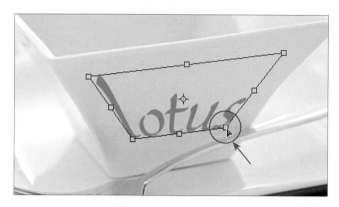

A The final transformations were to Ctrl/Cmd drag the bottom right and left corner handles diagonally inward to distort the type, aligning it with the inward slant of the bowl; we double-clicked inside the transform box to accept the transformation.

➤ To scale type horizontally, drag either of the side middle handles.

B To blend the type with the surface of the bowl, we applied the Outer Glow and Satin layer effects and adjusted the Blend If sliders to add reflections and shadows (settings shown below).

C For the Outer Glow effect, we changed the Outer Glow color to a medium dark gray (to match the bowl color) and adjusted the Opacity.

D For the Satin effect, we chose Difference mode, lowered the Opacity, changed the color to a very light gray to match the bowl, and dragged the Size slider just far enough to minimize the dark areas. The effect will be enhanced by changes to the Blend Options settings in the next step.

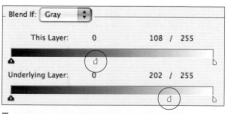

E Finally, in Blend Options, we Alt/Option dragged the white This Layer and white Underlying Layer sliders to reveal light colors and surface reflections from the image layer through the type layer.

Putting screened-back type on a bar

To create screened-back type on a bar:

1. Open a background image, then create editable type.

2. Ctrl-click/Cmd-click the type layer to create a selection from it, then hide it.

3. On the **Adjustments** panel,◉ click the **Levels** button.▦ ★ Move the gray slider to the left.**A** Note that the type shapes have become white shapes in the adjustment layer mask.

4. Choose the **Rectangular Marquee** tool,▢ then drag a narrow vertical rectangle. Create a second Levels adjustment layer, except this time move the gray slider to the right instead of to the left.**B–C** (Note: We renamed our adjustment layers.)

5. *Optional:* Apply layer effects to, or change the Opacity setting for, the topmost adjustment layer.**D**

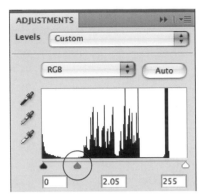

A We chose these settings for our "imagine" Levels adjustment layer...

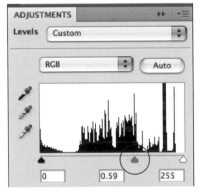

B ...and chose these Levels settings for our "bar" adjustment layer.

C The Levels adjustments are revealed only within the shapes in the layer masks.

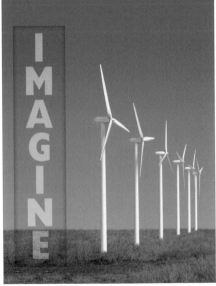

D To the topmost ("bar") adjustment layer, we applied the Inner Shadow layer effect (Distance 8, Choke 0, Size 60). We also lowered the layer Opacity to 60% and its Fill value to 15%.

6. On the Layers panel, Shift-click the two adjustment layers, then click the Link button 🔗 (Link icons appear).**A** Now you can transform (e.g., scale, move) them as a unit.**B–D**

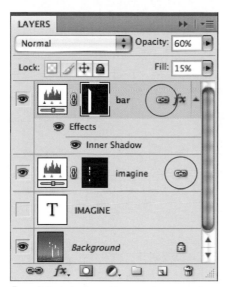

A We linked the two adjustment layers so they will transform as a unit.

B To narrow the bar and type shapes in the adjustment layer masks, we pressed Ctrl-T/Cmd-T, then dragged the center handle inward.

C Finally, to match the perspective plane of the wind turbines, we dragged the upper right handle downward with Ctrl-Alt-Shift/Cmd-Option-Shift held down, then pressed Enter/Return to accept the edit.

D Now the type and bar shapes are well integrated with the photo.

Creating skywriting

To create skywriting:

1. Open an image to be used as the background, and create a new blank layer.

2. With the **Pencil** tool, ✏ and with white chosen as the Foreground color, draw some letters. Right-click/Control-click the layer and choose **Convert to Smart Object**.

3. *Optional:* If you want to make the letters thinner, apply Filter > Other > **Maximum**.

4. Choose Filter > Blur > **Motion Blur**, choose a Distance setting of 20–30 pixels, then click OK.

5. Choose Filter > Stylize > **Wind**, click Wind and From the Right, then click OK.

6. Choose the **Gradient** tool ▥ (G or Shift-G). On the Options bar, click the Black, White preset on the Gradient preset picker, click the Linear Gradient button, set the Mode to Normal, set the Opacity to 100%, and uncheck Reverse.

7. Click the filter effects mask thumbnail (to the left of "Smart Filters"), then drag from the right edge of the document window halfway to two-thirds of the way across the type.**A–B**

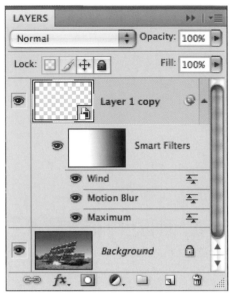

A This is the Layers panel for the final image. Note that the filter effects mask contains a gradient. (If you need to edit the settings for any filter, double-click the filter name.)

B To produce this skywriting, we drew letters with the Pencil tool (15 px diameter tip), applied three filters, and masked part of the effect by applying a gradient to the filter effects mask.

In this chapter, you'll learn how to create vector masks, which serve the same purpose as layer masks except that they can be used on any kind of layer, have sharp and precise edges, and occupy less storage space than layer masks or channels. You'll also learn how to use the shape tools to quickly create vector shapes.

Creating vector masks

Like layer masks, vector masks hide areas of a layer, except in this case the mask shape is delineated by a clean, sharp-edged path. We'll show you how to create the path to be used for a vector mask by using a type tool and a shape tool. You can reposition the path that is being used for the mask, or discard the mask, at any time. Like a layer mask, each vector mask belongs to only one layer; it displays as a thumbnail on the Layers panel.

First, we'll show you how to use a vector mask to make it appear as if type shapes are filled with imagery.

To create a vector mask from type:

1. Have an image layer available (you won't be able to use the Background), and create a type layer.**A**

2. Right-click/Control-click the type layer listing and choose **Convert to Shape**.

Continued on the following page

VECTOR MASKS & SHAPES

13

A Type is created above an image layer.

THE VECTOR ADVANTAGE

Paths and shapes are resolution independent, which means they print at the resolution of the output device, not at the file resolution. And unlike pixel layers, they remain sharp when transformed.

3. Drag the **vector mask thumbnail** to an image layer, then delete the shape layer.**A–B**

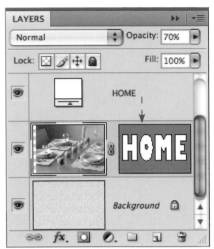

B The last step was to delete the shape layer. The image is visible only within the confines of the vector mask.

A We converted a type layer to a shape layer, then dragged its vector mask thumbnail downward to an image layer.

To create a vector mask from a custom shape:

1. On the Layers panel,◉ click an image layer that you want to add a vector mask to.

2. Do either of the following:

On the Layers panel, Ctrl-click/Cmd-click the **Add Vector Mask** button.◉ **C**

On the Masks panel,◉ click the **Add Vector Mask** button.◉ ★

3. Choose the **Custom Shape** tool ✐ (U or Shift-U). On the Options bar, click the **Paths** button ▩ and choose a shape on the **Custom Shape** preset picker.**D–E**

4. Shift-drag in the document.

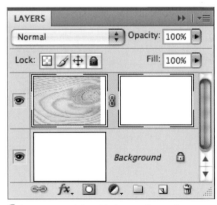

C A vector mask is added to an image layer.

D The vector mask is hiding part of the wood image layer (this shape is Arrow 17 in the Arrows library).

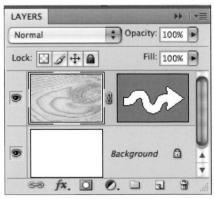

E The shape appears in the mask thumbnail.

Working with vector masks

A vector mask can be moved independently of its layer pixels at any time.

To reposition a vector mask:

1. Choose the **Path Selection** tool ▶ (A or Shift-A).

2. If the mask consists of multiple paths (such as type shapes) and you want to reposition them all, marquee them.

3. Drag the vector mask in the document window.**A** A different part of the image is now visible within the vector mask.**B**

To deactivate a vector mask:

Do either of the following:

On the Layers panel, Shift-click the **vector mask** thumbnail.

On the Layers panel, click the vector mask thumbnail, then on the Masks panel, click the **Disable/Enable Mask** button.👁 ★

A red X will appear over the thumbnail, and the entire layer will now be visible.**C**

➤ To remove the X and restore the masking effect, repeat either method above.

To copy a vector mask to another layer:

Alt-drag/Option-drag a vector mask thumbnail to another layer (not the Background). A duplicate vector mask appears.

A A vector mask is moved.

B Now a different part of the image is visible within the mask shape.

C The vector mask is deactivated, as indicated by the red X.

To reverse the visible and hidden areas in a vector mask:

1. Choose the **Path Selection** tool ↖ (A or Shift-A).

2. On the Layers panel, click the thumbnail for a vector mask that you created by following the steps on page 303 or 304. The vector outline displays in the document.

3. Click the vector mask in the document window, or if the mask contains multiple shapes (such as shapes created from type), marquee them. Its anchor points and segments will become selected.**A**

4. Click the **Subtract from Shape Area** button ⬜ on the Options bar, or press – (the minus key).**B**

   To switch the revealed and hidden areas again, click the **Add to Shape Area** button ⬜ on the Options bar, or press + (the plus key).

You can delete any vector masks that you no longer need. You won't recoup much file storage space by doing so, though.

To discard a vector mask:

Do one of the following:

On the Layers panel, click the thumbnail for the vector mask to be removed, click the **Delete Layer** button, 🗑 then click OK in the alert dialog (or Alt-click/Option-click the button to bypass the prompt).

On the Layers panel, right-click/Control-click the vector mask thumbnail and choose **Delete Vector Mask**.

On the Layers panel, click the vector mask thumbnail, then on the Masks panel, click the **Delete Mask** button.🗑 ★

A The segments and anchor points display when a vector mask is selected in the document.

B We switched the hidden and visible (masked and unmasked) areas by pressing – (the minus key).

Using the shape tools

A shape layer is a precise geometric or custom-shaped clipping path that reveals a solid-color, gradient, or pattern fill within its contour. At any time, you can reposition, transform, or reshape a shape layer; modify its fill content or change it to a different type; and apply the usual Layers panel settings to it, such as layer effects and blending modes. Every shape layer automatically has a vector mask that controls which parts of the layer are visible and hidden. The easiest way to create a shape layer is by using a ready-made shape, as in these instructions.

To create a shape layer:

1. Click a layer on the Layers panel for the new shape layer to appear above.

2. Choose a Foreground color for the shape's fill.

3. Choose one of the **shape** tools on the Tools panel (U or Shift-U).**A** Once a shape tool is selected, you can switch to a different one by clicking one of the six shape tool buttons on the Options bar.**B**

4. On the Options bar, do the following:

   Click the **Shape Layers** button.⊡

   For the Rounded Rectangle tool,◻ choose a **Radius** value; for the Polygon tool,◯ choose the desired number of **Sides;** for the Line tool,╲ choose a **Weight;** or for the Custom Shape tool,⌖ choose a shape from the **Custom Shape** preset picker.**C**

Continued on the following page

A Choose a shape tool.

PASTING SHAPES FROM ILLUSTRATOR

To paste a path from Adobe Illustrator to Photoshop as a shape layer, in Illustrator, copy a vector object. In Photoshop, choose Edit > Paste. In the Paste dialog, click Paste As: Shape Layer, then click OK. The current Foreground color will appear within the shape, and it will have a stroke of None.

Shape Layers   Paths   Fill Pixels   **B** Shape tool buttons   **C** Custom Shape preset picker (for the Custom Shape tool only)

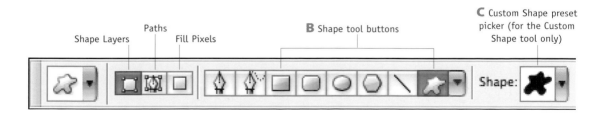

5. Drag in the document window to create the shape.**A** While dragging, you can hold down Shift to preserve the proportions of the original shape; or hold down Alt/Option to draw it from its center; or hold down Alt-Shift/Option-Shift to do both.

A new "Shape 1" layer will be listed on the Layers panel.**B** It will have an adjustment layer thumbnail that controls its fill content and a vector mask thumbnail that controls its contour and location. You can choose the usual Layers panel settings (blending mode, opacity, fill) for it.

➤ To append other libraries to the Custom Shape preset picker, choose a library name from the bottom of the Custom Shape preset picker menu, then click Append.

➤ When the Custom Shape tool 🐾 is selected, you can right-click/Control-click the image to open an "on-the-fly" shape preset picker.

➤ To choose default options for a shape tool, click the Geometry Options arrowhead 🔳🔲 on the Options bar. For example, we like to keep the Defined Proportions option on for our Custom Shape tool so we don't have to bother using the Shift key.

A We chose the Custom Shape tool, clicked the World preset on the Custom Shape preset picker (from the Symbols library), chose a Foreground color, then dragged in the document window to create this shape.

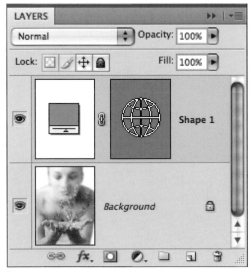

B The shape layer appeared on the Layers panel, complete with its own vector mask.

Recoloring shape layers

To recolor a shape layer:

Do either of the following:

To apply a new **solid-color** fill, double-click a shape layer thumbnail on the Layers panel;**A** or choose any shape tool (U or Shift-U), click the mask thumbnail, then click the Color swatch on the Options bar. Choose a color from the Color Picker, then click OK.

To apply a **stroke** color or a **gradient** or **pattern** fill, double-click the layer to open the Layer Style dialog, then apply the **Stroke** effect or an **Overlay** effect.

To apply a **style** to a shape layer, click the layer, then click a style on the Style preset picker (on the Options bar) or on the Styles panel.*fx* **B**

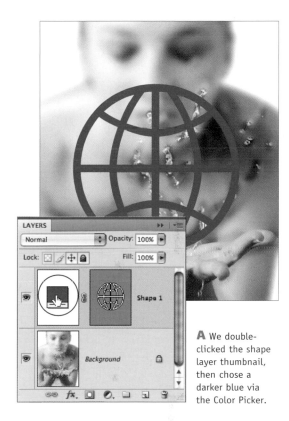

A We double-clicked the shape layer thumbnail, then chose a darker blue via the Color Picker.

DRAWING AND RESHAPING CUSTOM SHAPES

If you're adept at drawing with the Pen tool in Adobe Illustrator, you have the skills to draw custom shapes in Photoshop. Choose the Pen tool, click the Shape Layers button on the Options bar, then draw a shape. To reshape its contour, click the mask for the shape layer, then with the Direct Selection tool, manipulate the points and segments.

SAVING SHAPES

After editing the contour of a preset shape, pasting in a shape from Adobe Illustrator, or drawing a custom shape, you can save the results to the Custom Shape preset picker for future use. On the Layers panel, click the mask thumbnail for a shape layer, choose Edit > Define Custom Shape, enter a name in the Shape Name dialog, then click OK. The new shape appears at the bottom of the Custom Shape preset picker and is available for use in any document.

B With the shape layer chosen, we clicked the Blue Glass (Button) style on the Style preset picker (it's in the default style library).

Using shapes to create pixel areas

Finally, using the Fill Pixels function for any shape tool, you can create an area of pixels on an image layer in any predefined shape—without having to use a selection marquee or draw a path.

To create an area of pixels with a shape tool:

1. On the Layers panel, create a new blank layer, and keep it selected.

2. Choose a Foreground color.

3. Choose one of the **shape** tools (U or Shift-U).

4. On the Options bar, do the following:

   Click the **Fill Pixels** button.▢

   If you're using the **Custom Shape** tool,✐ choose a shape from the Custom Shape preset picker. For any other shape tool, choose tool options.

5. Drag in the document to create the shape (or hold down Shift as you drag to keep its proportions). A filled area of pixels will be created.**A**

   You can use brushes, editing tools, filters—whatever—to modify the pixels, or change the Layers panel settings (e.g., blending mode or Opacity). It's just a regular ol' layer. (Note: Click the Lock Transparent Pixels button ▢ on the Layers panel to restrict your edits to just the new shape.)

➤ To add a shape to a layer mask, first Alt-click/Option-click the Add Layer Mask button (on the Layers panel) to create a black mask. Choose a shape tool, click the Fill Pixels button on the Options bar, then with white as the Foreground color, drag or Shift-drag in the document.**B**

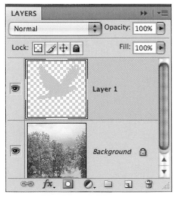

A The bird, created by using the Custom Shape tool with the Fill Pixels button clicked on the Options bar, is a standard image layer. (The Bird 2 preset shape is in the Animals library.)

B We created a Hide All layer mask. We chose white as the Foreground color and the Custom Shape tool, clicked the Fill Pixels button, then Shift-dragged in the document window.

To automate repetitive (and boring!) editing steps and tasks, you can record a sequence of commands in an action and then replay the action on one image or on a batch of images. Actions can be used to execute anything from one simple editing step, such as converting files to a different format or color mode, to a complex sequence of commands, such as running a series of adjustment commands or filters or a series of preflight steps to ready files for output. Actions can boost your productivity, relieve your life of drudgery, and standardize your edits. Photoshop ships with dozens of ready-made actions, some of which you may find useful (including those in the Default Actions set on the panel). In this chapter, you'll learn how to create, play, and edit custom actions.

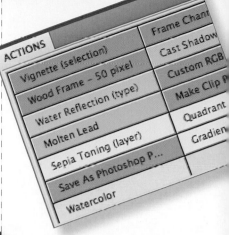

Features of the Actions panel

Using the Actions panel, you can record, store, edit, play, delete, save, and load actions. The panel has two modes: **List** (edit) **A** and **Button** (**A**, page 313). In List mode, you can expand or collapse a listing of all the commands in an action; toggle a dialog control on or off; add, exclude, delete, rerecord, or change the order of commands; or save actions and action sets to an actions file. To switch to List mode, uncheck **Button Mode** on the panel menu.

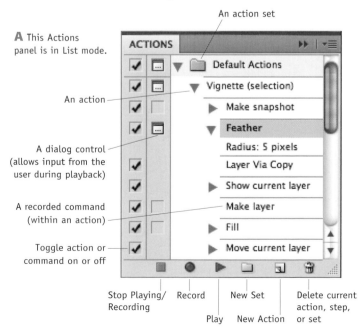

A This Actions panel is in List mode.

An action set

An action

A dialog control (allows input from the user during playback)

A recorded command (within an action)

Toggle action or command on or off

Stop Playing/ Recording

Record

Play

New Set

New Action

Delete current action, step, or set

Recording actions

To create an action, you click the Record button, execute a series of commands, then click the Stop button. Recorded commands are nested below the action name on the Actions panel. Actions, in turn, are saved in sets.

To record an action:

1. *Optional:* To create a new set for the action you're about to record, click the New Set button ⬜ at the bottom of the Actions panel, ▶ type a descriptive Name, then click OK.

2. Open a document or create a new one. Just to be on the safe side, copy the document using File > Save As.

3. Click the **New Action** button ⬒ at the bottom of the Actions panel.

4. In the New Action dialog, **A** enter a **Name** for the action, and from the **Set** menu, choose either the set you created in step 1 or a different one.

5. *Optional:* Assign a Function Key (keyboard shortcut) and/or display Color to the action. The color will display when the panel is in Button mode.

6. Click **Record**.

7. Execute the commands that you want to record, as you would normally apply them to any image. When you enter values in a dialog and click OK, your settings will be recorded (unless you click Cancel).

8. When you're done recording, click the **Stop Playing/Recording** button ⬛ on the Actions panel.

9. The new action will appear on the panel. (With the panel in List mode, click the arrowhead next to the action name to expand or collapse its list of commands.)

➤ When recording the Save As command in an action, be especially careful not to enter specific file names that could be overwritten when the action is played. We recommend that you either avoid changing the name or add a modal control to make the action pause at the Save As command (see page 319).

➤ To change the shortcut that is assigned to an action, click the action name, then choose Action Options from the panel menu to open the dialog.

SOME LIMITATIONS OF ACTIONS

➤ Some edits are not recordable, such as the following: specific strokes made by tools that use a brush (such as the Brush, Pencil, Healing Brush, Clone Stamp, Blur, and Dodge tools); some menu commands; and some Options bar and panel fields, menus, and sliders. However, you can record the selection of a specific tool, then insert a Stop into the action that includes a message for the user to choose specific settings for the tool and directions on how the tool is to be used (see page 317).

➤ An action can't include conditional logic, meaning you can't program it to execute one command if a specific situation exists and another command when it doesn't.

RULER UNITS MATTER FOR ACTIONS

Position-related operations (such as using a selection tool or the Gradient, Magic Wand, or Path tool) are recorded based on the current ruler units. The units can be actual (e.g., inches or picas) or relative (a percentage). An action that is recorded when the default measurement unit is actual can be played back on a file of the same size or smaller relative to the one in which it was recorded, provided the document contains enough canvas area for the commands in the action to be executed. An action recorded when a relative unit is chosen will work in any other relative space and on a file of any dimensions. To change the units, go to Edit/ Photoshop > Preferences > Units & Rulers and then, from the Units: Rulers menu, choose either a specific unit or Percent.

A Use the New Action dialog to assign a name and set to your action, as well as an optional function key or color, and to begin recording.

Playing actions

Actions can be triggered in various ways: via the Play button on the Actions panel; via the keyboard shortcut that has been assigned to it; by dragging a file or folder full of files onto a droplet icon (a mini-application that was created from the action); or by using the Batch command. We'll explain the Play button and shortcut methods first.

To play an action on one image:

1. Open an image.

2. *Optional:* Create a snapshot of your document for the History panel. This will give you the option to restore it quickly to its preaction state.

3. Do one of the following:

   If the Actions panel is in **List** mode, click an action name, then click the **Play** button.

   If the panel is in **Button** mode, 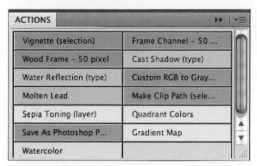 click the button for the action to be played.

   Execute the keyboard **shortcut**, if one has been assigned to the desired action.

▶ To play an action starting from a specific command in the action, put the panel in List mode, click the command name, then click the Play button. Or to play just one command in an action, click the command name, then Ctrl-click/Cmd-click the Play button; or simply Ctrl-double-click/Cmd double click the command.

▶ When creating layers or alpha channels in a document, assign them descriptive, nongeneric names to prevent the wrong edits from occurring when the action is played.

▶ To load other action sets onto the panel, see page 322.

To exclude a command from playback:

1. Put the Actions panel in List mode (actions can't be edited in Button mode).

2. Expand the list for the action to be edited.

3. Click in the leftmost column for the command to be **excluded** from playback, to remove the check mark.

   Beware! If you click the check mark for an entire action or action set, as an alert will tell you, any individual commands that you've painstakingly checked will become unchecked.

▶ To reinclude a command at any time, click in the same spot again to restore the check mark.

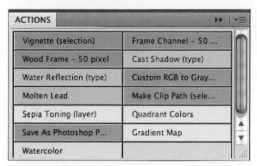

A When the Actions panel is in Button mode, a brightly colored button displays for each action, as well as its shortcut, if one was assigned.

CHOOSING PLAYBACK OPTIONS

To choose an option for playback, put the Actions panel in List mode, choose Playback Options from the panel menu, then click one of the following options in the dialog:

▶ Accelerated: The fastest playback option.

▶ Step by Step: The list for the action expands on the panel, and the name of each command or edit becomes highlighted as it's executed.

▶ Pause for [ ] seconds: This option works like Step by Step, except that a user-defined pause occurs after each step.

B The Unsharp Mask step within this action is unchecked, so it's currently excluded from playback.

The ability to play an action on multiple files is a super timesaver. You can do this quickly by dragging a folder of files onto a droplet (see "To create a droplet for an action" on page 316). Or if you need to choose a destination, a file-naming scheme, or other options for the files to be processed by the action, use the Batch command instead, as described below.

Note: If you choose Folder as the Destination in step 6, further options will become available for naming the resulting files so they don't replace the original ones.

To play an action on a batch of images:

1. In Bridge, put all the files to be processed into one folder and display the folder contents (or to limit which images are to be processed, select their thumbnails), then choose Tools > Photoshop > **Batch**.

2. The Batch dialog opens (**A**, next page). Under Play, choose a set from the **Set** menu and an action from the **Action** menu.

3. For the **Source**, make sure **Bridge** is chosen.

4. *Optional:* If the action contains an Open command, you can check Override Action "Open" Commands to have the batch command ignore the specific file name in the Open step.

5. Check **Suppress File Open Options Dialogs** and/or **Suppress Color Profile Warnings** to have the command bypass any dialogs or alerts that appear onscreen as source files are opened.

6. From the **Destination** menu, choose one of the following options:

   None to keep all the files open after processing.

   Save and Close to have the files save after processing and then close.

   Folder to have the files save to a new folder and to access the File Naming options. Click Browse/Choose, then choose a destination folder.

   Optional: If the action contains a Save As command, you can check Override Action "Save As"

   Commands to have the batch command save the file while ignoring the name and location specified in that command.

7. If you chose Folder as the Destination, you can do the following:

   Choose options from the menus in the **File Naming** area, or type the text to be included in the name. Make sure the **Example** displays the desired naming convention.

   If you chose a naming option that uses sequential (serial) numbers, enter a 1- to 4-digit starting number in the **Starting Serial #** field.

   Check any or all of the file name **Compatibility** options for the platforms you need the files to be compatible with.

8. *Optional:* By default, Photoshop will end the Batch process if it encounters an error. To have it play the whole action and keep track of error messages in a text file instead, from the Errors menu, choose Log Errors to File, then click Save As. In the Save dialog, type a name for the text file, choose a location for it, then click Save. If errors are encountered, you will be alerted via a prompt that errors were logged into the designated error log file.

9. Click OK to start the batch processing.

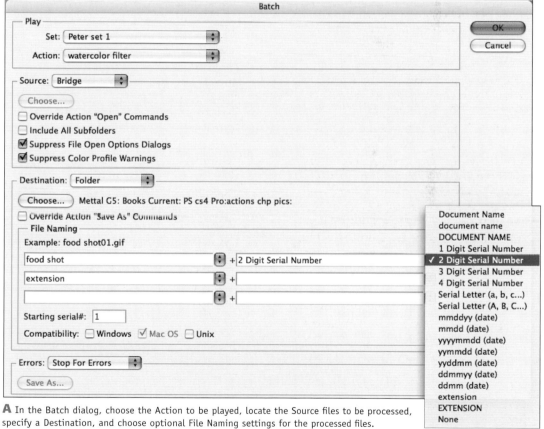

A In the Batch dialog, choose the Action to be played, locate the Source files to be processed, specify a Destination, and choose optional File Naming settings for the processed files.

An action can be turned into its own little mini-application, called a droplet, **A** that sits out on the Desktop or in a folder, waiting to be triggered. If you drag a file or a folder full of files onto a droplet icon, Photoshop will launch (if it's not yet running), and the action that the droplet represents will be played on those files. Droplets can be shared with other Photoshop users.

To create a droplet for an action:

1. Choose File > Automate > **Create Droplet**. The Create Droplet dialog opens. **B**

2. Click **Choose**. A Save dialog opens. Enter a name in the Save As field, choose a convenient location for the droplet, then click Save.

3. Back in the Create Droplet dialog, choose an action set from the **Set** menu, then choose the **Action** to be saved as a droplet.

4. Check any **Play** options to be included in the droplet, and choose **Destination** and **Errors**

options for the processed files (see steps 3–8 on page 314).

5. Click OK. The droplet will appear in the designated location. To use the droplet, drag a file or a folder full of files onto it, and the action will begin.

A This is a droplet icon for an action.

> **MAKING DROPLETS COMPATIBLE**
> ► To make a droplet that was created in Windows usable in Macintosh, drag it onto the Macintosh Photoshop CS4 application icon.
> ► To make a droplet that was created in Macintosh usable in Windows, save it with an ".exe" extension.

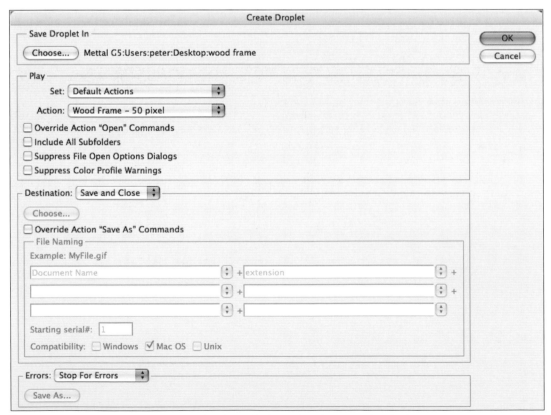

B Use the Create Droplet dialog to choose a location and other options for your action droplet.

Editing actions

You can insert a variety of special commands into your actions. For example, if you insert a Stop, the playback will pause at that point in the action to allow the user to perform a manual or nonrecordable edit, such as the use of the Brush or Clone Stamp tool. When the manual edit is completed, the user clicks the Play button again to resume the playback. A Stop can also include a text message for the user, which displays in an alert dialog.

To insert a Stop in an action:

1. Do either of the following:

   As you're creating an action, pause at the point at which you want the Stop to appear.

   To add a Stop to an existing action, on the Actions panel, click the command name after which you want it to appear.

2. Choose **Insert Stop** from the Actions panel menu. The Record Stop dialog opens.

3. Type an instructional or alert message.**A** We recommend spelling out in the message that after performing the desired edit, the user should click the Play button to resume the playback.

4. *Optional:* Check Allow Continue to include a Continue button in the alert dialog.**B** This will give the user an easy way to continue the action playback without performing the requested manual edits. Without this option, the user will still be able to resume the playback by clicking Stop when the alert dialog appears, then clicking the Play button on the panel.

5. Click OK. The Stop listing will appear below the command you paused after or clicked in step 1.**C**

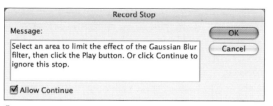

A In the Record Stop dialog, type an instructional message for the user. The Allow Continue option creates a Continue button that the person replaying the action can click to quickly resume the playback.

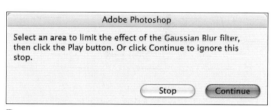

B The Continue button lets the user continue the playback of the action without performing the requested manual tasks.

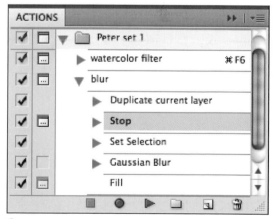

C The Stop command appears as a listing within the action.

If you forgot to include a particular command or editing step in an action, or you want to improve an action by adding a command, here's your second chance.

To add a command or edit to an action:

1. On the Actions panel, expand the list for the action the edit is to be added to, then click the command name after which you want the new one to appear.

2. Click the **Record** button.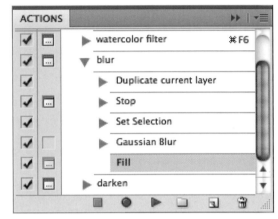

3. Execute the desired command(s). Note: You can't add a command that's available only under certain conditions (e.g., the Feather command requires an active selection) unless the creation of those conditions is also included as steps in the action.

4. Click the **Stop Playing/Recording** button ▪ to stop recording.

➤ To expand or collapse all the steps that are nested within an action, Alt-click/Option-click the arrowhead next to the action name.

Some dialog features aren't recordable, but there's a next best option. Via the Insert Menu Item command, you can force the dialog for a particular menu command to open and pause onscreen during playback, allowing the user to choose custom settings.

To insert a menu item in an action:

1. Expand the listing for an existing action, then click the command after which you want the new menu command to be inserted.

2. From the Actions panel menu, choose **Insert Menu Item**. The Insert Menu Item dialog opens.

3. From the Photoshop menu bar, choose the command to be added to the action. The command name will appear in the Insert Menu Item dialog.**A**

4. Click OK.**B** The ability to display a dialog and allow user input may be disabled for inserted menu commands. To allow a particular dialog in an action to pause onscreen, use a modal control, as discussed on the next page.

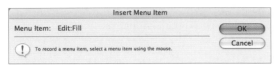

A When we chose the Fill command from the Edit menu, the command name magically appeared in the Insert Menu Item dialog.

B The menu item that we inserted appears as a listing on the Actions panel.

COPYING COMMANDS WITHIN OR BETWEEN ACTIONS

➤ To copy a command from one action to another, expand the listings for both, then Alt-drag/Option-drag the command to be copied from one list to the other (if you don't hold down Alt/Option, you'll cut the command from the original action). Note: Be careful when copying a Save command, as it may contain information that pertains only to the original action.

➤ To duplicate a command within an action, either drag the command over the New Action button 🔲 or Alt-drag/Option-drag it to the desired location.

A modal control, or pause, in an action, can be enabled for any command that uses a dialog, any tool that requires pressing Enter/Return in order to be executed, or for other edits. If users encounter a modal control for a dialog upon playing an action, they can either enter different settings in the dialog or simply click OK to proceed with the settings that were recorded originally.

To add a modal control for a command in an action:

1. With the Actions panel in List mode, expand the list for the action in question.

2. For any individual listing within the action, click in the second column; the **dialog** icon ⬚ appears.**A**

   When the action is played, it will pause when it encounters a command bearing a modal control. If the command involves using a dialog, the dialog will appear onscreen. The user can then enter new values, accept the existing values by clicking OK, or click Cancel. When the user exits the dialog, the playback resumes.

➤ To remove a modal control, click the dialog icon.

To enable or disable all modal controls for an action:

Click in the dialog column for an action name to turn all the modal controls in that action on or off. If the dialog icon for the action is red, it means that some modal controls in the action are off and some are on; click the red icon, then click OK in the alert dialog.

A Via the dialog icon, you give the user an opportunity to enter different settings in a dialog while playing the action.

If you want to experiment with an action or add to it without messing around with the original, work on a duplicate.

To duplicate an action:

Do either of the following:

Click an action, then choose **Duplicate** from the Actions panel menu.

Drag an action over the **New Action** button ⬒ on the Actions panel.

➤ To rename an action, double-click the name.

To rerecord an action using different dialog settings:

1. Click the name of the action that contains the settings to be edited.

2. From the Actions panel menu, choose **Record Again**.

3. The action will play back, stopping at each command that uses a dialog. Enter new settings, if desired, then click OK. Each time you close a dialog, the rerecording continues.

4. To stop the rerecording, either click **Cancel** in a dialog or click the **Stop Playing/Recording** button ■ on the panel.

To change the settings for a command in an action:

1. Expand the listing for an action on the Actions panel, then double-click a command that uses a dialog (or alert dialog) that you want to change the settings for.

2. Enter new settings.

3. Click OK. (Click Cancel to have your revisions disregarded.)

BE RESPONSIBLE FOR YOUR ACTIONS

Before editing an action, we recommend that you duplicate it first and edit the duplicate (see the instructions at left). Barring that, you should at least save the set to a file beforehand, so you'll be able to reaccess it at any time (see page 322).

This may seem obvious, but remember that if you change the order of edits in an action, the revised action may produce different results from the original.

To change the order of edits in an action:

1. On the Actions panel, expand the list for an action, if it's not already expanded.

2. Drag a command upward or downward on the list. Easy.

Deleting commands and actions

You can delete a whole action, or merely delete individual commands from it.

To delete an action or delete a command from an action:

1. *Optional:* To save the current actions on the panel as a set for future use, before deleting any actions or commands, follow the instructions on the next page.

2. Do either of the following:

   Click the **action** to be deleted.

   Click the individual **command** to be deleted. Ctrl-click/Cmd-click to highlight additional commands, if desired.

3. Click the **Delete** button 🗑 on the Actions panel, then click OK (or to bypass the prompt, Alt-click/Option-click the Delete button).

Saving and loading action sets

Each time you create a new action, you need to choose a set for it to be stored in. You can save a set of actions to a separate file for use on another computer or as a backup for safekeeping.

To save an action set to a file:

1. Click the action set to be saved.

2. Choose **Save Actions** from the panel menu.

3. In the **Save** dialog, type a name for the action set file, keep the default location (see the sidebar at right), then click **Save**. The new file will be regarded as one set, regardless of how many actions it contains.

4. When you relaunch Photoshop, your newly saved set will appear on the Actions panel menu. Note: If you edit any actions in the set, save the set again by following the steps above.

Photoshop includes many useful actions that don't appear on the panel by default. You can load them by following the instructions below, plus you can also load any user-created set.

To load a set onto the Actions panel:

1. Click the **set** name that you want the loaded set to appear below.

2. From the Actions panel menu, choose a predefined **action set** (Commands, Frames, Image Effects, Production, Text Effects, Textures, or Video Actions), or choose a user-saved set, if there are any, from the bottom of the menu.

If you prefer to have only one set on the Actions panel at a time, use the Replace Actions command instead of the Load Actions command.

To replace the current action set with a different set:

1. Choose **Replace Actions** from the Actions panel menu.

2. Locate and click the action set file to replace the existing sets, then click **Load**.

To load the default action set:

Choose **Reset Actions** from the panel menu, then click Append in the alert dialog to add the default set to the existing sets on the panel, or click OK to replace the existing sets with the default one.

WHERE ARE ACTIONS STORED?

Action sets are stored in the following locations:

► The predefined action sets are stored in Adobe Photoshop CS4 > Presets > Actions.

► In Windows, user-saved action sets are stored in C: Documents And Settings\user name\Application Data\Adobe\Adobe Photoshop CS4\Presets\Actions.

► In the Mac OS, user-saved action sets are stored in Users/user name/Library/Application Support/Adobe/Adobe Photoshop CS4/Presets/Actions.

Whether you're planning to print your document directly from Photoshop to a desktop printer, place it in a page layout application for commercial printing, or import it into a Web page layout application for display online, Photoshop provides a variety of output options.

To obtain a quality color print from an inkjet printer that closely matches your onscreen image, you'll need to follow up on the color management workflow that you began in Chapter 1 by selecting the proper printer profile. With that in place, you'll be ready to choose options for your printer and send your document to print.

If you're planning to export your file to a page layout application that can read Photoshop PSD files, see page 334. If, on the other hand, your target application doesn't read Photoshop PSD files, find out from your client or output service provider which format (and settings) will work for your particular output scenario, then follow the instructions in this chapter to save the file in the Photoshop PDF, Photoshop EPS, or TIFF format.

By using the Web Gallery controls (in the Output workspace) in Bridge, you can create a gallery for displaying your photos on a website. Not only does it give you many options for creating and customizing a gallery, but it also has an optional feature that will upload the gallery to a Web server.*

With so many print and output options available in Photoshop, your files can be prepped for use in a wide variety of media. In fact, multiple versions of the same file can be saved in various sizes and formats for different purposes.

Instructions for optimizing files in the GIF and JPEG formats are included in our Photoshop CS4, volume 1: Visual QuickStart Guide.

OUTPUT

15

IN THIS CHAPTER

Preparing a file for print output

By now, your "master" Photoshop document may contain multiple image, adjustment, shape, or Smart Object layers, and possibly also a few masks. Before reaching for the Print command, you need to prepare the file for printing (or, rather, prepare a copy of the file) by flattening layers, changing the bit depth, possibly changing the dimensions, and applying output sharpening.

To prepare an RGB file for printing:

1. Open a high-resolution RGB file that you intend to print. Choose File > **Save As** (Ctrl-Shift-S/ Cmd-Shift-S). Choose a location in which to save the new file, and enter a different name in the File Name/Save As field.

   Leave any options in the Save area that are already checked as is. In the Color area, check **ICC Profile/Embed Color Profile** [profile name] to preserve the profile in the new file. Click Save.

2. If the Photoshop Format Options alert displays, uncheck Maximize Compatibility, then click OK.

3. The new file will appear in the document window. You need to flatten the layers to prepare the file for sharpening. Right-click/Controlclick a layer and choose **Flatten Image**, and click OK in any alert dialogs.

4. On the Image > **Mode** submenu, make sure 8 Bits/Channel is checked.

5. To make sure the image has the proper dimensions for the chosen paper size, choose Image > **Image Size** (Ctrl-Alt-I/Cmd-Option-I), and note the Width and Height under Document Size.**A** If that size will fit on the paper size, you're all set; click Cancel.

   If you need to modify the dimensions, check Resample Image to prevent the Resolution value from changing (it should already be set to the necessary high resolution for your printer). Change just the **Width** or the **Height** value to fit the paper size. From the menu at the bottom, choose **Bicubic Smoother (Best for Enlargement)** if you enlarged the dimensions, or **Bicubic Sharper (Best for Reduction)** if you reduced the dimensions, then click OK.

6. Apply output sharpening by following the instructions on the next page.

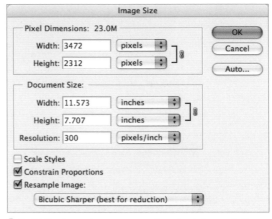

A To fit the image to your paper size, check Resample Image in the Image Size dialog, change the Width or Height, then choose an interpolation method from the menu at the bottom.

On pages 56–58, we showed you how to apply capture sharpening in Camera Raw, and in Chapter 9, we showed you how to apply sharpening in Photoshop. Before printing your file, you should apply a last round of sharpening to help compensate for potential "softening" from dot gain (the slight spreading of printing inks on paper).

To apply output sharpening:

1. Keep the high-res RGB file that you prepared for printing open onscreen (see the previous page).

2. Press Ctrl-J/Cmd-J to duplicate the Background.

3. Double-click next to the duplicate layer name to open the Layer Style dialog.

4. You'll use the **Blend If** sliders **A** to hide the highlight and shadow pixels on the duplicate layer in order to prevent any sharpening from affecting those areas (this technique was also used on pages 214–215):

   Move the **black Underlying Layer** slider to 10, then Alt-drag/Option-drag the right part of that slider to 20.

   Move the **white Underlying Layer** slider to 245, then Alt-drag/Option-drag the left part of that slider to 235.

   Click OK.

5. Next, you'll set the zoom level to help you judge the sharpening. Click the status bar at the bottom of the document window and note the pixel dimensions of your file. **B** ★ If it's 2000 x 3000 pixels (6 megapixels) or smaller, zoom to 100%; if it's 2400 x 3600 pixels (8 megapixels) or larger, zoom to 50%.

6. Choose Filter > Sharpen > **Unsharp Mask**. In the Unsharp Mask dialog, **C** check Preview, then set the **Amount** value to around 200, the **Radius** to between 0.7 and 1.0, and the **Threshold** to 3 or 4. Don't worry if the image now looks too sharp. This final sharpening should be judged from the print output, not from how the image looks onscreen. Click OK.

7. To limit the sharpening to just tonal values, **D** on the Layers panel, choose Luminosity as the blending mode for the duplicate layer; also lower the layer Opacity to 80%.

8. Save your file, then print it (see the next section). If the image looks too sharp on the printout, lower the Opacity of the duplicate layer to lessen the sharpening effect, then print it again.

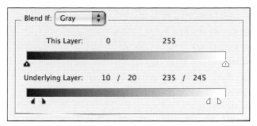

A In the Layer Style dialog, set the Blend If sliders to the positions shown above.

B Click the status bar to view the file's pixel dimensions (Width and Height).

C In the Unsharp Mask dialog, choose values similar to those shown above.

D On the Layers panel, choose Luminosity as the blending mode, and lower the Opacity.

Printing from Photoshop

Before printing a document on any type of device, via the Properties/Page Setup dialog, you need to tell Photoshop which printer model and paper size you're going to use. The available options will vary depending on your printer driver and operating system.

In this section, we'll focus on desktop inkjet color printing, to produce either initial test prints before a commercial print run or photo prints as final output.

To choose a paper size for inkjet printing:

1. Choose File > **Print** (Ctrl-P/Cmd-P). The Print dialog opens.

2. From the **Printer** menu, choose the printer you're planning to use.

3. Click **Page Setup** to open the [printer name] Properties dialog in Windows **A** or the Page Setup dialog in the Mac OS. **B**

4. In Windows, from the **Source** menu, choose the tray that holds the media you want to print on, and from the **Type** menu, choose the specific kind of media to be used (the menu names may differ, depending on your printer model).

   In the Mac OS, from the **Format For** menu, choose your inkjet printer once again.

5. From the **Size** or **Paper Size** menu, choose a paper size for printing. If your device can print borderless pictures, choose one of the sizes that is listed as "(borderless)."

   Leave the Scale value at 100% (because you already adjusted the image size on page 324).

6. Click OK. To choose settings for your printer, follow the instructions that begin on the next page.

A This is the Properties dialog (for an Epson printer) in Windows.

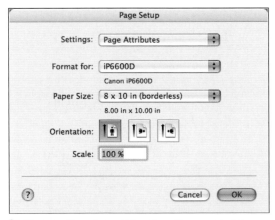

B This is the Page Setup dialog (for a Canon printer) in the Mac OS.

In these instructions, you'll choose settings for your printer via the Print dialog in Photoshop, incorporating color management as you do so. In addition to showing you a preview of the image on your chosen paper size, this dialog lets you choose print size and color management settings, and also lets you control the position of the image on the paper.

To choose settings for an inkjet printer:

1. If you completed the preceding task, the Print dialog is still open. If not, choose File > **Print** (Ctrl-P/Cmd-P). The white area in the dialog preview represents your chosen paper.**A**

2. Make sure the correct output device is listed on the **Printer** menu, and click a portrait or landscape orientation button.

3. If you haven't chosen page settings yet, follow steps 3–6 on the preceding page.

4. Check **Center Image** to position the image in the center of the paper. Or to reposition the image on the paper, uncheck Center Image and enter new Top and Left values using the scrubby sliders (note the preview).

KEEP YOUR FILE IN RGB COLOR MODE

When printing to a desktop inkjet printer, keep the image in RGB Color mode. Although these devices use six or more ink colors, their drivers are designed to receive RGB data, and they perform the conversion to printing ink colors internally.

---

5. *Optional:* To scale the print output slightly (not the actual saved image), do one of the following:

   Check **Scale to Fit Media** to have the image fit automatically to the paper size you chose in Properties/Page Setup.

   Change the **Scale** percentage or enter a specific **Height** or **Width** value (choose a unit from the Units menu). These three values are interdependent; changing one causes the other two to change.

Continued on the following page

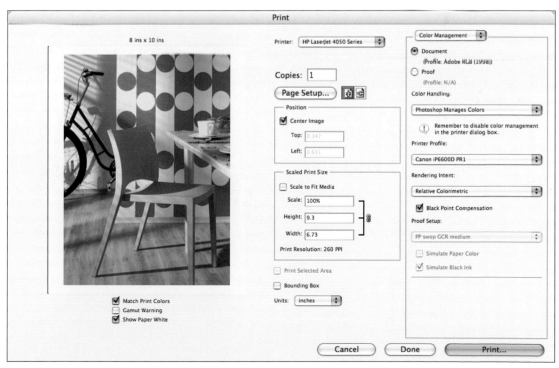

A In this Print dialog, the Color Management panel is displayed.

Check **Bounding Box** to display the image boundary in the preview, then drag a handle or the side of the box to scale the print slightly.

Note: Use the scaling features to scale the print by a small amount (i.e., fractions of an inch or a few percentage points). To scale more than that, cancel out of the dialog and use Image > Image Size to scale your image (see page 89).

6. From the menu in the top right corner of the dialog, choose **Color Management** (**A**, next page). Here, you will tell Photoshop to use the profile for your specific printer and paper.

7. Click **Document** to use the color profile that's embedded in the image, which will be Adobe RGB (1998) if you're continuing with the color management workflow that we began in Chapter 1.

8. From the **Color Handling** menu, choose **Photoshop Manages Colors** to let Photoshop handle the color conversion. Assuming you downloaded and installed a profile for your specific printer, ink, and paper (see the instructions on page 8), this option will ensure optimal color management.

9. Next, from the **Printer Profile** menu, choose the printer, ink, and paper profile that you downloaded and installed.

10. From the **Rendering Intent** menu, choose the same intent that you used when you created the soft-proof setting for your inkjet printer, which is likely to be either Perceptual or Relative Colorimetric (see the sidebar on page 10).

   ➤ You could run one test print for the Perceptual intent and one for the Relative Colorimetric intent, and see which one produces better results.

11. Check **Black Point Compensation**. This option preserves the darkest blacks and shadow details by mapping the full color range of the document profile to the full range of the printer profile, and is recommended for printing RGB images.

12. Below the preview, check **Match Print Colors** to display a color-managed soft proof of the image in the preview, based on the chosen printer and printer profile settings; uncheck **Gamut Warning**; and check **Show Paper White** to set any white in the preview to the color of the paper, also based on the current print profile. ★

13. Click **Print** to access the systemwide Print dialog, then carefully follow the steps on page 330 for Windows or 331 for the Mac OS to turn off color management for your printer before sending the file to print.

   ➤ Click Done in the Print dialog if you want to preserve most (but not all) of your settings and close the dialog.

   ➤ For technical information and documentation on specific printer models, see Photoshop Help.

   ➤ To print a 16-bits-per-channel file from the Mac OS (to a printer that can print such files), choose Output from the menu in the upper right corner of the Print dialog, and under Functions, check Send 16-Bit Data. The result will be a print with finer details. ★

OTHER COLOR HANDLING CHOICES

Other options on the Color Handling menu in the Color Management pane of the Print dialog are as follows:

➤ Printer Manages Colors sends all of the file's color information to the printer along with the document profile; the printer, not Photoshop, manages the color conversion. This isn't a good choice if you use either custom profiles or paper from a company other than the printer manufacturer, because (depending on the features and quality of the printer driver) the printer may not be aware of your custom choices. If you do use this option, be sure to enable color management options in the printer driver for the chosen printer.

➤ No Color Management prevents color values from being converted by Photoshop or the printer. Choose this option if you're planning to print a color target from which a color reading device will scan and generate a custom printer and paper profile. (We don't mean to be cryptic, but to explain color targets fully would take a whole chapter in itself…)

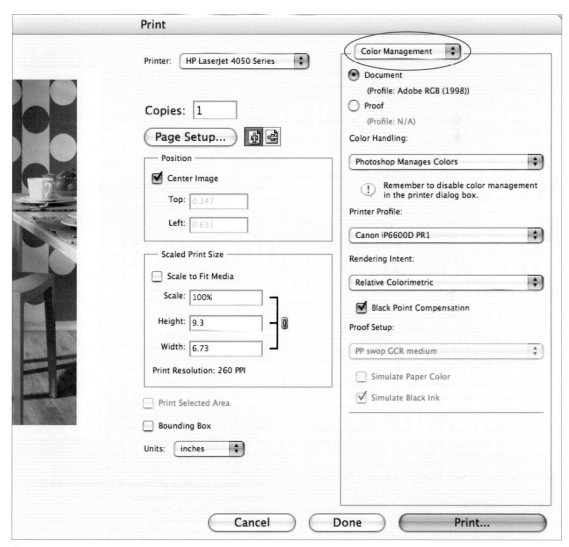

A To optimize the color accuracy of your printout, choose Color Management settings in the Print dialog in Photoshop.

The last step before outputting your file from an inkjet printer is to turn off color management for that device to allow Photoshop to manage the color conversion.

In Windows, the dialog that contains color management settings for printing is part of the printer driver software, not part of the system software. Therefore, the names and locations of the controls will vary depending on the manufacturer. In these instructions, printer color management will be turned off for an Epson printer driver. If you have a different printer model, research how to access print quality and color management settings for it, and use our steps as general guidelines.

To turn off color management for your printer in Windows, and print the file:

1. Open the File > **Print** dialog in Photoshop, then click **Print** to get to the Print dialog for your system.

2. In the **Select Printer** area of the **General** tab, click the name of your inkjet printer.

3. Click **Preferences A** to open the **Printing Preferences** dialog for your printer, which is identical to the Properties dialog that you used to specify the size and media type.

4. On the **Main** tab of the Printing Preferences dialog, click **Advanced.B** A different set of options will appear, including controls for color management.

5. In the **Color Management** area, click **ICM C** to switch color management from the Epson driver to the color management system that's built into Windows XP.

6. In the **ICC/ICM Profile** area, click **Off (No Color Adjustment)** to turn off color management for the printer (**A**, next page).

7. Click **OK** to close the Printing Preferences dialog and return to the Print dialog. Now you're ready to click **Print**. Phew!

➤ When you need to enable printer-based color management in Windows, follow steps 1–7 above, except in step 6, click Applied by Printer Software.

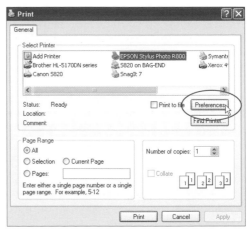

A In the Print dialog in Windows (here, for an Epson printer), click Preferences to open the next dialog.

B On the Main tab of the Printing Preferences dialog for an Epson printer, click Advanced.

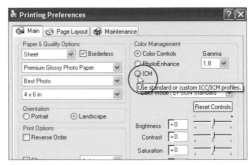

C These Color Management options display when you click the Advanced button.

In the Mac OS, the dialog that contains color management settings for the printer builds its list of options from both the system and the printer driver. Therefore, option names in the dialog will vary depending on the printer manufacturer. In these instructions, printer color management will be turned off for a Canon or Epson printer driver. If your printer is a different model, research how to access quality and color management settings for it, and use our steps as general guidelines.

To turn off color management for your printer in the Mac OS, and print the file:

1. Open the File > **Print** dialog in Photoshop, then click **Print** to get to the Print dialog for your system.

2. From the **Printer** menu, choose the name of your inkjet printer.

3. From the third menu, for a Canon printer choose **Quality & Media,B** or for an Epson printer choose **Print Settings**.

4. Choose the **Media Type** (the kind of paper to be used) and the **Paper Source** (how the paper feeds into the printer).**C**

5. In the **Print Mode** area, click the highest print quality option.

6. Returning to the third menu from the top, choose **Color Options** (Canon) **D** or **Color Management** (Epson). A new set of options displays in the dialog. Choose **None** from the **Color Correction** menu (Canon), or click **Off (No Color Adjustment)** (Epson).

7. Click **Print**. Congratulations!

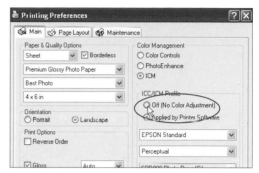

A In Windows, click Off in the ICC/ICM Profile area to turn off color management.

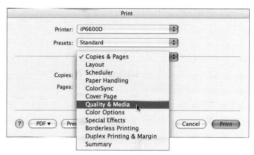

B In the Print dialog, we chose the Canon Pixma iP6600D printer from the Printer menu and are now choosing Quality & Media from the third menu.

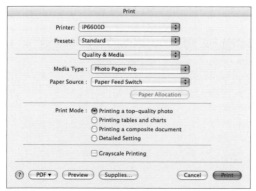

C For the Quality & Media settings, choose your paper type and source, and click the desired Print Mode.

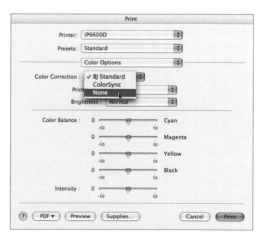

D From the third menu, choose Color Options, then choose Color Correction: None.

The Proof option in the Print dialog instructs your desktop printer to simulate the output of a commercial, four-color press. This "hard" proof won't match the press output exactly, but it will give you an idea of how the image will look in the restricted color range (color gamut) of a commercial press.

To output a CMYK proof from an inkjet printer:

1. For the best results, create a custom CMYK proof setup for your RGB file via View > Proof Setup > **Custom** (see pages 9–10).**A**

2. Open the File > **Print** dialog, display the **Color Management** pane, then click **Proof.B**

3. Make sure the **Color Handling** menu is set to **Photoshop Manages Colors** and the **Printer Profile** menu is set to the correct profile for your inkjet printer.

4. From the **Proof Setup** menu, **C** choose a profile for proofing, preferably the one you saved

via View > Proof > Custom (the same profile will also appear on the View > Proof Setup submenu).

5. Below the Proof Setup menu, check **Simulate Paper Color** (see page 9) and/or **Simulate Black Ink** to mimic those commercial printing conditions. See also Photoshop Help.

6. Click Print, then follow the steps on page 330 for Windows or 331 for the Mac OS.

> **GIVE THE PRINT TIME TO CURE**
>
> Before judging the true colors in an inkjet print, especially when printed on matte paper, allow about an hour for the inks to stabilize and the final colors to develop.

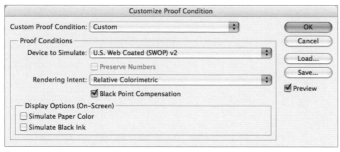

A Use the Customize Proof Condition dialog to create a custom CMYK proof.

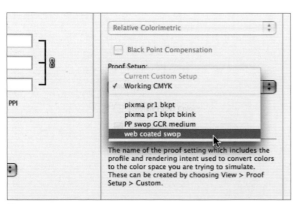

C Choose a proofing profile from the Proof Setup menu in the Print dialog.

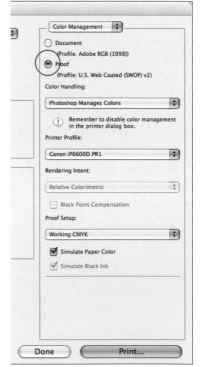

B In the Color Management pane of the Print dialog, click Proof, then choose Color Handling and Printer Profile menu options.

Preparing a file for commercial printing

Computer monitors display additive colors by projecting red, green, and blue (RGB) light, whereas commercial presses print subtractive colors using CMYK (cyan, magenta, yellow, and black) and/or spot color inks. Obtaining good CMYK color reproduction of digital images from a commercial press is an art.

Nowadays, with print shops creating their own profiles for their commercial presses, you don't need to concern yourself with creating a profile; you can leave this step to the pros. Do concern yourself with saving the custom profile from your print shop to the correct folder (as we showed you on page 7) so it can be accessed from the Color Settings dialog.

When you're ready to convert your file for commercial printing, you need to set the current CMYK working space to either the custom profile your print shop provided or to a predefined prepress profile. This CMYK profile will control the conversion of your images from RGB to CMYK color mode.

To choose a predefined CMYK profile:

1. Choose Edit > **Color Settings** (Ctrl-Shift-K/ Cmd-Shift-K).

2. Do either of the following:

   From the **Settings** menu, choose the .csf profile that you received from your commercial printer.**A**

   From the **CMYK** menu in the Working Spaces area, choose either the .icc predefined prepress profile that your print shop sent you or a profile that matches your chosen press and paper type.**B**

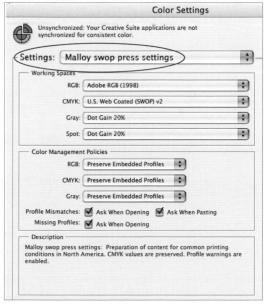

A From the Settings menu in the Color Settings dialog, choose the .csf profile you received from your print shop.

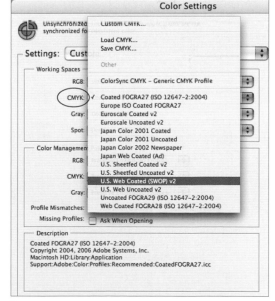

B From the CMYK menu in the Color Settings dialog, choose either a custom .icc profile that you received from your print shop or a preset CMYK profile that they recommend.

Exporting Photoshop files to Adobe InDesign and Adobe Illustrator

If you're going to export your Photoshop file to Adobe InDesign or Adobe Illustrator, be aware that **Photoshop (PSD)**, **TIFF**, **Photoshop PDF**, and the less practical **Large Document (PSB)** are the only formats that preserve Photoshop features such as multiple layers, Smart Objects, adjustment layers, etc. Because you can import a Photoshop PSD file into InDesign or Illustrator via the Place command, or into Illustrator via the Open command, exporting files to those programs is a cinch. If you decide to allow layers to be converted to objects, each layer will appear as an object on its own editable layer, nested within a group.

Photoshop to InDesign

To speed up performance when importing a Photoshop PSD file into InDesign, save a flattened, composite preview of the file with the layered version. To ensure that a flattened, composite preview of the layered file is always included when the Save or Save As command is used, go to Edit/ Photoshop > Preferences > File Handling, and on the Maximize PSD and PSB File Compatibility menu, choose Always. With this option on, a rasterized copy of any vector art will also be included for applications that don't support vector data. This option produces larger files that take longer to save, but it ensures compatibility for applications that don't support Photoshop-specific features.

Or if you prefer to decide on a file-by-file basis whether to include the additional flattened version with your layered file, choose Ask from the Maximize PSD and PSB File Compatibility menu instead. With this setting chosen, if you create one or more layers and then save your file using the Save or Save As command, an alert dialog will appear, giving you the option to include the composite preview or not.

If you need to preserve the possibility of editing a 16-bits-per-channel Photoshop file after importing it into InDesign, don't change the bit depth. Or if you're ready to lower the bit depth now, before exporting the file, from the Image > Mode submenu, choose 8 Bits/Channel.

InDesign can import Photoshop PSD files and color-separate them (both RGB and CMYK files), and it can also read embedded ICC color profiles. In InDesign, you can turn the visibility of Photoshop layers on or off at any time, as well as view layer comps. Since alpha channels, layer masks, and transparency are preserved, you won't need to create a clipping mask when you want to block areas of an image from printing. And like other programs in the Adobe Creative Suite, InDesign lets you use Adobe Bridge for file and color management.

Photoshop to Illustrator

It's also a cinch to get Photoshop files into Illustrator.

► If you **drag and drop** a Photoshop selection or layer into Illustrator, in Windows the imagery will appear on the Layers panel in Illustrator as an image layer, whereas in the Mac OS it will appear as a group with a generic clipping path and an image layer. Opacity settings are reset to 100% but are preserved visually, the blending mode is reset to Normal, and layer and vector masks are applied to their respective layers. Transparent areas surrounding the imagery are ignored, whereas transparent areas within the imagery are filled with white.

► Via File > **Place** in Illustrator, you can place either a whole Photoshop image or just a single layer comp. If you place a Photoshop image with the Link option checked, the image will appear on the Layers panel on a single image layer, and any masks in the file will be applied. If you embed the Photoshop image as you place it (uncheck the Link option), you'll be given the option to convert layers into objects or flatten them into one layer.

► The presence of **adjustment layers** in a Photoshop image will prevent the underlying layers from becoming individual layers in Illustrator. To work around this limitation, merge any adjustment layers downward before opening or placing the file into Illustrator.

► If you **flatten** the Photoshop layers into one layer, all transparency, blending modes, and layer mask effects will be preserved visually but won't be editable in Illustrator.

► Illustrator can't import 16-bit files. If you don't reduce the bit depth of your file to 8-bit via the Image > Mode menu in Photoshop, Illustrator will flatten the layers and lower the bit depth when it imports the file.

Exporting a silhouetted image from Photoshop

To place just a portion of a Photoshop PSD image into InDesign or Illustrator, the first step is to isolate it to a separate layer.

To create a silhouetted image in Photoshop:

1. Do either of the following:

    With an area of a layer selected, create a layer mask.**A**

    Select the area to be silhouetted, and put it on its own layer by pressing Ctrl-J/Cmd-J.**B**

2. *Optional:* Hide the Background by clicking its visibility icon. You'll also have the option to hide the Background once the file is imported into InDesign or Illustrator (see the next page).

3. Choose File > Save As, check As a Copy in the dialog to save a copy of the file, then follow either set of instructions on the next page.

➤ Instead of creating a path or text in Photoshop, consider using the File > Place command in Illustrator to import your Photoshop image, then create your vector paths or text on top of the image in Illustrator.

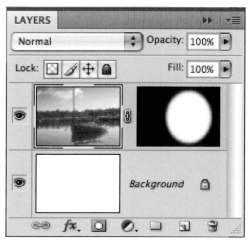

A In Photoshop, we created a layer mask to hide part of an image layer, then saved the file in the Photoshop PSD format.

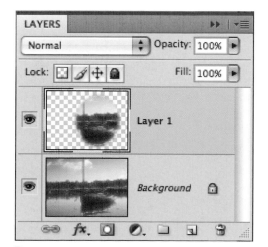

B In Photoshop, we created a silhouette by copying a selected area to a new layer, then saved the file in the Photoshop PSD format.

To place a Photoshop file into InDesign as a silhouette:

1. In InDesign, open or create a document, then import the Photoshop file via File > **Place**.

2. Choose Object > **Object Layer Options**.

3. In the dialog,**A** check Preview, show the layer that contains the **layer mask**, hide any other layers, then click OK.**C–D**

To import a Photoshop file into Illustrator as a silhouette:

1. In Illustrator, open the file via File > **Open**, or import it via File > **Place** with the Link option unchecked.

2. In the Photoshop Import Options dialog, click **Convert Layers to Objects**, then click OK. On the Layers panel, the image will appear on editable nested layers, within a group.**B–D** Note: When a Photoshop layer is converted into an Illustrator object, transparency and blending mode settings are preserved (and are listed as editable appearances), and any layer masks become opacity masks, as identified by a dashed line under the layer name.

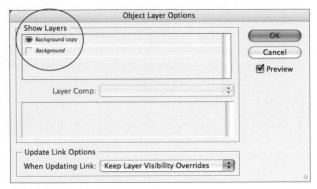

A In the Object Layer Options dialog in InDesign, we clicked the visibility icon for the Background to hide it.

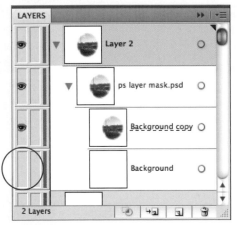

B In Illustrator, we chose File > Place, then chose Convert Layers to Objects in the Photoshop Import Options dialog. On the Layers panel, we hid the Background by clicking its visibility icon.

C This is the imported Photoshop PSD file with the Background visible.

D Here it is with the Background hidden.

E And here it is with both layers hidden. ;0)

Saving files in the TIFF format

TIFF files are versatile in that they can be imported into most applications and are usable in many color management scenarios. Both InDesign and QuarkXPress can color-separate a CMYK color TIFF.

To save a file in the TIFF format:

1. If the document will be printed on a four-color press and your print shop requests that it be a CMYK file, choose Image > Mode > CMYK Color.

2. Choose File > **Save As**.

3. In the Save As dialog, do the following:

   Enter a name and choose a location for the file.

   Choose Format: **TIFF**.

   Optional: Although you could check Layers to preserve any layers in your file, few image or layout programs can work with layered TIFF files, and those that don't will flatten them upon import. You can also choose to save Alpha Channels, Notes, or Spot Colors; or check ICC Profile/Embed Color Profile [profile name] to include the currently embedded color profile with the file.

   Click Save. The TIFF Options dialog opens.**A**

4. In the **TIFF Options** dialog, do the following:

   If the file is going to be color-separated, click **None** under **Image Compression** because output service providers usually prefer uncompressed files. If you do need to compress the file, LZW and ZIP are the preferred methods because they don't cause data loss. Note that some programs can't open compressed TIFF files.

   For the **Pixel Order**, keep the default setting of **Interleaved (RGBRGB)**.

   For the **Byte Order**, click **IBM PC** or **Macintosh** (the platform the file will be used on).

   Optional: Check Save Image Pyramid to include multiple resolutions in one file. Photoshop doesn't offer options for opening image pyramids, whereas InDesign does.

   Optional: If the file contains transparency that you want to preserve, check Save Transparency. Bear in mind that some applications can't open TIFF files containing transparency.

   If the file contains layers, click one of the **Layer Compression** options.

   Click OK.

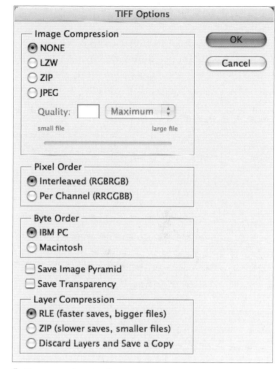

A Choose settings in the TIFF Options dialog.

Saving files in the Adobe PDF format

PDF (Portable Document Format) files can be opened in many Windows and Macintosh applications, and in Adobe Reader (available as a free download), Acrobat Standard, and Acrobat Professional.

There are two different PDF formats to choose from. The default format, Photoshop PDF, preserves image, font, layer, and vector data but saves only one image per file. To create this type of file, check Preserve Photoshop Editing Capabilities in the Save Adobe PDF dialog.

The other format is a generic PDF file, which provides backward compatibility with Photoshop versions CS and earlier. To create this type of file, uncheck Preserve Photoshop Editing Capabilities in the Save Adobe PDF dialog. The file will be flattened and rasterized, which will make your reediting choices in Photoshop quite limited.

Adobe has simplified the process of choosing settings for a PDF file by offering an array of presets.

To save a file as a PDF using a preset:

1. Open an 8-bit or 16-bit file (not a 32-bit file), choose File > **Save As**, enter a file name, choose a location, choose Format: **Photoshop PDF**, then click Save. If an alert appears, click OK.

2. The Save Adobe PDF dialog opens.**A** From the **Adobe PDF Preset** menu, choose a settings preset that's appropriate for the intended output medium (press, Web, etc.). The High Quality Print and Press Quality presets embed all fonts

automatically, compress the file using JPEG at Maximum quality, and create a large Photoshop PDF file that is compatible with Adobe Acrobat 5 and later. Also, the Preserve Photoshop Editing Capabilities option (discussed at left) is selected for these two presets automatically.

High Quality Print (the default preset) is for desktop printers and color proofing devices. The printer driver handles the color conversion, and the profile for the chosen printer is included.

Press Quality is for high-quality prepress output. Colors are converted to CMYK using the current CMYK workspace profile.

The following presets produce a generic PDF file:

PDF/X-1a: 2001, **PDF/X-3: 2002**, **PDF/X-4: 2007**, and **PDF/X-4: 2008** files will be checked for compliance with specific printing standards, to help prevent printing problems. PDF/X-4 files are compatible with Acrobat 5 and later; the others are compatible with Acrobat 4 and later.

Smallest File Size uses higher levels of JPEG compression to produce very compact files for output to the Web, e-mail, etc.

➤ You can read about the currently selected preset in the Description field.

3. Click **Save PDF**. If an alert appears, click Yes.

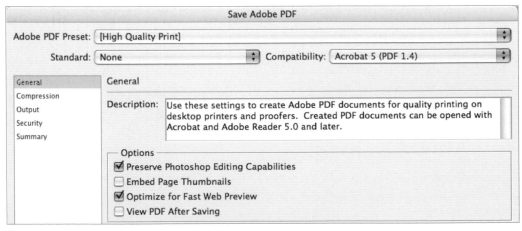

A In the Save Adobe PDF dialog, choose a preset from the Adobe PDF Preset menu.

To save a file as a PDF using custom settings:

1. Via the **Standard** menu, you can apply a PDF/X compliance standard to any non-PDF/X preset to ensure printing compliance. If you opt not to do this, from the Compatibility menu, choose which version of Acrobat you need your file to be compatible with, bearing in mind that not all applications can read Acrobat 7 or 8 files. (As of this writing, Acrobat 9 isn't an available option.)

   If you change any settings from the preset defaults, "[Preset Name] (Modified)" becomes the listing on the Adobe PDF Preset menu.

2. Under **Options**, check any of the following:

   Preserve Photoshop Editing Capabilities to allow the PDF file to be reopened and edited in Photoshop CS2 or later. Photoshop data —such as layers, alpha channels, and spot channels—are preserved.

   Embed Page Thumbnails to save a thumbnail of the file for display in the Open and Place dialogs.

   Optimize for Fast Web Preview to enable the file to display quickly in a Web browser.

   View PDF After Saving to have your system's default PDF viewer (usually Adobe Reader or Acrobat) launch automatically and display the file after you click Save PDF.

To choose more custom options, follow the remaining steps.

3. If you need to reduce the image resolution, click **Compression** on the list of panels on the left side of the dialog, **A** then choose options to control how your image will be compressed (downsampled). From the first menu under Options, choose an interpolation method for downsampling:

   Do Not Downsample keeps the image at its present resolution.

   Average Downsampling To divides the image invisibly into sample areas, averages the pixels in each area, and substitutes the average values for the original ones.

   Subsampling To replaces a sampled area with pixel data taken from the middle of that area, producing a smaller but possibly less accurate file.

   Bicubic Downsampling To replaces the sampled area with an average of that area's values, which usually produces a more accurate result than average downsampling.

   For any of the interpolation methods, enter the desired ppi resolution and the minimum resolution the image must have for downsampling to occur.

Continued on the following page

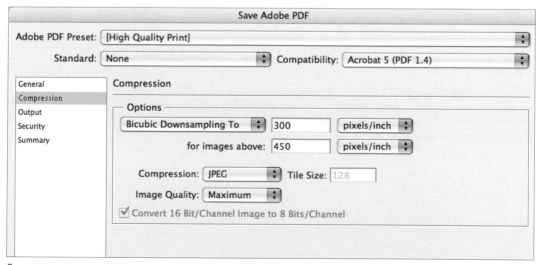

A In the Save Adobe PDF dialog, click Compression, then choose compression options for your image.

Choose other **Compression** settings:

Choose a compression type from the **Compression** menu: None for no compression, ZIP, or either of the JPEG options. JPEG2000 is available only when Acrobat 6 or higher is chosen on the Compatibility menu.

The ZIP option is lossless. If you chose a JPEG option, choose an **Image Quality** for the amount of compression. Maximum applies very little compression (a minimal reduction in file size) but produces a higher-quality image, whereas Minimum applies more compression (and yields a smaller file size), but produces a lower-quality image. All the JPEG options are lossy (cause data loss), except for JPEG2000 when the Lossless option is also chosen.

If Acrobat 6 or higher is chosen on the Compatibility menu, you can convert your file to a lower color depth by checking **Convert 16 Bit/Channel Image to 8 Bits/Channel**.

4. Click **Output** on the left side of the dialog. There, you will see options for controlling the color conversion and profile inclusion in the PDF file. Unless you're experienced with using a color-managed workflow, it's best to either leave these menus on the default settings or ask your print shop which settings to choose. (For Web output, we suggest choosing Smallest File Size from the preset menu in the General panel; the Output options will be set correctly for your file.)

   Note: Although the PDF/X options will be available if you chose a PDF/X preset from the Standard menu, you should keep the default settings in these fields unless your press shop instructs you to do otherwise.

5. *Optional:* Click **Security** on the left side of the dialog to view features for restricting user access to the PDF (these are available only if None is chosen on the Standard menu):

Check **Require a Password to Open the Document** to protect the file with a password, and type a password in the Document Open Password field. (Note that this option doesn't offer complete protection.)

➤ The password can't be recovered from the document, so jot it down in a separate location.

Check **Use a Password to Restrict Printing, Editing and Other Tasks** if you wish to maintain control over these options. Type a password in the Permissions Password field. Also choose Permissions options:

Choose an option from the **Printing Allowed** menu to control whether users can print the file: None, Low Resolution (150 dpi), or High Resolution.

Choose an option from the **Changes Allowed** menu to control precisely what users can and cannot alter.

Check **Enable Copying of Text, Images and Other Content** to permit users to alter text or images.

Check **Enable Text Access of Screen Reader Devices for the Visually Impaired** to permit screen readers to view and read the file.

Check **Enable Plaintext Metadata** to enable the file's metadata to be searchable by other applications (available only for Acrobat versions 6 through 8).

6. Click **Summary** on the left side of the dialog, then expand any category in the Options scroll window to view a list of settings that you've chosen for that category.

7. Click **Save PDF**, click Yes in the alert dialog, then give yourself a nice pat on the back.

➤ To learn more about the PDF options, see Saving and Exporting Images > Saving PDF Files in Photoshop Help.

Saving files in the EPS format

If the drawing or page layout program you're planning to export your files to can't read Photoshop PSD or PDF files, the Photoshop EPS format is the next best option. Note that this format flattens layers and discards alpha channels and spot channels. To access it, your file can be in any color mode except Multichannel, but its color depth must be 8 bits per channel. Printing an EPS file requires a PostScript or PostScript-emulation printer.

To save a file in the EPS format:

1. *Optional:* If the file is going to be color-separated by another application and you want to see how it will be affected by the mode conversion, choose Image > Mode > CMYK Color, then choose Edit > Undo immediately.

2. Choose File > **Save As** (Ctrl-Shift-S/Cmd-Shift-S). The Save As dialog opens.

3. Enter a file name or keep the current name, choose Format: **Photoshop EPS**, and choose a location in which to save the file.

   Optional: Check ICC Profile/Embed Color Profile to have Photoshop embed the document color profile or current working color space in the file (see page 6).

   Click Save. All layers will be flattened. The EPS Options dialog opens.

4. From the **Preview** menu, choose **TIFF (1 bit/pixel)** to save the file with a black-and-white preview or **TIFF (8 bits/pixel)** to save the file with a grayscale or color preview. Mac OS users, choose one of the "Macintosh" previews only if you're sure you won't need to open the file on another platform.

5. If the file is to be used in the Mac OS, choose **Encoding: Binary**, the default method used by PostScript printers; binary-encoded files are smaller and process more quickly than ASCII files. You must choose **ASCII** or **ASCII85** if the file is to be used in Windows, or for applications, PostScript printers, or printing utilities that can't handle binary files. **JPEG** is the fastest encoding method, but it causes some data loss. A JPEG file can print only on a PostScript Level 2 or higher printer.

6. If you changed the frequency, angle, or dot shape settings in the Halftone Screen dialog in Photoshop, check **Include Halftone Screen**. (To get to the Halftone Screen dialog, choose File > Print, choose Output from the menu in the upper right corner of the dialog, then click Screen.)

7. The **PostScript Color Management** option converts the file's color data to the printer's color space. We recommend keeping this option off, especially if you're going to import the file into another color-managed application (such as InDesign), as unpredictable color shifts may result.

8. If your document contains vector elements, such as shapes or type, check **Include Vector Data**. Although saved vector data in EPS files is available to other applications, as an alert will tell you when you reopen the file in Photoshop, the vector data will be rasterized.

9. Check **Image Interpolation** to allow other applications to resample pixels in an effort to reduce jagged edges on a low-resolution printout.

10. Click OK.

Creating a Web gallery

One way to display your Photoshop photos on the
Web is via a gallery, in which the images display
as thumbnails on a colored or neutral background,
with viewer controls for displaying any thumbnail as a larger preview and for displaying images
sequentially. You can create a gallery by using the
Web Gallery controls in Bridge.

To create a gallery for the Web: ★

1. In Adobe Bridge, put all the files to be displayed
   in the gallery in the same folder, in the desired
   order.

2. On the workspace switcher, click **Output**,* then
   click **Web Gallery** at the top of the Output
   panel.**A** A large Preview panel and the Output
   panel display.

3. In the **Folders** panel on the left side, click the
   name of the folder that contains the images
   to be used, to display them as thumbnails at
   the bottom of the Content panel. Ctrl-click/
   Cmd-click around four or five thumbnails in
   the **Content** panel (so you won't have to wait
   for a lot of previews to render as you choose
   options).

4. Click **Refresh Preview**; the Output Preview
   panel displays. Double-click the vertical bar
   between the left and center panes to hide the
   Favorites/Folders panel (**A**, next page).

5. From the **Template** menu at the top of the
   Output panel, choose a layout (**B**, next page),
   then click **Refresh Preview**. It's important

to make this decision first. If you change the
layout later, you will lose the custom changes
you'll be making in other categories on the panel.

The **Standard** template displays the thumbnails
to the left of the large preview. From the Style
menu, choose a thumbnail size.

The **Filmstrip** templates display the thumbnails
either to the left of or below the large preview.
From the Style menu, choose a thumbnail size.

The **Journal** templates list metadata information
for the currently selected thumbnail.

The **Slideshow** template displays the large preview but no thumbnails.

For the **Lightroom Flash Gallery** template, you
have a choice of preset layouts that you can
choose from the Style menu.

6. Click the **Site Info** bar to expand that category.
   Click in a field to activate it, then enter text to
   be displayed on the left and right sides of the
   title bar (**C**, next page).

Instructions continue on page 344

A In Bridge, we clicked Output on the workspace switcher, then clicked Web Gallery at the top of the Output panel.

*If the Output workspace isn't listed, go to Edit/Adobe Bridge CS4 > Preferences > Startup Scripts, check Adobe Output
Module, then relaunch Bridge.*

A This is the Standard gallery template (Style: Medium Thumbnails). The left pane of the Bridge window is hidden.

B From the Template menu, we chose the Left Filmstrip layout for our gallery.

C Next, we clicked the bar for Site Info and entered data to be displayed in the Title and Menu areas of the gallery.

7. Click **Refresh Preview** again (you have to do this for every change) to generate a preview of the selected thumbnails and the data that you just entered.**A**

➤ Click any gallery thumbnail to view it as a large preview.

8. Click the Site Info bar to collapse that category, then click the **Color Palette** bar. To change the color for any of the components of the gallery—Background, Title, Menu (below the title), or Thumbnail—click the color swatch, choose a color from the system color picker, then click OK. Click (you guessed it!) **Refresh Preview** to preview your choices (**A**, next page).

9. Click the Color Palette bar to collapse it, then click the **Appearance** bar. Check Show File

Names if you want file names to display in the gallery (helpful for enabling clients to identify specific photos). Choose a Preview Size and Thumbnail Size (this will overwrite your Style menu choice), and choose Slideshow Duration and Transition Effect options (**B**, next page). Click **Refresh Preview**.

10. Click the **View Slideshow** button 🖼 below the large preview image to hide the thumbnails.

11. Click the **Play Slideshow** button 🖼 to start the slideshow and preview your settings; click it again to stop the show. Click the **View Gallery** button 🖼 to redisplay the gallery.

12. To view the gallery in your default browser, follow the instructions on page 346.

A After choosing the Left Filmstrip template and entering text in the Site Info fields, we clicked Refresh Preview to preview our changes.

A In the Color Palette category, we chose new colors for the Title Bar and Menu Text, then clicked Refresh Preview to view our choices.

B In the Appearance category, we left the preview and thumbnail settings as is, but chose custom Slide Duration and Transition Effect options for the slideshow. Note: The Extra Large previews and thumbnails take longer to update.

To view the gallery in your default browser: ★

1. Select all the thumbnails to be included in the gallery.

2. In the Output panel, click **Preview in Browser** (next to Refresh Preview), then pause for processing. The gallery will open in your default browser, conveniently scaled to fit the window.

3. When you're done looking at the gallery and playing with the buttons,**A** exit/quit the browser, then click in the Bridge window.

   To save the gallery, follow the instructions on the next page.

➤ A maximum of 10 thumbnails can display in the Output Preview panel and in the browser preview, but all the thumbnails that you selected will display in the "actual" gallery.

➤ To change the order of images in a gallery, before saving it, rearrange the thumbnails in the Content panel.

A You can click the thumbnails or the navigation buttons as you preview the gallery in your default browser.

Once you've finalized your gallery, be sure to save it!

To save a Web gallery: ★

1. Select all the thumbnails you've decided to include in the Web gallery.

2. Click the **Create Gallery** bar to expand that category.**A**

3. Enter a Gallery Name for a folder to be created, click **Save to Disk**, click Browse and locate a destination folder, then click OK/Choose.

4. In the Create Gallery category, click **Save**. Pause for processing. All the necessary files for the gallery will be saved to the chosen folder.

You can even let Bridge upload your gallery to a Web server. What service!

To upload a Web gallery: ★

1. Verify that you've been authorized to upload data to a Web server.

2. Click the **Upload** button in the Create Gallery category.

3. Obtain the necessary data from your Web administrator, and enter it in the **FTP** (file transfer protocol) **Server**, **User Name**, **Password**, and **Folder** fields. (The folder is the location on the server
to which the gallery files will be uploaded.)

4. After entering all the necessary data, click the **Upload** button at the bottom of the Create Gallery category. Your gallery files will be sent to the server.

5. Give your viewers the address of the website so they can view your beautiful gallery.

A In the Create Gallery category, enter a Gallery Name for the folder to hold the images, click Save to Disk, choose a location, then click Save.

Using Zoomify

If you want to share a high-resolution image with viewers, but don't want to shrink it down to a speck in order to download it, check out Zoomify. This command creates an HTML file, along with a folder containing a Flash file, an XML file, and a series of JPEG tiles (slices) of the high-resolution image. Once the files are uploaded to a Web server, the viewer can zoom in on a detail. The slice for each area will display quickly because it's merely a segment of the larger image.

To create a Zoomify file:

1. With a high-resolution file open in Photoshop, choose File > Export > **Zoomify**. The Zoomify™ Export dialog opens.**A**

2. Do all of the following:

   Choose a preset **Template** for the background color behind the image in the browser. The Navigator templates include a blue frame that the viewer can click to display a different area of the image, which is very handy.

   For **Output Location**, click **Folder**, choose a location for the file, then click OK/Choose; also enter a one-word **Base Name** for the tile folder and HTML file.

   Under **Image Tile Options**, choose a **Quality** setting for the tiles (slices).

   For **Browser Options**, you can either keep the default pixel **Width** and **Height** dimensions for the image when viewed in a browser or enter slightly larger values.

   Check **Open in Web Browser** to have the file open in your default browser automatically after you click OK, so you can see how it looks.

   Click OK.

3. The HTML page will open in your default Web browser.**B** To **zoom** in or out, use the plus and minus buttons or the slider. To **pan** (bring a different area of the image into view), use the arrows; or if you chose one of the Navigator templates, you can also click or drag the blue frame inside the thumbnail.

4. Upload the files to your Web server, making sure that the HTML file and [base name]_img folder are located in the same folder.

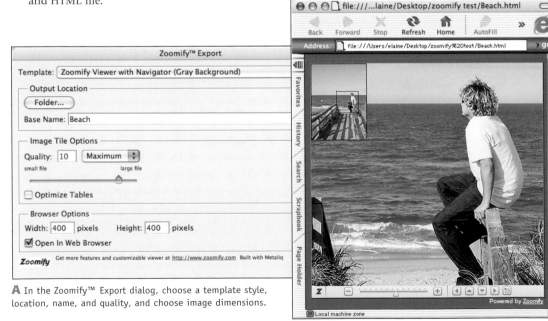

A In the Zoomify™ Export dialog, choose a template style, location, name, and quality, and choose image dimensions.

B In the browser, you can use the controls below the image to zoom and pan, or click or drag the navigation frame (if the template you chose offers that option).

Note: The listings in this index pertain to Photoshop, except where Bridge or Camera Raw is specified.

Photography credits

The photographs on the following pages are © ShutterStock.com:

i, v, vii, 1, 11, 15, 16, 17, 18, 20, 21, 23, 27, 28, 36, 45, 46, 60, 62, 64, 70, 73, 80, 81, 91, 93, 99, 100, 101, 115, 116, 117, 120, 121, 125, 128, 131, 135, 136, 138, 144, 146, 148, 152, 154, 156, 159, 160, 162, 166, 168, 170, 172, 174, 175, 176, 177, 179, 180, 184, 186, 189, 192, 194, 200, 203, 204, 209, 211, 213, 214, 218, 223, 227, 228, 230, 232, 234, 238, 243, 250, 266, 278, 280, 284, 285, 288, 290, 292, 294, 298, 302, 303, 304, 305, 308, 310, 323, 327, 346

The photographs on pages 122 and 194 are © 2007 JupiterImages.com.

All other photographs in this book are © Elaine Weinmann and © Peter Lourekas. (For the photographs on pages 50, 51, access to the garden was courtesy of firstbornmultimedia.com.)